SUPPLICANT EMPIRES

Supplicant Empires

Searching for the Iberian World in Global History

Edited by
EDWARD JONES CORREDERA

BREPOLS

Cover illustration: Exvoto del milagro realizado a Adrian Guapo Autor: desconocido óleo sobre lámina 1912 Colección del Museo Nacional de las Intervenciones – INAH. D.R. Instituto Nacional de Antropología e Historia

D/2025/0095/96
ISBN 978-2-503-61121-1
eISBN 978-2-503-61122-8
DOI 10.1484/M.HW-EB.5.137135
ISSN 2565-8476
eISSN 2565-9545

Printed in the EU on acid-free paper.

Contents

Part 2
Testimonials

Acknowledgments

The idea for this book first emerged at a time during Covid-19, when we all turned into comparative historians surveying the different national responses to a global pandemic. At the time I was affiliated to British and German institutions, Clare Hall, at the University of Cambridge, and the Max Planck Institute for Comparative Public Law and International Law, in Heidelberg. I worked with lawyers and historians, but I never saw the methodological differences between the various fields I was contributing to as an obstacle to the development of new ideas. In many ways, comparativism requires one to speak up and clarify one's ideas. My comparative outlook widened further when I joined the History Department at the Universidad Nacional de Educación a Distancia (UNED). In editing this book, I have incurred debts with a number of scholars and colleagues, such as Mark Somos, José Javier Rodríguez Solís, Marta García Garralón, Marcos Reguera, Yonatan Glazer-Eytan, Francesca Iurlaro, Juan Luis Simal and Nuria Salles Vilaseca. I owe my greatest debt of gratitude, however, to José María Iñurritegui and Pablo Fernández Albaladejo who understood, even if I had come to these themes from a different perspective to their own, that my comparative gaze was a valuable addition to the historiography in Spain. Born in Spain to an English father and a Spanish mother, my life has always been an exercise in comparative history and cultural translation. Returning home after living in France, the Netherlands, China, and Britain, has been a complex exercise in cultural translation, made easier by conversations with colleagues and peers. I am grateful to all of the contributors to this book for their excellent chapters and testimonials. Finally, I would like to thank the book's reviewers, Violet Soen, Chris Vandenborre, and the editors of the Habsburg World Series for their helpful suggestions and for their assistance with the production of this book.

EDWARD JONES CORREDERA   _____

Introduction

Who Prayed for the Iberian World? Incomparable Empires in Global History

The early modern Iberian World is out of joint. Siloed and atomised, its scholarship remains unable to acquire, as scholars have noted, a 'paradigmatic' or 'normative' power of its own.[1] This book, I hope, will allow scholars to escape the gravitational pull of exceptionalism. This volume is a collection of reflections from senior and younger historians regarding the merits of comparativism in the study of Iberian history. It encourages scholars of the Iberian Empires to reassess how they analyse the broader history of the early modern and the modern world. It prompts scholars of other regions in global history to consider the recent literature on the Iberian Empires anew, and to move beyond the tropes of the Black Legend and narratives of growth, splendour, and decline. The goal of the book is to rethink the Iberian World's place in global history.

In a series of chapters and testimonials, contributors were encouraged to consider the role of linguistic divides in the growth of historiographical strands and to speak plainly about the silos that have emerged in the field. The chapters and testimonials in this book assess the state of the field and offer new ways to rewrite the course and character of four centuries of Iberian history. Comparative historical studies in this volume – on gender and labour, corporations, citizenship, food history, and a naturalistic theory of empire drawn from the *rhizome* – all bridge the study of Iberian Empires and global history. In a number of testimonials, historians explore changes and continuities in the field, including new trends in the history of witch-hunts, the history of science, material history, the history of coffee and chocolate, postcolonial history, and environmental history,

---

1 See Tamar Herzog's observations below and, on the pursuit of a paradigmatic model of the Portuguese Empire, see Ananya Chakravarti, 'Zoltán Biedermann, (Dis)connected Empires: Imperial Portugal, Sri Lankan Diplomacy, and the Making of a Habsburg Conquest in Asia', *The American Historical Review* 126:2 (2021), pp. 781-83.

Edward Jones Corredera • Universidad Nacional de Educación a Distancia

Supplicant Empires, ed. by Edward Jones Corredera, Habsburg Worlds, 8 (Turnhout: Brepols, 2025), pp. 9–34

BREPOLS ❧ PUBLISHERS   10.1484/M.HW-EB.5.145062

from Angola through Salvador da Bahia to the Basque Country. The following pages feature a critical introduction to this edited volume. This introduction explores a number of themes: the problems and possibilities embedded in our understanding of these territories as supplicant empires, the historical anthropology of non-statist views of justice in the Iberian World, the two siloed strands that dominate the study of the Iberian World, their roots in the politics of Atlantic history, and the Atlanticist and Eurosceptic politics behind the myth of the Spanish composite monarchy. This chapter concludes by emphasising that only comparative historical research can generate a global history of the Iberian World.

Supplicant Empires

The Iberian Empires ruled republics of supplicants. These republics of supplicants were united in and by prayer. They coalesced around their shared belief in arbiters of piety that governed through ecumenical crowns and courts. The economy of oblation, captured in ex-votos like the one depicted on this book's cover, shaped the moral economy of these empires.[2] The Iberian Crowns merely deciphered the unknowable and revealed to these subjects in search of redemption what their arbiters were owed. These supplicants were far from pliant and subservient – they were subversive in their demands and laid claim to saints as sinners. Predictably, in a battle of expectations between rulers and subjects, a litigious culture emerged across these territories and turned chartered corporations into seminaries for the study of lawsuits.[3]

Supplicant kings were tormented by one question: what did Catholic sovereigns owe God? This question burned its way into the mind of

---

2 On ex-votos see Marianne Bélard and Philippe Verrier, *Los exvotos del occidente de México* (Mexico City: Centro de estudios mexicanos y centroamericanos, 2013).

3 An impression formed by reading Adrian Masters, *We, the King: Creating Royal Legislation in the Sixteenth-Century Spanish New World* (Cambridge: Cambridge University Press, 2023); Max Deardorff, *A Tale of Two Granadas: Custom, Community, and Citizenship in the Spanish Empire, 1568-1668* (Cambridge: Cambridge University Press, 2023); Miguel Valero, *Sovereign Joy: Afro-Mexican Kings and Queens, 1539-1640* (Cambridge: Cambridge University Press, 2022); Christina. H. Lee, *Saints of Resistance: Devotions in the Philippines under Early Spanish Rule* (New York: Oxford University Press, 2022); Karen B. Graubart, *Republics of Difference: Religious and Racial Self-Governance in the Spanish Atlantic World* (New York: Oxford University Press, 2022); Stuart M. McManus, *Empire of Eloquence: The Classical Rhetorical Tradition in Colonial Latin America and the Iberian World* (Cambridge: Cambridge University Press, 2021). Erin Rowe, *Black Saints in Early Modern Global Catholicism* (Cambridge: Cambridge University Press, 2019).

Philip II.[4] Perhaps the runes of his empire's future could be found in his ever-expanding stockpile of sacred relics in El Escorial.[5] Like all of the other collectors of devotional debris across these empires, Philip was just another eager supplicant. Impelled by the hope that another conquest would redeem more souls and bolster God's support for his kingdom, he ruled over a supplicant empire.[6] For the subjects across these vast empires were not bound across space. They were bound by time. Great expectations of the future, where the last judgement would one day be delivered, united these empires: prayer, conversion, redemption, miracles, and the promise of profit turned these territories into holy empires that were forced to regulate the profane economy of waiting. And yet, we only know half of this history. For we know about life in these empires by day, but the systematic study of the night – the other half of human history – has entirely eluded the historiography of the Iberian World and Latin America.

Focusing on prayer appears to subvert traditional imperial narratives and nuance the focus of recent studies on the power of the petitioner. A supplicant culture implied a constant negotiation of power under threat of subversion from its own promissory logic: the immanent critique of the daily elements of royal authority was built into a system that promised to deliver salvation through devotion, debt, and distributive justice. The relational ritual of prayer generated a concentric system of power which regulated the symbolic and the quotidian reparation of injustice: vassals, towns, corporations, indigenous communities, and monarchs operated the levers of pleading and grievance. Prayer served to articulate demands: it shaped political affect, structured political communication, and served to litigate the limits of imperial rule and legitimate its authority. This reading of the Iberian Empires as supplicant empires emerges from a comparative overview of the latest research in the field. But how distinct were these dynamics from those of other contemporary empires? And how do these dynamics relate to the Atlantic World and other historiographical pillars that support the study of the Iberian World?[7] In addressing these questions we

---

4 On how the question of *ars moriendi* tormented his father, Charles V, see Violet Soen, "Charles V", in *Martin Luther in Context*. Edited by David M. Whitford (Cambridge: Cambridge University Press, 2018), pp. 232-39.

5 Guy Lazure, 'Possessing the Sacred: Monarchy and Identity in Philip II's Relic Collection at the Escorial', *Renaissance Quarterly* 60:1 (2007), pp. 58-59.

6 Geoffrey Parker, *Imprudent King: A New Life of Philip II* (New Haven: Yale University Press, 2014), p. 236.

7 Drawing on Graubart's pioneering work, *Republics of Difference*, and other outstanding works by Mina García Soormally, *Idolatry and the Construction of the Spanish Empire* (Denver: University Press of Colorado, 2018); Patrick J. O'Banion, *The Sacrament of Penance and Religious Life in Golden Age Spain* (University Park: Pennsylvania State University Press, 2012).

must not treat historiography as the dead weight of a bygone era. We must first study the origins of the current dividing lines in our historiography – for the scholarship's feet of clay are unlikely to lead us down new paths. Indeed, scholars of the Iberian Empires have failed to critically engage with the historiographical foundations, and the foundational terms, that structure the study of the Iberian Empires, and which are still drawn from the literature on the Atlantic World. These terms are often at odds with the focus of today's scholarship: after all, as Ian Steele once noted, 'no one ever lived, prayed, or died for the Atlantic World'.[8] Scholars have reinforced a worldview drawn from the North Atlantic Treaty Organization (NATO). But there is a fundamental incompatibility between this Atlanticist world-view of great power politics and the study of the spiritual economy that animates the scholarship of the Iberian World today. As the field grows more interested in how early modern violence and belonging informed the rise of nineteenth-century visions of rights, status, and citizenship, the Atlanticist tendency to entirely overlook this century, a vast gap in an accepted sequence on the path to irenic internationalism, is gradually exposed. Its once intuitive spatial model, which might remain valuable for the study of migration and trade, masks the shortcomings of its approach to historical time. It once served the Atlantic Order's sense of mission: the aim was to foreclose the revolutionary violence that shaped the nineteenth century, not to study its roots. As the Atlantic Order wanes, we ought to be able to denaturalise its rise.

The spectre of state violence: historical anthropology in the Iberian World

Once tied to the study of great power politics, economics, and law, the anglophone study of the Iberian Empires is increasingly, like so many areas of historical research, dominated by anthropologists.[9] In this context, the neglected old can seem strikingly new. The work of the late Bartolomé Clavero, which had a huge influence in Spain, Portugal, and Italy, is cited by many of the European contributors to this volume.[10] It was almost

---

8   Ian K. Steele, 'Review of Bernard Bailyn's American Atlantic, *History and Theory* 46:1 (2007), pp. 48-58, p. 48.
9   Freddy Foks, 'Finding modernity in England's past: Social anthropology and the remaking of social history in Britain, 1959-77', *History of the Human Sciences* (2024) (Online First).
10 His recent death generated a number of reassessments of his work; see, for example, Carlos Garrica, 'En memoria de Bartolomé Clavero', *Revista de Historia del Derecho* 65 (2023), pp. 1-11; Marta Llorente and Jesús Vallejo, 'Bartolomé Clavero, un referente en la Historia del Derecho', *El País*, 13 October 2022. Federico Fernández Crehuet, 'En recuerdo y nostalgia de Bartolomé Clavero', *Anales De La Cátedra Francisco Suárez* 57 (2023), pp. 287-89. These texts built on some of the themes of his Festschrift. Jesús Vallejo Fernández

entirely ignored by the anglophone scholarship. But his historical anthropology illuminates many of the areas that are currently of interest to scholars in the United States. Where anglophone scholars were once students of state formation, US historians in particular have become disillusioned with the capacity of the nation state to deliver justice. Statist models are out: many anglophone scholars are now more focused on subjectivity and the internal experience of power and tyranny. In this soul-searching mission to find salvation in the study of the past, scholars in the United States have folded the study of empire into an analysis of the subaltern resistance against top-down authority and racial hierarchies. Ideas of compassion, care, resistance, and salvation are now the focus of many studies.

Clavero spent his entire career studying these values. He was a prolific and profoundly creative historian. His works were dense and rich in irony, full of compelling and wry observations – and they were sometimes criticised by anglophone scholars for their inattention to analytical terms.[11] Clavero's work studied the role of Catholicism in creating a moral economy that underpinned and transcended the rule of law. In his most influential work, *Antidora*, Clavero showed that, in the Spanish Empire, economic ideas emerged from Catholic doctrines of salvation; money and debt were salvific gift exchanges.[12] In his writings on the *mayorazgo*, or entail, and the main systems of land ownership in medieval Castile which would shape the dynamics of socioeconomic power across the Spanish Americas, Clavero drew attention to dynamics of power and space.[13]

Spain and Portugal, in this reading, were emphyteutic monarchies from the top down – they had a temporary hold on their territories, which they ruled on behalf of God.[14] Under the *encomienda* and the *repartimiento*, landholders nominally leased the land from the Crown, while indigenous people paid a tribute, a never-ending debt, to the landholder for his protection. One of the merits of Clavero's work was that it allowed scholars to connect the early modern to that period that Atlantic historiography always overlooked, the nineteenth century. In his work on the Cádiz Constitution, Clavero made what ought to have been a field-defining intervention when he noted that, at the Cádiz Cortes, Spanish officials drew on Jeremy Bentham and not on John Locke to retain and entrench existing

de la Reguera and Sebastián Martín Martín eds., *Antidora. Homenaje a Bartolomé Clavero* (Navarra: Thomson Reuters Aranzadi, 2019).

11 James S. Amelang, 'Tantas personas como estados: Por una antropología política de la historia europea. Bartolomé Clavero', *The Journal of Modern History* 60:4 (1988), pp. 734-35.

12 Bartolomé Clavero, *Antidora: Antropología católica de la economía moderna* (Milán: Giuffrè Editore, 1991).

13 Bartolomé Clavero, *Mayorazgo: Propiedad feudal en Castilla 1369-1836* (Madrid: Siglo XXI, 1989).

14 See Edward Jones Corredera, *Odious Debt: Bankruptcy, International Law, and the Making of Latin America* (Oxford: Oxford University Press, 2024).

colonial property rights – and the inequalities they guaranteed.[15] It is hard to overstate the significance of this insight for the study of nineteenth-century property rights in those Mediterranean and Atlantic constitutions that were influenced by the Cádiz charter.[16] In these discussions, he noted, the terms 'souls', or '*almas*', and '*vecinos*' were used instead of 'citizens' to describe subjects, and in order to avoid opening up the question of the relationship between citizenship, property, and representation.[17] Women's rights remained subject to the needs of patriarchal structures, and this patriarchal logic endured in many of the states that were carved out of this empire – in nineteenth-century Mexico, as Erika Pani has shown, Mexican nationality for those born abroad was passed down through the father, not the mother.[18] On the basis of, and in dialogue with, many of Clavero's ideas, José María Portillo developed his own narrative about the Spanish Atlantic, one that showed that Spain emancipated itself from its monarchy but never from the Church and its values.[19] Portillo's work followed a different approach to the study of the Spanish Atlantic from the one espoused by many scholars in the US – Portillo's Atlantic is not one of circulation and trade, but one that denotes the centripetal power of religion.[20]

Clavero was a comparative historian. He read widely and across historiographical boundaries. Many of his works were published by Italian publishers. Countless Atlanticist historians boarded the ships of those conquistadors that made their voyages across the ocean and seized on their excitement to elide the complexity of their soteriological beliefs.[21] Clavero, and a number of other comparative historians of Spain and Portugal, like António Manuel Hespanha, Pedro Cardim, Tamar Herzog, and David Martín Marcos, instead found that the uneven and fluid rules of the borderlands shaped the law of the land in Iberia and the Americas. These scholars stuck to the study of the dynamics of porous lands and

---

15 Bartolomé Clavero, *Razón de estado, razón de individuo, razón de historia* (Madrid: CEPC, 1991), pp. 192-231.

16 Maurizio Isabella, *Southern Europe in the Age of Revolutions* (Princeton: Princeton University Press, 2023).

17 Bartolomé Clavero, 'Antropología del sujeto de derechos en Cádiz, con particular atención al trabajo y al género', *Revista Española de la Función Consultiva* 19 (2013), pp. 99-128, pp. 112-13; Tamar Herzog, *Defining Nations: Immigrants and Citizens in Early Modern Spain and Spanish America* (New Haven: Yale University Press, 2003), pp. 141-63.

18 Clavero, 'Antropología del sujeto', p. 102. Erika Pani '"Ciudadana y Muy Ciudadana?" Women and the State in Independent Mexico, 1810-30', *Gender & History* 18:1 (2006), pp. 5-19, p. 9.

19 José María Portillo, *Una historia atlántica de los orígenes de la nación y el Estado: España y las Españas en el siglo XIX* (Madrid: Alianza, 2022).

20 As noted by Juan Luis Simal in 'Una perspectiva atlántica para la historia española en la Era de las revoluciones', *Ayer* 89 (2013), pp. 199-212.

21 Elliott, *Atlantic Empires*; John Elliott, *Imperial Spain, 1469-1716* (London: Penguin, 1963).

considered how they shaped America – Clavero's last works focused on how colonial genocides shaped modern international law.[22] This meant that their work carried into the nineteenth century; whereas the Atlantic sublimated its crowning feat, the United States of 1787, into the shining example of modern statehood – a melting pot of migrants who, through common interest and purpose, would eventually forge the modern nation state – the study of borderlands drew on nineteenth-century US history to explore the violent, incoherent, and contested continuities that truly forged the modern nation state.[23] Herzog's work is, after all, a study of that idea that was already salient in the fifteenth century and would come to shape modern states: citizenship.

It is worth noting that the threat of state violence and the experience of terrorism shaped the Southern European historical anthropology of Clavero, Hespanha, and countless other historians.[24] In the second half of the twentieth century, Clavero stimulated a thriving dialogue – and some of the main themes of this historiographical strand are captured in Cardim's chapter on corporate structures – which emerged among historians in Italy, Spain, Portugal, and France as they sought to study the relationship between Catholicism and statehood.[25] The writings of these historians, which reflected on the experience of war and totalitarianism in Southern Europe, were haunted by the state's monstrous potential for violence – and its equally gruesome counterinsurgent responses. Historians sought to find bonds that united communities beyond statist visions of history – and sought to exorcise the ghosts of their nation's past. The relentless search for a model of the state beyond the nation was diagnosed by Clavero in his own historiographical analysis of the writings of Pablo

22 Bartolomé Clavero, 'Colonial genocide and the historiography of international law: A paradigm shift? (Apropos of Dirk Moses' Problems of Genocide and beyond)', *Quaderni fiorentini per la storia del pensiero giuridico modern* 51:1 (2022), pp. 517-57 and Bartolomé Clavero, *Genocide Or Ethnocide, 1933-2007: How to Make, Unmake, and Remake Law with Words* (Milan: Giuffrè Editore, 2008); David Martín Marcos, *People of the Iberian Borderlands: Community and Conflict between Spain and Portugal, 1640-1715* (London: Routledge, 2023).

23 A. J. R. Russell-Wood, *A World on the Move: The Portuguese in Africa, Asia, and America 1415-1808*. (New York: St. Martin's Press, 1993), pp. 63-64.

24 António M. Hespanha, *La Gracia del Derecho: Economía de la Cultura en la edad Moderna*. Edited by Bartolomé Clavero (Madrid: CEPC, 1993).

25 Paolo Grossi, 'Un Diritto senza Stato (La nozione di autonomia come fondamento della costituzione giuridica medievale)', *Quaderni Fiorentini per la Storia del Pensiero Giuridico*, 25 (1996), pp. 267-84; Bartolomé Clavero, 'Religión y Derecho. Mentalidades y Paradigmas', *Historia, Instituciones, Documentos*, 11 (1985), pp. 1-26; António Manuel Hespanha, *Poder e instituições na Europa do Antigo Regime* (Lisbon: Fundação Calouste Gulbenkian, 1984); Piedro Costa, *Lo Stato Immaginario. Metafore e Paradigmi nella cultura Giuridica Italiana fra Ottocento e Novecento* (Milan: Giuffrè, 1986); Jean-Frédéric Schaub, 'La Penisola Iberica nei secoli XVI e XVII: la questione dello Stato', *Studi Storici* 36:1 (1995), pp. 9-49.

Fernández Albaladejo, a leading historian of early modern Spain, who coined, among other things, the term pastoral sovereignty to describe the Abrahamic relationship between the Crown and the people.[26] The monumental works of Javier Fernández Sebastián, who has, with the help of a coterie of researchers, created the largest group of scholars of conceptual history in the world, and Portillo's own oeuvre on the never-ending Hispanic pursuit of conciliatory constitutionalism, bear the mark of the legacy of terrorism and violence in modern Spain.[27]

The old, then, is new: the ghosts of Southern Europe's past haunt the US. Can a connected and comparative historical anthropology unite our atomised field? The answer is simple: not without an acknowledgement of the political roots of historiography, and a dialogue between and across these subfields, both of which are sorely missing. This historiographical review is both a belated analysis, for it should have been carried out decades ago, and yet it is, I hope, a timely one, since the field might today agree on a certain set of first principles. In his last publication to appear during his lifetime, Elliott lamented the tendency sketched across recent historiographical overviews to decry all past efforts to study the Iberian Empires as studies that were insensitive to the lived experience of empire.[28] One may then say that the old is only new because the new has failed to study the old. But the old was uncritical in its attachment to its foundational texts: Elliott's work was never subjected to a single systematic and urbane critique during his entire lifetime – something that has not happened with foundational works in any other regional area of twentieth-century historical research.[29]

---

26 Bartolomé Clavero, "España antes de España (Éxito y derrota de Pablo Fernández Albaladejo)", in *Historia en fragmentos. Estudios en homenaje a Pablo Fernández Albaladejo*, edited by Julio Pardos, Julen Viejo, José María Iñurritegui, José María Portillo, Fernando Andrés (Madrid: UAM, 2017), pp. 47-66; Pablo Fernández Albaladejo, *La crisis de la monarquía* (Barcelona: Crítica, 2009), p. 367-93.

27 Javier Fernández Sebastián, *Diccionario político y social del mundo iberoamericano. La era de las revoluciones, 1750-1850*. Two volumes (Madrid: CEPC, 2009/2014); José María Portillo, *Fuero indio. Tlaxcala y la identidad territorial entre la monarquía imperial y la república nacional, 1787-1824* (Mexico City: El Colegio de México, 2014).

28 John Elliott, Review in *Journal of Early Modern History* 26 (2022), pp. 154-62, of D.A. Levin Rojo and C. Radding eds., *The Oxford Handbook of Borderlands in the Iberian World* (Oxford: Oxford University Press, 2019); Y. Martínez-San Miguel and S. Arias eds., *The Routledge Hispanic Studies Companion to Colonial Latin American and the Caribbean (1492-1898)* (New York: Routledge, 2020); Bouza, Cardim and Feros, eds, *Iberian World*; I. del Valle, A. More and R.S. O'Toole, eds, *Iberian Empires and the Roots of Globalization* (Nashville: Vanderbilt University Press, 2019); Â. Barreto Xavier, F. Palomo and R. Stumpf eds., *Monarquias Ibéricas em Perspectiva Comparada (Sécs. XVI–XVIII): Dinâmicas Imperiais e Circulação de Modelos Administrativos* (Lisbon: Instituto de Ciências Sociais, 2018).

29 With one exception: Pablo Fernández Albaladejo, "El problema de la 'composite monarchy' en España", in Isabel Burdiel and James Casey eds., *Identities: nations, provinces and regions (1550-1900)* (Norwich: University of East Anglia, 1999), pp. 185-201.

Most other historiographical clusters are better and more critically informed about their past. The lack of historiographical debate has hindered the development of the field. As Herzog notes in her study, Spain and Portugal do not carry a 'normative' power in the study of global history – where, for all of the merits of the global turn, the Reformation in Germany or the French Revolution and, increasingly, the Haitian Revolution, continue to serve as turning points in global history, the research on Iberian Empires in global history is the study of empires that exist outside of time and space. We run the risk of repeating the well-intentioned mistakes of our forebears: so much of the twentieth-century European and Latin American scholarship on the Iberian Empires was a study of nationalism masking as a study of the failure to build stable nations: the making of patriotism in the Spanish-speaking world, countless studies concluded, created worlds of *caudillos* and revolutions. Patriotism failed to create the modern nation – but it fuelled the flames of political fanaticism and therein lay the roots of the Hispanic *Sonderweg*.[30] Today, as the US turns its attention to the search for forms of patriotism, nationalism, and unity without the nation, we risk repeating this mistake.

Establishing a global dialogue, in an age of open access and online publications that are, in principle, easily available, is critically important for the future of the field. There are many benefits to the anthropological approach that dominates today's research: for one, it can reconcile the insights generated by studies of scholars in late-twentieth-century Southern Europe with the research emerging in the United States, where historians who are growing sceptical of the state's capacity to deliver justice are also seeking alternative forms of communitarianism. But the language we use has to be consistent and the anthropological turn has very little to do with the course and the character of Atlantic historiography. As we will see, Atlantic history emerged to inform a triumphalist vision of twentieth-century geopolitics that was not particularly interested in Iberia's long nineteenth century. And while the study of the Pacific Ocean may slowly displace the dominance of the Atlanticist worldview, its framework survives in modern studies of slavery, commodities, and identities in the Iberian World.[31]

Today, we need to engage in more historiographical debates that allow us to assess the state of the field. Atlantic scholarship once believed that while Protestant empires created exclusionary sacred covenants and narrowed the scope of communities, the Iberian Empires, shaped by ideas of

---

30 Edward Jones Corredera, *The Diplomatic Enlightenment: Spain, Europe, and the Age of Speculation* (Leiden: Brill, 2021), pp. 6-17.

31 See, for example, Mariano Ardash Bonialian, *El pacífico hispanoamericano. Política y comercio asiático en el imperio español (1680-1784). La centralidad de lo marginal* (Mexico City: Colegio de México, 2012); Matt K. Matsuda, *Pacific Worlds: A History of Seas, Peoples, and Cultures* (Cambridge: Cambridge University Press, 2012).

charity and a paternal love for the Crown, deployed saints to demonstrate the Crown's all-encompassing grace.[32] But recent research has challenged this view. Devotion to Philippine 'saints of resistance' and Black saints took place, and these practices were deeply subversive in the Spanish Empire.[33] In Goa, indigenous peoples subverted practices of conversion and created structures of defiance.[34] What does this suggest about the Iberian contributions to that touchstone of global history, the Reformation? And what of Iberian trade in global history? Were Iberian Empires, as Cardim asks in his chapter, actually corporate empires? The vision that Black confraternities, religious communities, and confessional bodies had an autonomous life of their own is confirmed by recent studies of the dawn of the rise of independent movements in Latin America.[35] Does this focus on confessionalism and corporations encourage us to reconsider the generalised view in the historiography that Spain was an communal empire of law and Britain was an individualistic empire of trade?[36] Or were corporations precisely the means through which Iberian officials reconciled the rise of political economy with their systems of law?[37] Thiago Krause's ongoing work on the global history of Salvador da Bahia would certainly suggest that alienated local corporate interests understood the economics of Iberian trade.[38]

For a comparative historian, these radical re-readings of these empires raise a sobering question: how distinctive were these supplicant empires?

---

32 Cornelius Conover, "Catholic Saints in Spain's Atlantic Empire", in Linda Gregerson and Susan Juster eds., *Empires of God: Linda Gregerson and Susan Juster* (Philadelphia: University of Pennsylvania Press, 2011), pp. 87-105.

33 Lee, *Saints of Resistance*.

34 Ângela Barreto Xavier, *Religion and Empire in Portuguese India: Conversion, Resistance, and the Making of Goa* (Albany: SUNY Press, 2022).

35 Marcela Echeverri, *Indian and Slave Royalists in the Age of Revolution* (Cambridge: Cambridge University Press, 2016); Ben Vinson, *Bearing Arms for His Majesty: The Free-Colored Militia in Colonial Mexico* (Stanford: Stanford University Press, 2002); Eric van Young, *The Other Rebellion: Popular Violence, Ideology, and the Mexican Struggle for Independence* (Stanford: Stanford University Press, 2001), pp. 75-90. See also Javiera Jaque Hidalgo and Miguel A. Valerio eds, *Indigenous and Black Confraternities in Colonial Latin America: Negotiating Status through Religious Practices* (Amsterdam: Amsterdam University Press, 2022).

36 On Spain as an empire of law as a foil for Britain's empire of trade see Elliott's Atlantic Empires. On Portugal's maritime empire see Francisco Bethencourt, 'The Portuguese Empire (1415-1822)', in Peter Fibiger Bang, C. A. Bayly, and Walter Scheidel eds., *The Oxford World History of Empire: Volume Two: The History of Empires* (New York: Oxford, 2021), pp. 832-61.

37 Corredera, *Diplomatic Enlightenment*, pp. 36-37.

38 See also Cátia Antunes's project at the University of Leiden, funded by a NWO Vici grant, on "Exploiting the Empire of Others: Dutch Investment in Foreign Colonial Resources, 1570-1800" and Francisco Bethencourt, *Strangers Within: The Rise and Fall of the New Christian Trading Elite* (Princeton: Princeton University Press, 2024).

How common were forms of confessional resistance across these ecumenical unions of Iberian polities against local authorities in the Age of the Reformation? Studies of the Reformation are now referring to the plural *Reformations,* and frequently integrate the Catholic responses to global confessional debates as part of this process.[39] Paradoxically, as more and more scholars of the Protestant world are drawing attention to the ways Catholic authors influenced modern ideas of private property and sovereignty, scholars of Iberia insist on entrenching the distinction between Protestantism and Catholicism.[40] Exceptionalist readings will not help us contextualise the course and character of Iberian Empires in global history. The historiography on the Lusophone world has traditionally been more transparent, critical, and self-reflexive about its space in global history – some have even described Portugal as a 'forgotten empire'.[41] But when this historiography is integrated into the comparative study of the Iberian Empires, this self-reflexivity fades and its critical edge is frequently blunted.

The politics of translation have also generated new inequalities in today's scholarship. An important methodological aspect that contributors of this volume allude to, and which merits further attention, is the matter of the anglophone approach to the historiography written in Spanish and Portuguese. As Tomás Pérez Vejo and José María Portillo have recently argued, Spanish is a 'language for sources, not bibliographies'.[42] The same may be said for the scholarship written in Portuguese: as the internet has facilitated the possibility for dialogue between institutions across the world, as scholarship becomes more global and equitable, the paradoxes of the global are thrown into stark relief. This tension between the availability

---

39 Carlos Eire, *Reformations: The Early Modern World, 1450-1650* (New Haven: Yale University Press, 2016); Simon Ditchfield, "Catholic Reformation and Renewal", in *The Oxford History of the Reformation.* Edited by Peter Marshall (Oxford: Oxford University Press, 2022).

40 David M. Lantigua, *Infidels and Empires in a New World Order: Early Modern Spanish Contributions to International Legal Thought* (Cambridge: Cambridge University Press, 2020); Andrew Fitzmaurice, *Sovereignty, Property and Empire, 1500-2000* (Cambridge: Cambridge University Press 2014), pp. 59-84; Jorge Cañizares-Esguerra, 'How the "Reformation" Invented Separate Catholic and Protestant Atlantics', *Archive for Reformation History* 108:1 (2017), pp. 245-54.

41 As noted by Roquinaldo Ferreira, 'Taking Stock: Portuguese Imperial Historiography Twelve years after the e-JPH Debate', *Journal of Portuguese History* 14:1 (2016) (Online). For the broader context behind the original observation see Giuseppe Marcocci, *A Consciência de um Império: Portugal e seu Mundo* (s. XV-XVII) (Coimbra: Imprensa da Universidade de Coimbra, 2012).

42 Tomás Pérez Vejo and José María Portillo Valdés, 'La Monarquía hispánica En Las Revoluciones atlánticas: Nuevos Enfoques', *Araucaria* 24:49 (2022), 429-50, p. 445. See also Roberto Breña, 'Tensions and Challenges of Intellectual History in Contemporary Latin America', *Contributions to the History of Concepts* 16:1 (2021), pp. 89-115 and Barcia, 'Into the Future', p. 189.

of information and the terms of the debate, between innovation and use, serves to draw greater attention to the importance of debating the origins, means, and ends of the international and global world we live in today.

Convivencia: reconciling the two main strands in Iberian history

The study of the early modern Iberian World is divided into two historiographical strands. On one side, the study of the European dimensions of the Iberian Empires remains anchored in a question that shaped the Atlantic scholarship of the twentieth century: why was the Iberian World late to the process of European modernization? In this reading, early modern Iberia lost its north when it continued to fight to rule the seas, only to find itself moored in a distant past. Scholars on this side of the debate have portrayed the two empires as the cradle of globalisation. Yet many of their works rely on an undefined use of the term "globalisation".[43] Trade was global prior to the rise of the Iberian Empires, early modern Iberian visions of the global were imperial, not international, and the Inquisition, the Jesuits, and the Franciscans did not favour the equality of states, empires, or peoples.[44] In this reading, the challenge for Iberian rulers and rebels was never the construction of transcontinental economic networks,

---

43 An exception to the rule, however, is Serge Gruzinski's compelling oeuvre, where globalisation is depicted as an imperial project; see his *Les quatre parties du monde. Histoire d'une mondialisation* (Paris: La Martinière, 2004) and *A passagem do século: 1480-1520: as origens da globalização* (São Paulo: Companhia das Letras, 1999). Readings of Iberia and globalisation often build on earlier tropes that saw the international as a step prior to the emergence of a universal empire. See Rafael Valladares, *"Por toda la Tierra": España y Portugal: globalización y ruptura (1580-1700)* (Lisboa: CHAM, 2016), pp. 23-84; Christian Hausser and Horst Pietschmann, 'Empire. The Concept and Its Problems in the Historiography on the Iberian Empires in the Early Modern Age', *Culture and History Digital Journal* 3:1 (2014), pp. 1-10.

44 Then again Hugo Grotius did not accept this premise either, see Inge van Hulle, 'Grotius, Informal Empire and the Conclusion of Unequal Treaties', *Grotiana* 37:1 (2016), pp. 43-60. On the transnational collaboration of the Inquisition beyond Rome see François Soyer, 'An example of collaboration between the Spanish and Portuguese Inquisitions: the persecution of the Converso Diego Ramos and his Family (1680-1683)', *Cadernos de Estudos Sefarditas* 26 (2006), pp. 317-40 and 'The extradition treaties of the Spanish and Portuguese Inquisitions (1500-1700)', *Estudos de Historia de España* 10 (2008), pp. 201-38. Francisco Bethencourt, *The Inquisition. A Global History, 1478-1834* (Cambridge: Cambridge University Press, 2009); Dauril Alden, *The Making of an Enterprise: The Jesuits in Portugal, Its Empire and beyond, 1540-1750* (Palo Alto: Stanford University Press, 1996); João Fragoso, Roberto Guedes, Thiago Krause eds., *A América Portuguesa e os Sistemas Atlânticos na Época Moderna: Monarquia Pluricontinental e Antigo Regime* (Rio de Janeiro: FGV, 2013); João Fragoso, Maria Fernanda Bicalho, Maria de Fátima Gouvêa eds., *O Antigo Regime nos trópicos: A dinâmica imperial portuguesa* (Rio de Janeiro: Civilização Brasileira, 2001).

but the generation of norms that could govern both intra-imperial and inter-imperial relations.[45] Modern Latin American revolutionaries, faced with this dilemma, turned to international law to craft new empires under monarchical, imperial, amphictyonic, federative, and transnational constitutions.[46]

On the other side of the historiographical spectrum, research on the global Caribbean, Pacific, and Atlantic dimensions of the Iberian World, long unmoored from these older interpretations, has now reached new shores. It has gradually grown more connected to, and in dialogue with, regional, trans-imperial, and postcolonial strands of history. Terms like the Pacific World or Vast Early America, and the study of the relationship between gender, race, taxation, and legal representation have all challenged the coordinates of the Iberian Atlantic, all while the broader category of the Atlantic has undergone a revision of its own.[47] Caroline Dodds Pennock's brilliant article on the "Indigenous Atlantics" reconsidered its temporal and geographical parameters and shed light on the political and social agency of the Aztec peoples in the Spanish Empire.[48]

Yet in the study of the pursuit of freedom, ordinary people have come alive while sovereigns have turned wooden. The monarchical courts of the Iberian Peninsula, in these readings, appear not as vibrant imperial centres but as static political actors that were periodically rankled and jolted into action by crises; agents that were responsive and reactive to challenges that forced them to claw back control over their overseas territories. Confessional principles and institutions, and administrative structures of negotiation, compromise, and coercion, shaped the law of the land. Such studies seek to show how and why the architects of the idea of modernity forgot,

---

45 Corredera, *The Diplomatic Enlightenment*.

46 Marcela Ternavasio, *Los juegos de la política: las independencias hispanoamericanas frente a la contrarevolución* (Zaragoza: Siglo XXI, 2021); Corredera, *Odious Debt*. On some of these continuities see Jeremy Adelman ed., *Colonial Legacies: The Problem of Persistence in Latin American History* (New York: Routledge, 1999). Lauren Benton's 2004 study on the role of Latin America in global history remains relevant today: Lauren Benton, 'No Longer Odd Region Out: Repositioning Latin America in World History', *Hispanic American Historical Review* 84:3 (2004), pp. 423-30.

47 Katrina Gulliver, 'Finding the Pacific World', *Journal of World History* 22:1 (2011), pp. 83-100; Nicole Poppenhagen & Jens Temmen, 'Across currents: Connections between Atlantic and (Trans)Pacific studies', *Atlantic Studies* 15:2 (2018), pp. 149-59; Karin Wulf, 'Vast Early America: Three Simple Words for a Complex Reality', *Humanities* 40:1 (2019), pp. 26-47.

48 Caroline Dodds Pennock, 'Aztecs Abroad? Uncovering the Early Indigenous Atlantic', *American Historical Review* 125:3 (202), pp. 787-814. Building on earlier seminal works like Susan Kellogg, *Weaving the Past: A History of Latin America's Indigenous Women from the Prehispanic Period to the Present* (Oxford: Oxford University Press, 2005) and Alejandra B. Osorio, *Inventing Lima: Baroque Modernity in Peru's South Sea Metropolis. The Americas in the Early Modern Atlantic World* (New York: Palgrave Macmillan, 2008).

misrepresented, and erased the Iberian foundations of power, culture, and economics – and the indigenous bedrock on which they rested – from global and local history.[49] Vague visions of globalisation and modernity that neglect the history of international politics colour the field: in 2021, the quincentennial of the Spanish invasion of Mesoamerica of 1521 was described in an otherwise excellent book on the topic as a violent clash which, by virtue of 'connecting trans-Atlantic and trans-Pacific colonial exchange networks', constituted 'a key event in creating the globalised world we inhabit'.[50]

When and where did the Iberian Empires happen? Pursuing the study of the global on the back of forced analogies without drawing on the tools of comparison makes this question harder to resolve.[51] Global and imperial historians working in an anglophone context waged a protracted debate about the merits of comparison in the turn towards the global and largely excluded the Iberian World from this discussion.[52] This omission speaks to the limits of comparison and should encourage a reflexive use of this tool. But comparison can also disarm provincialism, and the global turn can sometimes cast the concerns and the characteristics of a region upon

---

49 On the denial of Coevalness see Johannes Fabian, *Time and the Other How Anthropology Makes Its Object* (New York: Columbia University Press, 2014). On certain problematic aspects of the term see Kevin Birth, "The Creation of Coevalness and the Danger of Homochronism". *The Journal of the Royal Anthropological Institute* 14:1 (2008), pp. 3-20.

50 David M. Carballo, *Collision of Worlds: A Deep History of the Fall of Aztec Mexico and the Forging of New Spain* (New York: Oxford University Press, 2020), p. 2.

51 Some scholars have noted how 'the Global Turn' has shown little interest in comparison see Michael Adas, "Global and Comparative History", in Ross E. Dunn, Laura J. Mitchell and Kerry Ward eds., *The New World History: A Field Guide for Teachers and Researchers* (Berkeley: University of California Press, 2016), pp. 335-37, p. 335. Only analogous things can be compared, argued Charles V. Langois in his 'The Comparative History of England and France during the Middle Ages', *English Historical Review* 5:18 (1890), pp. 259-63, p. 260, an article praised by Marc Bloch as a model for the study of comparative history. See Marc Bloch, *Land and Work in Medieval Europe* (Routledge Revivals) (London: Routledge, 2015), p. 76 n. 2. The question then is why there has been so little interest among historians in the Iberian World in finding analogous polities beyond Britain.

52 Best summarised in Durba Ghosh, 'Another Set of Imperial Turns', *American Historical Review* 117:3 (2012), pp. 772-93, Sanjay Subrahmanyam, 'Historicizing the Global, or Labouring for Invention?', *History Workshop Journal* 64 (2007), pp. 329-34 and Frederick Cooper, 'What Is the Concept of Globalization Good for? An African Historian's Perspective', *African Affairs* 100:399 (2001), pp. 189-213; Simon J. Potter and Jonathan Saha, 'Global History, Imperial History and Connected Histories of Empire', *Journal of Colonialism and Colonial History* 16:1 (2015). It featured important contributions from Charles Tilly: *Big Structures, Large Processes, Huge Comparisons* (New York: Russell Sage Foundation, 1984), and Kenneth Pomeranz: *The Great Divergence: China, Europe, and the Making of the Modern World Economy* (Princeton: Princeton University Press, 2000).

the rest of the world.[53] Other approaches have also been tested. Instead of pursuing a comparative approach, many historians of the Iberian World turned to *histoire croisée* and relied on the existence of a common enemy: the idea of modernity.

French scholars of the Iberian World mastered this task.[54] *Histoire croisée* promised to deal with 'specific subjects' that escaped 'comparative methodologies and studies of transfers', but a reflexivity is required to understand why past and present interests in these 'specific subjects surfaced': as the late Bruno Latour remarked, 'the sorting' makes 'the times', the times do not make 'the sorting'.[55] What determines the modern today, or whether there is even a shared vision of modernity within the field, has not yet been subjected to debate.[56] Even the question of what period we viably compare the modern to has changed over time: the last historiographical review on the Atlantic published in the journal *Atlantic Studies* noted the relative dearth of fifteenth, sixteenth, and seventeenth century studies on the topic, centuries that were once the main topic of study by scholars interested in the implementation of Iberian medieval norms in the Americas.[57] The work of Jorge Canizares-Esguerra, and the Red and Black Atlantics, expanded the scope of the field. But religion continues to puzzle historians: in one reading, under these empires subaltern actors could make subversive uses of devotional practices and engage in a 'conversion to modernity'.[58] According to many institutional historians, however, zealous devotion delayed the rise of modern values and institutions until the twentieth century.

Scholars of the Iberian World working on these two strands of history who fail to speak to one another, or to historians in other fields, about

---

53 A critique with its own history, see Edward Jones Corredera, 'Carlo Denina's *Lettres Critiques*: Transnational History in an Age of Information Overload', *Journal of Early Modern History* 23 (2019), pp. 519-41.

54 See the work of Jean-Frédéric Schaub and Gruzinski's *Les quatre parties du monde*.

55 Michael Werner and Bénédicte Zimmermann, '*Histoire Croisée*: Between the Empirical and Reflexivity', *Annales. Histoire, Sciences Sociales* 58:1 (2003), pp. 7-36. Bruno Latour, *We Have Never Been Modern* (Cambridge: Harvard University Press, 1993).

56 Comparison can render 'absences' in teleologies of the modern 'more visible'. It has encouraged scholars working on China and Russia to reconsider the mechanics of modernity. See Peter Burke, 'Comparative History and Comparative Sociology', *Serendipities* 1 (2016), pp. 82-88, p. 84. See also the valuable volume Balázs Trencsényi, Constantin Iordachi, Péter Apor eds., *The Rise of Comparative History* (Vienna: CEU Press, 2021).

57 Manuel Barcia, 'Into the future: A historiographical overview of Atlantic History in the twenty-first century', *Atlantic Studies* 19:2 (2022), pp. 181-99, p. 188.

58 A concept recovered by Barreto Xavier in her book *Religion and Empire* but, in fact, reinterpreted by this author, since Peter van der Veer originally meant to use the term to criticise the colonising belief that 'the colonized had to be converted to modernity'. See Peter van der Veer, 'Introduction', in *Conversion to Modernities: The Globalization of Christianity* (London: Routledge, 1996), pp. 1-23, p. 4.

their operative frameworks may find themselves tilting at windmills, albeit windmills of their choosing. Moreover, as the field has grown more confident of its historiographical foundations, and more self-referential in its outlook, the appeal of pursuing an expansive comparative history has decreased. How can we bring these two strands together? In the absence of modernity as a foil or a lodestar, in the absence of the fabled narrative of imperial growth and decline, it is not obvious how one would synchronise all-encompassing – and not just fragmentary – histories of the early modern Iberian Empires with the history of the rest of the world.[59] The obsession with historiographical turns can also overshadow continuities in historical writing.[60] Historians once obsessed over the ways that Iberian officials, dressed in the garb of their Roman predecessors, sought to escape the cycle of imperial decline by turning to the study of history, thus spurring authors to revolutionise law, chorography, and history in the process.[61] In the context of the global turn, this imperial effort to escape imperial eschatology through expansion is reconfigured and cast as an antiquarian interest in the globe.[62]

Perhaps an unravelling of the field is necessary before the threads can be pulled back together – histories on the bottom-up construction of imperial legislation in the Spanish Empire, for example, promise to reconstruct a coherent narrative about its administration, but continue to draw on the language of the Atlantic World.[63] Scholars of the Iberian World, after all, cannot quite figure out whether law was fundamental or meaningless in shaping power relations: some have questioned whether, in empires increasingly shaped by legal pluralism from without, laws crafted from within mattered at all. Others have asked whether they mattered so much that a far more careful study of their crystallisation is required to understand the political dynamics of these societies.[64]

---

59 On synchronisation and global history see the interest in the German academy fostered by Margrit Pernau; Margrit Pernau and Helge Jordheim, 'Global history meets area studies. A workshop report', H-Soz-Kult, November 14, 2017.

60 See Gary Wilder, 'From Optic to Topic: The Foreclosure Effect of Historiographic Turns', The American Historical Review 117:3 (2012), pp. 723-45, Peter Burke, "Overture: The New History: Its Past and its Future", in Peter Burke ed., New Perspectives on Historical Writing (University Park, PA: Pennsylvania State University Press, 1992), pp. 1-25.

61 See for example David A. Lupher, Romans in a New World: Classical Models in Sixteenth-Century Spanish America. History, Languages, and Cultures of the Spanish and Portuguese Worlds (Ann Arbor: University of Michigan Press, 2003).

62 Guiseppe Marcocci, The Globe on Paper: Writing Histories of the World in Renaissance Europe and the Americas (Oxford: Oxford University Press, 2020).

63 Jorge Cañizares-Esguerra and Adrian Masters, The Radical Spanish Empire: Petitions and the Creation of the New World (Harvard University Press, forthcoming).

64 An issue that was discussed in a number of historiographical debates in the context of Portuguese and Spanish history; see, for instance, António M. Hespanha, "Justiça e Administração entre o Antigo Regime e a Revolução", in António M. Hespanha ed., Justiça

One way to address these questions is to study the roots of the field. The historiographical origins of the Atlantic turn, as opposed to the anthropological turn that has shaped recent scholarship, were profoundly indebted to political science and international relations.[65] This was a comparative type of history that emphasised continuities and commonalities. It spoke to a belief that progress could secularise difference: Iberia's role in the Atlantic was understood as part of a modern transatlantic military and economic network that owed 'more to NATO than Plato'.[66] In today's geopolitical debates, the interpretative power of this political framework has faded, but its ideas remain lodged deep in the historiographical foundations of the study of the Iberian Empires.[67] Built on the back of the Atlantic turn, the most influential explanatory historiographical model in the field was the concept of the composite monarchy.[68]

From composite monarchy to globalisation: nationalism without the nation

The last major anglophone historiographical effort to explain the political logic of the Iberian World took place in the context of imperial fragmentation and national reconfiguration. In the 1990s, the popularisation of

---

e Litigiosidade: História e prospectiva (Lisbon: Fundação Calouste Gulbenkian, 1992), pp. 381-468; Jesús Bohorquez, 'Book review: Bianca Premo, The Enlightenment on trial: Ordinary litigants and colonialism in the Spanish Empire', Nuevo Mundo Mundos Nuevos 1 (2020), [Online book reviews and essays]; Christopher Albi, "Law and Colonial Reform in the 18th Century Spanish World: The Life of Francisco Xavier Gamboa, Mexican Lawyer", in Atlantic Biographies (Leiden: Brill, 2014), pp. 235-62. The debate influenced discussions on the relevance of the term 'corruption' in the Iberian World. See Christoph Rosenmüller, Corruption and Justice in Colonial Mexico, 1650-1755 (Cambridge: Cambridge University Press, 2019), pp. 1-13 and Tamar Herzog, Upholding Justice: Society, State, and the Penal System in Quito (1650-1750) (Ann Arbor: University of Michigan Press, 2004), p. 157. More broadly, see Ronald Kroeze, Pol Dalmau and Frédéric Monier eds., Corruption, Empire and Colonialism in the Modern Era: A Global Perspective (London: Palgrave, 2021).

65 The field of Atlantic history is vast. For a general overview see the Oxford Bibliographies on the topic edited by Trevor Burnard. For the most recent historiographical overview see Barcia, 'Into the future'.

66 David Armitage, "Three Concepts of the Atlantic World", in David Armitage and Michael Braddick eds., The British Atlantic World (New York: Palgrave, 2002), pp. 11-27.

67 Some scholars have tried to integrate it into global history; see, most recently, Trevor G. Burnard, The Atlantic in World History, 1490-1830 (London: Bloomsbury Academic, 2020). On the view that the Spanish Atlantic remains relevant see, for instance, Gabriel Paquette, Manuel Lucena-Giraldo, Gonzalo M. Quintero Saravia & Oriol Regué-Sendrós, 'New directions in the political history of the Spanish-Atlantic world, c. 1750-1850', Journal of Iberian and Latin American Studies 24:2 (2018), pp. 175-82.

68 Helmut Koenigsberger, 'Monarchies and Parliaments in Early Modern Europe: Dominium Regale or Dominium Politicum et Regale', Theory and Society 5:2 (1978), pp. 191-217; John Elliott, 'A Europe of Composite Monarchies', Past and Present 137 (1992), pp. 48-71.

the term composite monarchies and the exponential growth of Atlantic history reshaped the field.[69] As he was drafting his vision of Spain as a composite monarchy, John Elliott, the leading Hispanist of the twentieth century, delivered his inaugural lecture as the new Regius Chair at Oxford. The topic of the lecture was comparative and national history. Elliott suggested that modern scholars had forgotten about the importance of the historical study of national characters. He proposed the establishment of a Centre for Atlantic Studies and he warned that European integration should not force the countries of the United Kingdom into becoming 'anonymous partners in a civilisation reduced to composite commonness'.[70] This view was shared by other leading Atlantic historians, like J.G.A. Pocock, who a few months later observed that the 'accession of the United Kingdom to the European Community entailed a rejection by that kingdom's peoples of the former global capacity of their culture; it was a confession of defeat, and at the same time a rejection of the other nations of that culture'.[71] The European Union threatened to undermine Britain's national character – and the bonds that united this union. By contrast, the Atlantic reflected the British capacity for expansion and renewal. A year later, Elliot published his seminal article, 'A Europe of Composite Monarchies'. The term encapsulated a monarchical system of government that was shared by post-Franco Spain and modern Britain.[72]

Elliott's use of the term was unashamedly presentist. This *trompe l'oeil* elided the Enlightenment and its reconfiguration of Western ideas about sovereignty, federalism, and diplomacy – it discarded the need to study the composite materials with which modern nineteenth-century nation states were forged. But this was a deeply political use of the early modern world, for the Enlightenment's law of nations and its federal ambitions, upon which modern European and North and South American states based their sovereignty, were predicated on the convincing demonstration by enlightened thinkers that Spain was a patrimonial, and not a composite, monarchy.[73] There was then a fundamental incompatibility between an

---

69 The sharpest reflections on the relationship between the Atlantic and the Iberian World have come from Jean-Frédéric Schaub; see for instance his "The Imperial Question in the History of Ibero-America: The Importance of the Long View", in Kalypso Nicolaïdis, Berny Sebe, and Gabrielle Maas eds., *Echoes of Empire: memory, identity and colonial legacies* (London: Taurus, 2014), pp. 63-80.

70 John Elliott, *National and Comparative history. An Inaugural Lecture delivered before the University of Oxford on 10 May 1991* (Oxford: Clarendon Press, 1991), p. 13.

71 J.G.A. Pocock, 'Deconstructing Europe', *London Review of Books*, 19 December 1991.

72 Elliott, 'A Europe of Composite Monarchies', pp. 48-71.

73 Jan Waszink, 'Hugo Grotius on the Agglomerate Polity of Philip II', *History of European Ideas* 46 (2020), pp. 276-91; Vattel was even more critical of Spain's patrimonial monarchy and characterised it as a 'chimera'. See Emer de Vattel, *The Law of Nations, Or, Principles of the Law of Nature, Applied to the Conduct and Affairs of Nations and Sovereigns, with Three*

enlightened European federation of states and Spain's composite union of nations. Spain's future was Atlantic, not European.

Elliott failed to explain the causal relationship between the end of the composite monarchy and the rise of the nation states in the Hispanic world – indeed, it remained unclear, in his own reading, when or how this composite monarchy ended and modern nation states emerged across these spaces.[74] The growth of nation states in the eighteenth- and nineteenth-century Europe, the United States, and Latin America, was based on the rise of new models of diplomacy and international law that emerged in the seventeenth century.[75] In the law of nations, Catalan, Portuguese, and French officials found ways to undermine the strategic ambiguity that characterised Spain's aggregational empire – and Spain in turn played by the new rules of the game.[76] It therefore joined an Enlightenment built on federative expectations: the Holy Roman Empire, a true composite monarchy, inspired the federative peace plans of the abbé de Saint Pierre, Emer de Vattel, and Benjamin Franklin, and Simón Bolívar.[77] Spanish American and British American authors engaged with these schemes and the most significant result of irenic efforts to create a federation of states, based on the designs of authors like Saint Pierre, Vattel, and Immanuel Kant, was not to be found in Europe, but in the towering achievement of the Atlantic World, the United States.[78] The

---

Early Essays on the Origin and Nature of Natural Law and on Luxury. Edited and with an Introduction by Béla Kapossy and Richard Whatmore (Indianapolis, 2008), p. 104, p. 115*.

74 See Edward Jones Corredera, 'The End of Composite Monarchies: Hugo Grotius's *De iure belli ac pacis* and Mid-Seventeenth-Century Iberian Diplomacy', *English Historical Review* 139:601 (2024), pp. 1389-1413.

75 Beatrice de Graaf, *Fighting Terror after Napoleon: How Europe Became Secure after 1815* (Cambridge: Cambridge University Press, 2020); Glenda Sluga, '"Who Holds the Balance of the World?" Bankers at the Congress of Vienna, and in International History', *American Historical Review* 122:5 (2017), pp. 1403-30; Stella Ghervas, *Conquering Peace: From the Enlightenment to the European Union* (Cambridge: Harvard University Press 2021); Isaac Nakhimovsky, *The Holy Alliance: Liberalism and the Politics of Federation* (Princeton: Princeton University Press, 2024).

76 Upon reading more and more of Koenigsberger's work after the publication of my article, I noticed that in his earlier work he was rather explicit about how Spain failed to establish a consistent set of norms to its rule in Europe; see Helmut Koenigsberger, *The government of Sicily under Philip II of Spain: a study in the practice of Empire* (London: Staple Press, 1951), pp. 52-53, pp. 171-72, p. 196.

77 Nakhimovsky, *The Holy Alliance*, pp. 167-87. Peter Schröder, "The Holy Roman Empire as model for Saint-Pierre's Projet pour rendre la Paix perpétuelle en Europe", in Robert Evans and Peter Wilson eds., *The Holy Roman Empire, 1495-1806* (Leiden: Brill, 2012), pp. 35-50; Juergen Overhoff, 'Benjamin Franklin, Student of the Holy Roman Empire: His Summer Journey to Germany in 1766 and His Interest in the Empire's Federal Constitution', *German Studies Review* 34 (2011), pp. 277-86.

78 David Armitage, *The Declaration of Independence: A Global History* (Cambridge, MA, 2007); David Armitage, 'The Declaration of Independence and International Law', *William and*

obsession of the Founding Fathers with Vattel's writings on international law was matched by Latin American statesmen, who studied and debated the political economy of the law of nations to build their nations, unsuccessfully pursue the creation of a union of Latin American states, and successfully reform international law. Enlightened writings about diplomacy, in this process, changed how Europe and the Americas thought about modern statehood.

From the Catalan and the Portuguese revolts of the 1640s to the Cádiz Cortes, many Iberian and Spanish American officials drew on enlightened ideas as they tried to transform this patrimonial monarchy into a true composite monarchy or a global federation. The Spanish Empire, explained José Mejía Lequerica, a Peruvian deputy at the Cortes, should renounce its patrimonial structure, assume guise and shape of the Holy Roman Empire, a composite and negotiated polity with an imperial diet and a nested set of sovereign states, and accept the Americas for what they had become: *primus inter pares*. In the nineteenth century, in the aftermath of the failure to create composite states, Latin American states turned to federalism; often, they drew on the model of the *Zollverein* to coordinate their regional relations.

There was therefore nothing organic about the concept of the early modern Spanish composite monarchy – but there was also nothing organic about the parliamentary monarchy that governed Spain in 1992. Symbiotically, the two models stabilised each other. That same year, celebrations surrounding the signing of the Maastricht Treaty coincided with the five-hundredth anniversary of 1492 and the intensification of calls for Catalan national representation. Elliott's article offered a useful analysis of patterns in the formation and consolidation of early modern European empires. The concept of the composite monarchy bolstered the comparative political framework of the growing subfield of Atlantic history. The *longue durée* history of religious difference could be compared and prejudice could be overcome: the American societies built by Protestant Britain and Catholic Spain could be placed side by side, compared and contrasted as hypostasised historical models. America was not the product of federalism – or composite commonness – it was the child of composite empires.

This was the culmination of a long effort to bracket and distance the early modern world from the politics of the modern. Indeed, as Francesco Benigno and Maria José Rodriguez-Salgado noted, during this period historians sought to defeat sociologists and challenge their totalizing readings of the French Revolution as the harbinger of the modern state.[79] Elliott

---

Mary Quarterly 3:54 (2002), pp. 39-64; Anthony J. Bellia & Bradford R. Clark, *The Law of Nations and the United States Constitution* (New York: Oxford University Press, 2017).

79 Francesco Benigno, *Mirrors of Revolution: Conflict and Political Identity in early modern Europe* (Turnhout: Brepols, 2010); Maria José Rodriguez-Salgado, 'Koenigsberger, Helmut Georg,

and others, in fostering the popularisation of the category of the early modern world as a space between the medieval and the modern, sought to separate and isolate the early modern revolts of the seventeenth century from the politics of the Jacobins – the destabilising power of consent, the core principle of the revolution, was displaced, in this interpretative framework, by the mollifying study of the emergence of consensus.[80] Revolts were rebellions, not revolutions.[81] Southern European historians who sought to find a world that was not subject to the tyranny of the absolutist state found in this discourse a new rhetoric to articulate their views. And yet, as Helmut Koenigsberger noted with characteristic candour, the one revolt that could not be easily accommodated within the model of the composite monarchy was the Dutch Revolt.[82] Elliott overlooked the long-term impact of the Dutch Revolt, which fuelled the rise of ideas of consent and rights that would later inspire Enlightenment thought, and foreshortened instead the Catalan Revolt to emphasise the analogies with modern dissent and the making of the modern Spanish nation. This was, however, history by analogy.

In this context, the early modern world was a reservoir of patterns of aggregation that were alternatives to federalism. The term composite monarchy, used rather sparingly and uncritically by Koenigsberger and ultimately theorised by Elliott himself, had to compete with other historicised models that the Maastricht Treaty had recovered. One of these conceptual innovations had first emerged during the last days of the Holy Roman Empire – the distinction between *Staatenbund*, a federative organisation of states with composite parts that retained their sovereignty, and *Bundesstaat*, where powers were devolved to the composite parts but where sovereignty remained centralised, played an important structuring role in German political debates about the organisation of the European Union.[83]

1918-2014', *Biographical Memoirs of Fellows of the British Academy*, 14 April 2016, pp. 301-33. See also Jean-Frédéric Schaub, 'Révolutions sans révolutionnaires? Acteurs ordinaires et crises politiques sous l'Ancien Régime (note critique)', *Annales* 55:3 (2000), pp. 645-53; Calogero Messina, *Helmut Koenigsberger e Virgilio Titone* (Roma: Edizioni internazionali di letteratura e scienze, 1992).

80 Benigno, *Mirrors*, p. 64.

81 Benigno, *Mirrors*, p. 284.

82 Helmut Koenigsberger, 'Monarchies and Parliaments in Early Modern Europe: *Dominium Regale or Dominium Politicum et Regale*', *Theory and Society* 5:2 (1978), pp. 191-217, p. 208.

83 Reinhart Koselleck, *The Practice of Conceptual History: Timing History, Spacing Concepts*. Translated by Todd Samuel Presner. Foreword by Hayden White (Stanford: Stanford University Press, 2002), p. 285; Signe Rehling Larsen, *The Constitutional Theory of the Federation and the European Union* (Oxford: Oxford University Press, 2021), pp. 14-22; Nakhimovsky, *The Holy Alliance*, p. 49. In the 1980s and early 1990s, Felipe González leaned on Germany to advance his interests in Europe but understood the need to engage with Atlanticist politics. See Sanz, Rosa Pardo. "La Política Exterior de Los Gobiernos de Felipe

How did Iberian Empires relate to the wider world? Were their approaches to international relations set in stone? And how did nation states
emerge out of them? Diplomatic history, Elliott observed, had never truly
interested him.[84] Diplomacy was always the blind spot of the interpretative
model of the composite monarchy. In his original essay on the topic of
monarchies and parliaments, one of his many urbane and unsystematic
explorations on negotiated statehood, Koenigsberger pointed to the difficulty of integrating the impact on foreign affairs on the internal dynamics
of composite states: 'The most serious difficulty in the construction of an
overall theory is presented by the intervention of outside powers in the
struggles between kings and their parliaments. Such intervention would
alter the relative strength of the internal forces to an extent which is, I believe, unpredictable, even if we were to use game theory or a computer.'[85]
And yet, in an uncharacteristically muddled article, he blamed this type of
'intervention' for nothing less than the birth of the United States.[86]

Both composite monarchies and the Atlantic turn had, after all, grown
out of modern interpretations of international relations: the Atlantic turn
emerged in political science departments that saw the nineteenth century
as one characterised by great power politics and the triumph of peace over
revolution.[87] Walter Lippmann's idea of an Atlantic Community would
serve to advance international economic schemes that could accommo-
date wildly disparate political systems, including dictatorships and liberal
democracies.[88] Presentist discussions about universalism, a global balance
of power, the defence of Western civilisation, all informed conceptions of
the Atlantic Alliance, even if there was intense disagreement over which
one of these operative ideas should be the dominant one.[89]

Novel concepts like legal pluralism or legal patchwork sought to capture the overlapping legal norms at play, but failed to explain how the
tensions between these principles were resolved.[90] The lack of the interest

González: ¿un Nuevo Papel Para España En El Escenario Internacional?", *Ayer* 84 (2011),
pp. 73-97. I am grateful to José Javier Rodríguez Solís for drawing my attention to this point.

84 See a valuable summary in Pedro Cardim, Antonio Feros and Gaetano Sabatini, "The
Political Constitution of the Iberian Monarchies", in Fernando Bouza, Pedro Cardim and
Antonio Feros eds., *The Iberian World, 1450-1820* (London: Routledge 2019), pp. 34-61.
Elliott admitted to having 'no enthusiasm for diplomatic history': John Elliott, *History in the
Making* (New Haven: Yale University Press, 2012), p. 95.

85 Koenigsberger, 'Monarchies and Parliaments', p. 214.

86 Helmut Koenigsberger, 'Composite States, Representative Institutions and the American
Revolution', *Historical Research* 62:148 (1989), pp. 135-53, p. 153.

87 On its multiple histories see Armitage, "Three Concepts of the Atlantic World", pp. 11-27.

88 William O'Reilly, 'Genealogies of Atlantic history', *Atlantic Studies* 1:1 (2004), pp. 66-84, p.
68.

89 Bernard Bailyn, 'The Idea of Atlantic History', *Itinerario* 20:1 (1996), pp. 23-29.

90 Lauren Benton and Richard J. Ross eds., *Legal Pluralism and Empires, 1500-1850* (New York:
New York University Press, 2013); Antonio Hespanha, 'Savants et rustiques. La violence

in the ways that the similarity in the structures of Protestant, Catholic, and non-Christian composite monarchies may have accommodated and fostered transnational cooperation served to further perpetuate impressionistic outlooks.[91] Diplomatic efforts to create transnational unions and confederations, or attempts to create states in Latin America, did not receive a great deal of scholarly attention from scholars of the Iberian World.[92]

Decades later, the blind spot around the nature of Iberian connections to the wider world shaped one of the most recent trends in the field: the view of the Iberian World as the cradle of globalisation. As Julia McClure has noted in her excellent new book, *Empire of Poverty*, scholars have failed to study the tension in the claim that Spain fathered both globalisation and poverty at the same time. How did this come to pass?[93]

The historical writings of nineteenth-century postcolonial states in America contain some of the most remarkable answers to this question – and to broader questions about the sources of imperial aggregation. The historiography of the Iberian World began in nineteenth-century Latin America. In Latin America, rebels and rulers often understood the nature of Spanish colonial rule better than their peninsular contemporaries. And yet there is still an enduring tendency to end books about Iberian history not in the Americas or in Asia, but in Europe. By contrast, reading Juan Bautista Alberdi's writings on Spain's legacy in the Americas encouraged me to write a new history of the Hispanic World following the thread of that idea that characterised Western readings of early modern Habsburg monarchs and Latin American states: debt.[94] In this regard, the separation that was otherwise entirely enriching to the study of history and which Elliott fostered throughout his life, the distinction between early modern and modern history, masked and obscured continuities in the formation

---

douce de la raison juridique', *Ius commune. Zeitschrift für Europäische Rechtsgeschichte* 10 (1983), pp. 1-48.

91 Bailyn, 'The Idea of Atlantic History', p. 35; David Hancock, *Citizens of the World: London Merchants and the Integration of the British Atlantic Community, 1735-1785* (New York: Cambridge University Press, 1995).

92 A number of excellent studies have bucked the trend; see Zoltán Biedermann, *(Dis)connected Empires: Imperial Portugal, Sri Lankan Diplomacy, and the Making of a Habsburg Conquest in Asia* (Oxford: Oxford University Press, 2018), Matthew Restall ed., *Beyond Black and Red: African-Native Relations in Colonial Latin America* (Albuquerque: University of New Mexico Press. 2005), and Toby Green, *A Fistful of Shells West Africa from the Rise of the Slave Trade to the Age of Revolution* (Chicago: Chicago University Press, 2019).

93 Julia McClure, *Empire of Poverty: The Moral-Political Economy of the Spanish Empire* (Oxford: Oxford University Press, 2024).

94 See Corredera, *Odious Debt*. Jorge Mayer, *Alberdi y su tiempo* (Buenos Aires: Editorial Universitaria de Buenos Aires, 1963). See also the extensive work of Tomás Pérez Vejo on Latin American thought on its Iberian past and, in particular, Tomás Pérez Vejo, *España imaginada: historia de la invención de una nación* (Barcelona: Galaxia Gutenberg, 2015).

of Hispanic and Lusophone nations and how their founding fathers peri-
odised the modern and its rise.

This book shows how the latest groundbreaking research in the field
can offer time-tested and new elements with which to unify the study of
the Iberian World. As the chapters of this volume show – dazzling with
new insights from the history of science to the history of prostitution
– there are plenty of ways to rethink the relationship between the early
modern Iberian Empires and the global modern world we inhabit today.

A comparative historiography of the Iberian World

Perhaps the most fascinating new interpretation of the Iberian Empires
produced in the past few decades is the one that Fabien Montcher has
presented, for the first time in published form, in this volume.[95] Montcher
heeds Dipesh Chakrabaty's call to integrate natural and political history
and develops a sweeping comparative interpretation of the natural roots of
power in the early modern world.[96] This interpretation of the "rhizomatic
Iberian worlds", particularly when tied to the study of belief and unbelief in
these empires, promises to generate entirely new insights in the field.

David Martín Marcos, in turn, shows how Iberian and European ideas
of rusticity and barbarism were intimately connected. A comparative
analysis of writings in and on Iberian and American borderlands sheds
new light on counter-hegemonic and empowering uses of discriminatory
language. Pedro Cardim, in turn, contrasts the role of corporations and
normative pluralism in the construction of the Iberian Empires to that
of their Northern European rivals. In her particularly innovative and
enriching chapter, Bethany Aram compares the study of concubinage,
prostitution, marriage, gender, and sorcery in Spanish and British overseas
spaces. Marcos Reguera, challenging traditional views about the direction
of travel in the dissemination of political ideas, studies the way that the
idea of Manifest Destiny influenced Hispanic political debates before it
became a subject of intense debate in the Anglophone world. Reguera then
considers the reception of the American interpretation of Manifest Destiny in the Spanish-speaking world. Finally, my chapter on the nocturnal
draws attention to the fact that we know almost nothing about the night in
Iberian spaces – even though the nocturnal was a crucial building block in
the construction of the modern identities of Iberian and Ibero-American
nations.

---

95 See his excellent book *Mercenaries of Knowledge: Vicente Nogueira, the Republic of Letters, and
the Making of Late Renaissance Politics* (Cambridge: Cambridge University Press, 2023).

96 Dipesh Chakrabarty, 'The Climate of History: Four Theses', *Critical Inquiry* 35:2 (2009), pp.
197-222.

The testimonials in this volume address the question of the role, and the aptitude, of comparison in Iberian history to address questions on the exceptionality, the framing, and the nature of the scholarship on the Iberian World. In a series of conversational contributions, authors working on economic history, legal history, and environmental history, shed light on how comparative history has influenced the development of the field. Herzog explores how, through a comparative lens, she has challenged Spanish exceptionalism in order to establish what scholars of Spain can contribute to the study of the wider world. Comparison led Herzog to reconsider the periodisation of legal change not just in Iberia but in Europe, and to encourage other scholars to reconsider the boundaries of the field.

Amanda Scott evaluates how studies of Basque spaces are either the product of extremely specific case studies in microhistory or sweeping accounts of the region – and suggests that there are countless under-analysed sources across a number of archives which deserve greater scholarly attention. Scott provides a deft summary of the state of the field and the main strands in the historiography of Basque migration to – and from – the Americas, sheds light on exciting new scholarship on early modern witch-hunts across the Pyrenees, and alludes to a reorientation of the geographic focus of the field. Thiago Krause suggests that the last few decades have seen the gradual integration of the study of Iberian and overseas territories. Drawing attention to the works, *inter alia*, of Cardim and Kirsten Schultz, Krause notes that the sheer modern size and global weight of Brazil has balanced a field that was once focused on the Iberian Peninsula. Krause considers the ways that comparative history illuminated his exploration of the connections, parallels, and differences between Salvador da Bahia and Lisbon, and how it is proving instrumental in his collaborative project with Christopher Ebert on the global history of Salvador da Bahia (1580-1763). He also draws attention to the ways that new technologies can advance today's scholarship.

Juan Pimentel considers how historical accounts of Iberia's role in the history of science have changed over time, and particularly in light of the contributions of Jorge Cañizares-Esguerra. Maria Gago shows how the history of commodities in modern Portuguese spaces in Africa, and in Angola in particular, has changed over the past few decades. She analyses how Portugal's modern experience with dictatorship shaped historiographical depictions of these spaces as backward and how, thanks to comparative history, a number of academics began to reconsider the meaning of science and modernisation in Portuguese territories. Gago provides a critical reading of the Atlantic framework and suggests that material history, and postcolonial studies, can generate new readings of connected histories of science and power. As she notes, the 'epistemic zone where the history of science meets Iberian history is an especially fertile field' and can unite global and planetary histories. Marta Manzanares explores the relationship between gendered tastes and the sugar trade in the Spanish Atlantic, how comparative history allowed her to revolutionise the study of the politics of sugar in the Iberian World, and how the literature's lack of interest in Spain hindered her ability to generalise her conclusions. José María Portillo suggests that over the past few decades the study of the Age of Revolutions in the Iberian World has become 'de-nationalised'. The scholarship on nation-building in the Iberian Atlantic, he argues, has benefited from a generative debate regarding the suitability of the North Atlantic framework in the study of the Spanish Atlantic. Indeed, in Portillo's view, the revolutions across the Iberian Atlantic World were more Atlantic than those in the United States or France. Finally, Javier Rodríguez sheds light on how the scholarship on Spain and Portugal has grown more connected across national historiographies.

I hope these contributions will encourage young and senior scholars to transcend stale tropes about the Iberian World, critically engage with historiographies of times past, and engage in a dialogue that can harness the vibrant new historiographical insights that are emerging today. As this book shows, there is, after all, nothing incomparable about the Iberian World.

Part 1

PEDRO CARDIM

Corporations, Normative Pluralism, and Jurisdictional Culture

Explaining the Political Landscape of Early Modern Iberia[*]

Introduction

Since the mid-nineteenth century, scholars from different backgrounds have drawn attention to one particular aspect of Western European society before the Age of Revolutions: the corporate structure upon which the social and political order rested. By corporate structure, they essentially meant a society in which the basic unit was not the individual but social bodies endowed with various capacities for regulating collective life. This dimension of the European past was first systematically explored within the fields of anthropology (particularly studies on kinship) and legal history. The German legal historian Otto von Gierke is usually regarded as one of the founding figures in the study of corporate bodies.[1] Other pioneering contributions were made by the British legal historians Frederic William Maitland, John Neville Figgis, and Harold Laski, especially their surveys of the main features of corporative systems: pluralism, both

---

[*] My heartfelt thanks to all those who engaged with and commented on this work at the series of conferences «Methoden der Rechtsgeschichte», organised by the Max-Planck-Institut für Rechtsgeschichte und Rechtstheorie, as well as at the Helsinki Legal History Seminar Series at the Faculty of Law, University of Helsinki. Tamar Herzog kindly reviewed an earlier draft of this text, providing invaluable critiques that played a pivotal role in its development. Edward Jones Corredera, Pablo Sánchez León, Jorge Díaz Ceballos, and Max Deardorff also offered exceptionally thoughtful suggestions, greatly enriching the work. I am profoundly grateful for their insightful feedback.

1 Otto von Gierke, *Das deutsche Genossenschaftsrecht*. Volume 3. *Die Staats- und Korporationslehre des Alterthums und des Mittelalters und ihre Aufnahme in Deutschland* (Berlin: Weidmannsche Buchhandlung, 1881) and *Das deutsche Genossenschaftsrecht*; Volume 4. *Die Staats- und Korporationslehre der Neuzeit*. (Berlin: Weidmannsche Buchhandlung, 1913).

Pedro Cardim • Universidade Nova de Lisboa

Supplicant Empires, ed. by Edward Jones Corredera, Habsburg Worlds, 8 (Turnhout: Brepols, 2025), pp. 37–62

BREPOLS ❦ PUBLISHERS   10.1484/M.HW-EB.5.145063

political and normative.[2] Thereafter, the contribution of early twentieth-century German sociology became particularly influential, especially the seminal work of Ferdinand Tönnies. As is well known, Tönnies contrasted the nature of *Gemeinschaft* with another type of social formation, which he termed *Gesellschaft*.[3] Max Weber also devoted significant attention to corporations and their impact on collective life and governance.[4] Despite their controversial ideological stances, mid-twentieth-century historians Otto Hintze and Otto Brunner should also be mentioned as significant contributors to the research on the corporate framework of premodern European society.[5] Their studies called attention to the role of communal order and its capacity to shape politics and power relations. Chronologically, they regarded the Middle Ages as the apex of the corporate structure in Western Europe.

More recently, beginning in the 1980s, several legal historians from Italy, Spain, and Portugal (Paolo Grossi, Bartolomé Clavero, António Hespanha, Pierangelo Schiera, Paolo Prodi, Pietro Costa, Angela De Benedictis), along with a number of French medievalists and early modernists (Jacques Le Goff and Robert Descimon, to name just a few), also displayed a marked interest in the study of the corporate structure of Western European society and culture. Focusing on Southwestern Europe, they explored the corporate order and its many political dimensions from the perspective of what was then called "new legal history". As noted, one distinctive feature of this research strand was its reappraisal of the chronology of the corporate structure. Grossi, Clavero, and Hespanha, along with other legal historians of their generation, argued that, long after the Middle Ages and until the nineteenth-century creation of the state, the bulk of the political order continued to rely on corporate regulation.[6]

---

2 Frederick William Maitland, 'The Crown as Corporation', *The Law Quarterly Review* XVII (1901), pp. 131-46 and *The Constitutional History of England* (Cambridge: Cambridge University Press, 1909); John Neville Figgis, *Studies of Political Thought from Gerson to Grotius, 1414–1625* (London: Birkbeck Lectures, 1900); Harold Laski, *The Foundations of Sovereignty, and other essays.* (New York: Harcourt, Brace and Company, 1921).

3 Ferdinand Tönnies, *Gemeinschaft und Gesellschaft Untertitel: Abhandlung des Communismus und des Socialismus als empirischer Culturformen* (Leipzig: Fues, 1887).

4 Max Weber, *The Protestant Ethic and the Spirit of Capitalism: and Other Writings* (London: Penguin, 2002).

5 Otto Hintze, *The Historical Essays of Otto Hintze*, ed. *Felix Gilbert* (Oxford: Oxford University Press, 1975); Otto Brunner, *Land und Herrschaft: Grundfragen der territorialen Verfassungsgeschichte Südostdeutschlands im Mittelalter* (Baden-bei-Wien: Veröffentlichungen des Instituts für Geschichtsforschung und Archivwissenschaft in Wien, 1939).

6 Paolo Grossi, 'Un Diritto senza Stato (La nozione di autonomia come fondamento della costituzione giuridica medievale)', *Quaderni Fiorentini per la Storia del Pensiero Giuridico* 25 (1996), pp. 267-84; Bartolomé Clavero, 'Religión y Derecho. Mentalidades y Paradigmas', *Historia, Instituciones, Documentos*, 11 (1985), pp. 1-26; António Manuel Hespanha, *Poder e instituições na Europa do Antigo Regime* (Lisbon: Fundação Calouste Gulbenkian, 1984);

Within their studies, corporations were systematically understood as social bodies in which hierarchy, power, discipline, obedience, and belonging were closely interwoven. Taken together, their studies contributed to a profound renewal of the history of early modern European politics and power, shaping the scholarly agenda for years to come.

Clearly, the corporate character of early modern Western European societies is a longstanding subject of research. This essay seeks to highlight the contribution of one of the previously mentioned strands of scholarship: the study of corporations in Spain and Portugal. The reading of corporate logic carried out by the aforementioned Spanish, Italian, and Portuguese historians ultimately contributed to producing a specific way of understanding the political system of early modern Iberia. The key element of this scholarship is the close connection it established between corporations, political and normative pluralism, and jurisdictional culture. In addition, this research argued that, whereas in many regions corporations were gradually replaced by other power structures at the end of the medieval period, the Iberian Peninsula followed a distinct path. Rather than disappearing, corporations in Iberia either remained intact or were even strengthened, persisting well into the nineteenth century. These features came to be seen as specific characteristics of Iberian polities, almost as if they represented a unique trait of Spain and Portugal.

The aim of this essay is to examine the body of research developed by legal historians specializing in early modern Spain and Portugal. Its primary purpose is to assess how they forged this particular understanding of early modern Iberian politics. The essay begins by highlighting the main features of corporations in late medieval and early modern Iberia. It then analyses pluralism, both normative and political, as a key component within this corporate form of social organisation. In addition, it examines the close connection between corporate logic and the role of jurisdiction in policymaking across the Iberian monarchies. The third part of the essay reflects on the limits of corporatism as a framework for understanding the order upon which premodern Iberia rested. Even while pointing out some of the limitations of this approach, this essay ultimately advocates for the continuing importance of this analytical framework for understanding early modern politics and social order.

The present author's work has been – and remains – strongly shaped by this stream of research and its achievements. Nonetheless, this does not preclude him from acknowledging the limitations of this approach to understanding early modern Iberian politics.

Piedro Costa, *Lo Stato Immaginario. Metafore e Paradigmi nella cultura Giuridica Italiana fra Ottocento e Novecento* (Milan: Giuffrè, 1986); Jean-Frédéric Schaub, 'La Penisola Iberica nei secoli XVI e XVII: la questione dello Stato', *Studi Storici* 36:1 (1995), pp. 9-49.

The Corporate Structure of Social Order

In what ways has the aforementioned scholarship conceptualised the social and political roles of corporations across the Iberian world?

Firstly, it argued that, long after the medieval period, the basic unit of social life was not the individual but rather a series of collective bodies (*corpora*). In other words, it described a world where social interaction was rooted in a variety of corporate and associational bodies, bound together for a common purpose. Each of these bodies had the capacity to generate and uphold order within its own particular sphere. In addition to sharing a set of rules and norms, the autonomy of the corpora was also manifest in their capacity to settle internal disputes, levy dues, and establish standards of inclusion and exclusion.[7]

Most of these dimensions were present in medieval and early modern Western Europe. The Iberian context is not an exceptional case. However, within it, the corporate structure arguably had a more lasting influence. Over a very long period, the basic unit of Iberian society was not the individual human being but social bodies such as the family, the seigneurial domains of the Church and the nobility, urban institutions, artisan guilds and mercantile and financial corporations.[8]

Scholarship devoted to the widespread presence of corporate structures in Spain and Portugal also foregrounded their connection with kinship. Such studies underscored the fact that, during the late medieval and early modern periods, family units were regarded as natural and organic forms of collective life. Domestic groups were seen as corporations resulting from the natural impulse of human beings to live alongside others. The ultimate goal of such an impulse was to foster collaboration towards a shared purpose. The expression most frequently employed to describe this purpose or telos of collective life, was *bonus communis* (common good).[9]

According to this understanding of kinship, the family order was believed to be based on a natural 'constitution'. Determined by nature, it

---

7 Pietro Costa, *Iurisdictio. Semantica del potere politico nella pubblicistica medievale* (Milan: Giuffrè, 1969), pp. 1100-1433; Paolo Grossi, 'Un Diritto senza Stato (La nozione di autonomia come fondamento della costituzione giuridica medievale', *Quaderni Fiorentini per la Storia del Pensiero Giuridico* 25 (1996), pp. 267-84; Bartolomé Clavero, *Antidora. Antropologia Catolica de la Economia Moderna* (Milan: Giuffrè Editore, 1991); António Manuel Hespanha, 'Pré-compréhension et savoir historique. La crise du modèle étatiste et les nouveaux contours de l'histoire du pouvoir', *Rättshistorika Studier* XIX (1939), pp. 49-67.

8 Bartolomé Clavero, "Almas y cuerpos. Sujetos del Derecho en la Edad Moderna", *Studi in Memoria di Giovanni Tarello*. Volume 1 (Milan: Giuffrè, 1990), pp. 153-71; Ruth MacKay, *"Lazy Improvident People": Myth and Reality in the Writing of Spanish History* (Ithaca: Cornell University Press, 2006).

9 Clavero, 'Religión y derecho'; Daniela Frigo, *Il padre di famiglia. Governo della casa e governo civile nella tradizione dell' "economica" tra Cinque e Seicento* (Rome: Bulzoni, 1985).

was often regarded as ahistorical and essentially immutable. Authorities constantly stressed that individuals could not modify this institution, since they had not created it. Catholic theologians and jurists argued that the domestic order was God's will. Such a natural order thus carried strong religious overtones, making it even less malleable to human intervention.[10] The influence of the family as a corporate entity remained relatively intact in Iberia long after the medieval period, whereas in other parts of Europe, the state increasingly intervened in the norms governing the domestic sphere.

In addition to the Catholic component, studies on the corporate structure of Portugal and the Spanish Monarchy also underscored another fundamental feature of the domestic order: families were regarded as autonomous bodies with a particularly wide scope of action. The domestic unit covered and regulated the interactions among a broad group of individuals, including consanguineous kin, servants, and enslaved women and men. Families were also crucial identity markers for their members. A woman or a man was fundamentally identified by position within the kinship body, rather than by individual identity. The same applied to domestic servants and enslaved persons. Family units were therefore particularly influential for understanding belonging and identity, both individual and collective. Ultimately, the status of a person was largely determined by the domestic body into which they were born or entered, whether willingly or not (as in the case of enslaved persons). It was a corporate identity, with significant legal implications.[11]

As stated, families were regarded as corpora entitled to self-government and capable of upholding internal order.[12] Scholarship on the corporate character of Iberian social life, however, has also stressed that within the family unit, the primary mode of regulation was domestic discipline. This disciplinary force was a complex mix of moral norms emanating from the household hierarchy. The main authority within the household, the *pater familias*, exercised a power that was moral and organic rather than legal because it emanated from the allegedly natural constitution, itself regarded as the result of God's will. Late medieval and early modern theologians and jurists often stressed that, within the household,

---

10 Clavero, "Almas y cuerpos"; Bartolomé Clavero, *'Dictum beati. A proposito della cultura del lignaggio'*, *Quaderni storici* 86:2 (1994), pp. 335-63; António Manuel Hespanha, 'Carne de uma só carne: para uma compreensão dos fundamentos histórico-antropológicos da família na época moderna' *Análise Social* 28 (1993), pp. 951-73; António Manuel Hespanha, 'O Estatuto Jurídico da Mulher na Época da Expansão', *Oceanos* 21 (1995), pp. 8-16; Charlotte de Castelnau-L'Estoile, *Un catholicisme colonial. Le mariage des Indiens et des esclaves au Brésil, XVIᵉ-XVIIIᵉ siècle* (Paris: PUF, 2019).

11 Clavero, *Antidora*.

12 Romina Zamora, *Casa poblada y buen gobierno: oeconomía católica y servicio personal en San Miguel de Tucumán, siglo XVIII* (Buenos Aires: Prometeo, 2017).

no authority was created ('constituted') by human beings; there was no room for human voluntarism.[13]

In this system, the *pater familias* was regarded as the only emancipated member of the household, meaning he alone had the legal capacity to make independent decisions. All other members were considered unemancipated and subject to his authority. The *pater familias* governed the household with a specific form of authority, known as *patria potestas*. This authority encompassed jurisdiction, including the proclamation of law (*iuris dictio*), the definition of norms, and their application. It also involved the resolution of conflicts.

Another deeply ingrained belief in late medieval Iberia, which persisted into the early modern period, was that love was the true foundation of family life. Not exactly romantic love or affection linked to sexual desire, but Christian love, *charitas*, the voluntary giving of help and doing good to others.[14] This notion of love emerged from a longstanding discourse on communal life, rooted in the Christian understanding of salvation as a collective enterprise achievable through the practice of charity. As stated, the idea of justice was not central to family affairs. Love, not justice, was the main driving force within the domestic sphere, mostly because in its purest form there should be no conflicting interests within the family. Ownership of goods within the domestic sphere, for example, was intended to be primarily collective and to avoid conflicts of interest.

This discourse emphasised the primacy of the 'common good' over particular interests and fostered a persistent suspicion of individual material gain.[15] This represents a significant divergence from other European regions, where a growing emphasis on individual self-interest over collective well-being emerged as the primary driving force shaping society. In Iberia, by contrast, the emphasis on the 'common good' fostered a strongly group-oriented (and anti-individualistic) ethos, shaping specific attitudes

---

13 Bartolomé Clavero, *Usura. Del uso económico de la religión en la história* (Madrid: Tecnos, 1984); Clavero, '*Dictum beati*'; António Manuel Hespanha, *As Vésperas do Leviathan. Instituições e Poder Político. Portugal, Século XVII* (Coimbra: Almedina, 1995).

14 António Manuel Hespanha and Antonio Serrano, "La senda amorosa del derecho. *Amor y iustitia* en el discurso jurídico moderno", in *Las Pasiones del Jurista. Amor, memoria, melancolia, imaginación*. Edited by Carlos Petit (Madrid: Centro de Estudios Constitucionales, 1997), pp. 23-73; Emanuele Conte, 'Passioni', *Rechtshistorisches Journal* 17 (1998), pp. 53-59.

15 Paolo Grossi, '*Un altro modo di possederi*'. *L'emersione di forme alternative di proprietà alla coscienza giuridica postunitaria* (Milan: Giuffrè, 1977); Paolo Grossi, *Il Dominio e le cose. Percezioni Medievali e Moderne dei Diritti Reali* (Milan: Giuffrè, 1992); Carlos Petit, '*Mercatvra y ius Mercatorvm*. Materiales para una Antropología del Comerciante premoderno', in *Del Ius Mercatorum al Derecho Mercantil*. Edited by Carlos Petit (Madrid: Marcial Pons, 1997), pp. 15-70.

towards the use of family patrimony.[16] As legal historian Pietro Costa observed, for a very long time the individual remained barely detachable from the corporate community to which he belonged, and his liberty or immunity was rarely considered as separate from the pursuit of the common good.[17]

The family's corporate character manifested itself in two important ways. First, in its alleged self-sufficiency in settling disputes. The domestic sphere was said to have its own mechanisms for dispute resolution, based on discipline and paternal authority. As noted, the *pater familias* exercised both the authority to declare the law (*iuris dictio*) and to enforce it, which involved resolving conflicts. Second, the family was widely perceived as crucial in drawing the line between private and public spheres.[18] The public sphere referred to interactions occurring outside the bounds of the family, and thus beyond the domain of domestic regulation. Private affairs, by contrast, took place within the wide sphere of the family. Domestic discipline governed the internal life of the household, whereas public life was primarily regulated by justice, its norms (the law), its agents (the jurists), and its institutions (judicial courts).

However, family discipline also shaped collective life beyond the household, for two main reasons. First, because – as stated – the scope of the family in premodern European societies was much wider than today. Second, because the domestic unit and its corporate structure came to serve as a model for organising other, more complex forms of collective life. As such, it was eventually adopted across many spheres, both at the level of basic social interaction and within large political formations.[19] The household, the domestic economy, and the family paradigm all served as matrices for the early modern political framework.[20]

This corporate culture thus shaped the principal forms of collective life, including municipal powers, craft guilds, mercantile and financial guild-like associations (*consulados*), and even the self-perception and operations of estates such as the nobility and the clergy. Religious entities such as convents, chantries, and cathedral chapters were also based on corporate foundations. Royal power itself adopted a corporate configuration. As a

---

16 Emanuele Conte, 'Cose, persone, obbligazioni, consuetudini. Piccole osservazioni su grandi temi', in *Le sol et l'immeuble. Les formes dissociées de propriété immobilière dans les villes de France et d'Italie (XIIe-XIXe siècle). Actes de la table ronde de Lyon* (Rome: École Française de Rome, 1995), pp. 27-39.

17 Pietro Costa, 'Diritti', in *Lo Stato Moderno in Europa. Istituzioni e diritto.* Edited by Maurizio Fioravanti (Bari: Laterza, 2002), pp. 37-58; Bartolomé Clavero, *Tantas personas como estados: por una antropología política de la historia europea* (Madrid: Tecnos, 1986).

18 Clavero, "Almas y Cuerpos".

19 Xavier Gil Pujol, '"The Good Law of a Vassal". Fidelity, Obedience and Obligation in Habsburg Spain', *Revista Internacional de Estudios Vascos* 5 (2009), pp 83-106.

20 Clavero, "Almas y Cuerpos".

result, larger polities – such as the Western European kingdoms – were frequently portrayed as assemblages of corpora, the Crown itself being one of them. Significantly, royal rule was commonly regarded as an extension of *patria potestas*, implying that royal authority should be more distributive than unilaterally authoritative. No less important, the influence of the family and its hierarchical order on Iberian society was so strong that it helped naturalise two of its fundamental features: highly asymmetric power relations and the strikingly uneven distribution of wealth. As for Catholic Church authorities, they were instrumental in consolidating this corporate framework. Studies on the ecclesiastical milieu have demonstrated the importance of canon law and ecclesiastical political practices in the formation – and perpetuation – of family corporate bodies in general.[21]

Scholars working on the corporate structure of early modern Spain and Portugal have particularly underscored the Catholic element in writings on collective order and justice.[22] The very concept of *res publica* denoted a community ordered by a notion of *iustitia*, an ideal of justice with distinct religious overtones.[23] This assumption was reinforced from the mid-sixteenth century onwards. Neo-Scholastic doctrines underscored the notion of the 'common good', wherein religious morality was closely interwoven with communitarian ideals of justice. In addition, they also stressed the imperative of elevating collective well-being over individual interests.[24] The king himself was systematically portrayed as an intrinsic part of a collective based on cooperation and Catholic understandings of justice: a social body conceived not as a collection of competitive individuals, but as an ensemble of collaborative human beings, organised into corporate entities specifically designed to foster the common good.

Pluralism and Jurisdictional Culture

Parallel to emphasizing that premodern Spain and Portugal were based on corpora, scholarship on corporate bodies has also drawn attention to another striking feature: pluralism, both normative and political. A great number of historians working in this field have underscored that the

---

21 Clavero, 'Religión y Derecho'.
22 Bartolomé Clavero, "La Monarquía, el Derecho y la Justicia", in *Las Jurisdicciones*. Edited by Enrique Martínez Ruiz and Magdalena de Pazzis Pi (Madrid: Actas Editorial, 1996), pp. 15-38.
23 Carlos Petit, 'Iustitia y *Yudicium* en el reino de Toledo. Un estudio de Teología Jurídica Visigoda', in *La Giustizia nell'alto medioevo (secoli V-VIII)* (Spoleto: CISAM, 1995), pp. 843-932.
24 Xavier Gil Pujol, "Spain and Portugal", in *European Political Thought, 1450-1700. Religion, Law and Philosophy*. Edited by H. A. Lloyd, G. Burgess, S. Hodson (New Haven: Yale University Press, 2007), pp. 416-56.

corporate framework usually went hand in hand with a fundamentally plural system.[25] Pluralism did not merely refer to each corporation having its own distinct forms of government; it also pointed to a broader normative landscape that was inherently diverse and multifaceted.

Royal legislation was thus one among many overlapping forms of regulation, not all of which were legal in nature. In Iberia, the king's law coexisted with, and was articulated alongside, other sources of normativity, such as Roman Law, the *ius commune*, a wide range of consuetudinary norms, Christian morals, and domestic discipline.[26] In addition, the king also acknowledged – and relied upon – the norms issued by seigneurial lords, the various sectors of the Church, urban centres, artisan guilds, and mercantile-financial corporations.[27] Each one of these social bodies issued its own particular norms and regulated collective life within its respective sphere.

It is important to note, however, that this normative plurality existed within the same legal system. Pluralism was inherent to what was then understood as law. Across most jurisdictions, the laws in force were largely consistent and drew from shared sources such as customary law, Roman law, royal edicts, municipal codes, and canon law, among others. Possessing the authority to enforce the law within a particular group did not necessarily entail applying an entirely distinct legal framework. Rather, it reflected a variation in who held the authority to implement the law and, perhaps more significantly, in how the law was interpreted and applied within specific contexts.

The political implications of this conception of normative plurality are manifold. As stated, the king not only recognised the plurality of entities with normative capacity; he also depended on it to maintain societal organisation. This fact generated a political culture rooted in the

25 Bartolomé Clavero, *Temas de Historia del Derecho. Derecho común* (Sevilla: Publicaciones de la Universidad de Sevilla, 1979); Clavero, "Almas y Cuerpos"; António Manuel Hespanha, 'Da *Iustitia* à *Disciplina*. Textos, poder e política penal no Antigo Regime', in *Estudos em Homenagem ao Prof. Eduardo Correia*. (Faculdade de Direito da Universidade de Coimbra. Coimbra: Imprensa da Universidade, 1998); António Manuel Hespanha, 'Les autres raisons de la politique. L'économie de la grâce', in *Recherche sur l'histoire de l'État dans le monde ibérique (15ᵉ-20ᵉ siècle)*, edited by Jean Frédéric Schaub (Paris: Presses de l'École Normale Supérieure, 1993), pp. 67-86.
26 Hespanha, *As Vésperas do Leviathan*.
27 José Ignacio Fortea Pérez, 'Principios de gobierno urbano en la Castilla del siglo XVI', in *Las Jurisdicciones*, pp. 261-308; N. G. Monteiro, 'Os Poderes Locais no Antigo Regime'. In *História dos Municípios e do Poder Local (Dos finais da Idade Média à União Europeia)*. Edited by C. Oliveira. (Lisbon: Círculo de Leitores, 1996), pp. 17-175; Xavier Gil Pujol, 'Ciudadanía, patria y humanismo cívico en el Aragón foral: Juan Costa'. *Manuscrits*, 19 (2001), pp. 81-101 and Xavier Gil Pujol, "City, Communication and Concord in Renaissance Spain and Spanish-America", in *Athenian Legacies. European Debates on Citizenship*. Edited by P. Kitromilides (Florence: Leo S. Olschki, 2014), pp. 195-221.

fundamental interdependence between the monarch and the various social entities. This is precisely the reason why corporate authorities developed interdependent relationships among the coexisting normative spheres. Although largely sanctioned by the Crown and based on well-defined models, these entities subsequently operated with a significant degree of autonomy.

The concept of 'jurisdiction', in the sense that it was understood in early modern Spanish and Portuguese legal doctrine, was particularly apt for this corporative landscape and its peculiar understanding of order. *Iurisdictio* signalled an operation aimed at extrapolating from nature the norms that governed the world. As legal historian Pietro Costa put it long ago, magistrates were expected to explain an already existing natural order, and by *iuris dictio* – by dictating the law – they prescribed how it should be applied to the many concrete and particular circumstances.[28] Order was to be revealed and preserved by human beings, not created or transformed. By dictating an already existing norm, contemporary jurists reinforced the idea that the main objective of authority was to realize and maintain a preexisting natural order, not to change it.[29]

Paolo Prodi, Bartolomé Clavero, and António Hespanha, among many others, have also stressed that early modern jurists, alongside their doctrinal commitment to this corporate notion of law, were practitioners engaged in interpreting and shaping the world around them. As Tamar Herzog recently put it, jurists were deeply involved with social issues and everyday life: they constructed the law of persons, the meaning of things, and the purpose of action, both individual and collective.[30] This jurisdictional way of understanding the world permeated all fields of knowledge and social action, and eventually shaped the exercise of government. Justice thus became the principal foundation of all governance, and the main task of authorities was to exercise power by declaring and by applying the law.[31]

---

28 Pietro Costa, *Iurisdictio. Semantica del potere politico nella pubblicistica medievale, 1100-1433* (Milan: Giuffrè, 1969).

29 Jesús Vallejo, 'Power Hierarchies in Medieval Juridical Thought. An Essay in Reinterpretation', *Ius Commune. Zeitschrift für Europäische Rechtsgeschichte*, 29 (1992), pp. 1-29; Carlos Petit & Jesús Vallejo, 'La categoria giuridica nella cultura europea del Medioevo', in *Il Medioevo, secoli V-XV*, Volume 3 of *Storia d'Europa*. Edited by Gherardo Ortalli (Torino: Einaudi, 1994), pp. 721-60; Jesús Vallejo, "Derecho como cultura. Equidad y orden desde la óptica del ius commune", in *Historia de la Propiedad. Patrimonio Cultural*. Edited by Salustiano de Dios et al. (Madrid: SECR, 2003), pp. 55-70.

30 Tamar Herzog, "A Civil Law for a Religious Society", in *The Cambridge History of Latin American Law in perspective*. Edited by Thomas Duve & Tamar Herzog (Cambridge: Cambridge University Press, 2024); Tamar Herzog, 'The Uses and Abuses of Legal Pluralism: A View from the Sideline', *Law and History Review* 42:2 (2024), pp. 211-22.

31 I. A. A Thompson, 'Castile', in *Absolutism in Seventeenth Century Europe*. Edited by John Miller (London: Macmillan, 1990), pp. 69-98; Carlos Garriga, *Las Audiencias y*

This understanding of 'jurisdiction' – as *iurisdictio* – proved fundamental in establishing relations of interdependence in these pluralistic corporate societies. Most early modern Spanish and Portuguese jurists and theologians did not conceive of 'jurisdiction' as based on rigid, unilateral, and exclusive supremacy. On the contrary, intrinsic to their understanding of 'jurisdiction' was the idea that power was 'naturally' distributed among the different members of the body politic, each of whom possessed a certain degree of autonomy and self-government.[32] *Iurisdictio* thus served as the means of linking the various spheres of power. Instead of establishing strictly hierarchical relations of absolute superiority, jurisdiction articulated these bodies in a more balanced manner.

Rather than being an anomaly, political and normative pluralism was thus a fundamental feature of the Iberian legal system.[33] Upholding justice essentially meant giving each individual their due. In this framework, justice was equated with restoring the prevailing status quo and maintaining the established social and legal order.

The legal thinking just described was intrinsic to the corporate character of late medieval and early modern Iberia, and Spanish and Portuguese jurists widely shared this pluralistic conception of the political system. Its prevalence explains why more voluntaristic and individualistic visions of society were not easily accepted, particularly in Catholic Southern Europe. Not surprisingly, the idea of absolute rule clashed deeply with this pluralistic way of understanding normativity and power. Significantly, various late eighteenth-century jurists opposing royal authoritarianism argued that the best antidote to despotism was a strong corporate and pluralistic order, sanctioned by Catholicism.[34]

---

las *Chancillerías Castellanas (1371-1525). Historia Política, Régimen Jurídico y Práctica Institucional* (Madrid: Centro de Estudios Constitucionales, 1994); Vallejo, 'Derecho como cultura'; Mario Sbriccoli et al, *Ordo iuris. Storia e forme dell'esperienza giuridica* (Milan: Giuffrè, 2003); Carlos Garriga, 'Sobre el gobierno de Cataluña bajo el régimen de la Nueva Planta. Ensayo historiográfico', *Anuario de Historia del Derecho Español* 80 (2010), pp. 716-65.

32 I. A. A Thompson, "Absolutism, Legalism and the Law in Castile, 1500-1700", in Ronald G. Asch und Heinz Duchhardt eds., *Der Absolutismus – ein Mythos? Strukturwandel monarchischer Herrschaft in West- und Mitteleuropa (c. 1550-1700)* (Cologne: Böhlau, 1996), pp. 185–228; Gil Pujol, "City, Communication and Concord".

33 Costa, *Iurisdictio*; Luca Mannori & Bernardo Sordi, *Storia del diritto amministrativo* (Rome-Bari: Laterza, 2001).

34 José María Portillo, 'De la Monarquía Católica a la Nación de los Católicos', *Historia y Política* 17 (2007), pp. 17-35.

Political pluralism, Empire, and Colonial Rule

As legal history research into corporate structures progressed during the 1980s and 1990s, studies on the composite nature of early modern polities similarly gained momentum. Historians such as Helmut Koenigsberger, John H. Elliott, and Conrad Russell, among others, explored the pluralistic and corporate structure of early modern Western European political formations.[35] As the outcome of their ground-breaking work, European territorial conglomerates came increasingly to be regarded as composite corporate bodies, a mosaic of territories characterised by legal pluralism and decentralisation.[36]

This understanding of territorial conglomerates aligned with legal history's emphasis on normative and political plurality. Under a common monarch, different territories were preserved as distinct entities, as monarchical rule did not necessarily impose uniformity or centralisation. This was primarily due to two factors: these conglomerates were often established through corporate forms of territorial union, and each territorial unit was organised according to the corporate culture outlined earlier.

---

35 H. G. Koenigsberger, 'Monarchies and parliaments in early modern Europe – dominium regale or dominium politicum et regale', *Theory and Society* 5 (1978), pp. 191-217; John Elliott, 'A Europe of Composite Monarchies', *Past & Present* 137 (1992), pp. 48-71; Conrad Russell, *The Fall of the British Monarchies, 1637-1642* (Oxford: Clarendon. Press, 1990).

36 John Elliott, "Monarquía compuesta y Monarquía Universal en la época de Carlos V", in *Carlos V. Europeísmo y universalidad. Vol. V – Religión, cultura y mentalidad* (Madrid: SECCFC, 2001), pp. 699-710; John Elliott, 'Introduction – Forms of Union: the British and Spanish Monarchies in the Seventeenth and Eighteenth Centuries', *Revista Internacional de Estudios Vascos* 5 (2009) pp. 13-19; John Robertson, 'The conceptual framework of Anglo-Scottish Union', *Revista Internacional de Estudios Vascos* 5 (2009), pp. 125-37; Jon Arrieta Alberdi, "Las formas de vinculación a la Monarquía y de relación entre sus reinos y coronas en la España de los Austrias", in *La Monarquía de las Naciones. Patria, nación y naturaleza en la Monarquía de España*. Edited by Bernardo José García García and Antonio Álvarez-Ossorio Alvariño (Madrid: Fundación Carlos de Amberes & Universidad Autónoma de Madrid, 2004), pp. 303-26; Jon Arrieta Alberdi, "Ubicación de los ordenamientos de los reinos de la Corona de Aragón en la Monarquía Hispánica: concepciones y supuestos varios (siglos XVI-XVIII)", in *Il Diritto Patrio tra Diritto Comune e Codificazione (secoli XVI-XIX)*. Edited by Italo Birochi & Antonello Matone (Roma: Viella, 2006), pp. 127-71; Fernando Bouza, *Felipe II y el Portugal 'dos povos'. Imágenes de esperanza y revuelta* (Valladolid: Universidad de Valladolid, 2010); Pablo Fernández Albaladejo, "Unión de almas, autonomía de cuerpos: sobre los lenguajes de unión en la Monarquía Católica", in *Modernitas. Estudios en Homenaje al Profesor Baudillo Barreiro Mallón*. Edited by Manuel García Hurtado (A Coruña: Universidade da Coruña, 2008), pp. 111-19; Xavier Gil Pujol, *La Fábrica de la Monarquía. Traza y Conservación de la Monarquía de España de los Reyes Católicos y los Austrias* (Madrid: Real Academia de la Historia, 2016); Jean Frédéric Schaub, *Portugal na Monarquia Hispânica* (Lisbon: Livros Horizonte, 2001).

Such composite polities were, in the phrase of the late António Manuel Hespanha, essentially a 'legal patchwork'.[37]

As expected, the heuristic potential of the category "early modern state" was also particularly contested by historians who gave centre stage to corporations. Instead of a highly centralised royal structure prefiguring the modern nation-state, the sixteenth and seventeenth centuries became the stage for a persistent corporate and pluralist political culture.[38]

The interpretative framework that underscored the pluralistic structure of early modern polities, developed decades ago, became widespread in the early twenty-first century. In a recent analysis of the territorial conglomerate under Spanish rule in the early modern period, Gabriel Paquette stated that 'even after their union, each of the [Spanish] kingdoms continued to exist as a distinct political unit, maintaining its peculiar identity and status. Each was marked by a vast complex of corporate bodies, from the clergy to the nobility and to merchant guilds (*consulados*), each of which zealously guarded its own bundle of rights and privileges, known as fueros'.[39]

This conception of early modern Iberian monarchies fostered several multifaceted research strands. Italian historians Luca Mannori and Bernardo Sordi, for instance, highlighted the weight of corporate mentalities in early modern administrative (and political) culture.[40] The same emphasis can be found in Pablo Fernández Albaladejo's and Carlos Garriga's works on jurisdictional culture and its enduring influence in Spanish policymaking, even into the early nineteenth-century constitutional regimes.[41]

The evolution of republicanism also came to be seen in a different light. Early modern republicanism was traditionally associated with civic humanism and the emergence of an individualistic ethos in a world

---

37 António Manuel Hespanha, 'Savants et rustiques. La violence douce de la raison juridique. *Ius commune*', *Zeitschrift für Europäische Rechtsgeschichte* 10 (1983), pp. 1-48.

38 Bartolomé Clavero, 'Tejido de sueños: la historiografía jurídica española y el problema del Estado', *Historia Contemporánea* 12 (1996), pp. 25-47; António Manuel Hespanha, 'Précompréhension et savoir historique. La crise du modèle étatiste et les nouveaux contours de l'histoire du pouvoir', *Rättshistorika Studier* 19 (1993), pp. 49-67; Angela de Benedictis, 'Reggere e governare i sudditi in età moderna. Alcune "Carte" (fonti) per scriverne una "Storia" (non teleologica)', *Le Carte e la Storia* 2 (2020), pp. 5-14.

39 Gabriel Paquette, *The European Seaborne Empires: From the Thirty Years' War to the Age of Revolutions* (New Haven: Yale University Press, 2019), p. 48.

40 Mannori and Sordi, *Storia del diritto amministrativo*.

41 Pablo Fernández Albaladejo, "El problema de la 'composite monarchy' en España", in *Identities: nations, provinces and regions (1550-1900)*. Edited by Isabel Burdiel & James Casey (Norwich: University of East Anglia, 1999), pp. 185-201; Pablo Fernández Albaladejo, "Teoría y Práctica del Poder en la Monarquía del siglo XVII", in *Actas de las Juntas del Reino de Galicia*. Volume 7 (Santiago de Compostela: Xunta de Galicia, 2003), pp. 51-79; Carlos Garriga, 'Orden jurídico en el Antiguo Régimen', *Istor. Revista de Historia Internacional* 16 (2003), pp. 13-44; Carlos Garriga, 'Sobre el gobierno de la justicia en Indias (siglos XVI-XVII)', *Revista de Historia del Derecho* (Buenos Aires) 34 (2006), pp. 67-160.

hitherto dominated by corporate forces. However, new historiographical trends have shown that in the Iberian world and beyond, corporate logic did not preclude the development of strands of republican thought. Studies on urban politics have drawn attention to the various discourses on republicanism that emerged in the early modern Spanish and Portuguese corporate monarchies, ranging from the defence of urban liberties (based on the concept of urban commonwealths as self-sufficient political and jurisdictional units) to late seventeenth-century 'aristocratic republicanism'.[42]

Studies on Iberian representative institutions have likewise demonstrated the influence of corporate structures of society on both the concept of representation and the practice of representative government.[43] In early modern Spain and Portugal, representative institutions were profoundly shaped by the prevailing corporate culture, which defined not only their structure and function, but also the representation of the political body, the conduct of estate representatives, and the decisions they enacted.[44]

Scholars have explored many other aspects of corporate life, including its influence on forms of identity. Corporations shaped the articulation of discourses and symbols, the selection of distinctive names for the collective, the production of origin myths, and the construction of shared memory.[45] Historians have increasingly focused on the narratives generated

---

42 Marteen Roy Prak, *Citizens without Nations. Urban Citizenship in Europe and the World, c. 1000-1789* (Cambridge: Cambridge University Press, 2018); Elizabeth Penry, *The People are King: The Making of an Indigenous Andean Politics* (Oxford: Oxford University Press, 2019); Manuel Herrero Sánchez ed., *Repúblicas y republicanismo en la Europa moderna (siglos XVI-XVII)* (Mexico City: Fondo de Cultura Económica, 2017).

43 Pablo Fernández Albaladejo, "La Representación Política en el Antiguo Régimen", in *El Senado en la Historia* (Madrid: Temas del Senado, 1998), pp. 51-82; José Ignacio Fortea Pérez, "Las Ciudades, las Cortes y el problema de la representación política en la Castilla Moderna", in José Ignacio Fortea Pérez ed., *Imágenes de la Diversidad. El mundo urbano en la Corona de Castilla (s. XVI-XVIII)* (Santander: Universidad de Cantabria, 1997), pp. 421-45; Xavier Gil Pujol, 'Parliamentary Life in the Crown of Aragon: Cortes, Juntas de Brazos, and other Corporate Bodies', *Journal of Early Modern History* 6 (2002), pp. 363-95; Xavier Gil Pujol, "Republican Politics in Early Modern Spain: the Castilian and Catalano-Aragonese Traditions", in *Republicanism. A Shared European Heritage, vol. I – Republicanism and Constitutionalism in Early Modern Europe*. Edited by Martin Van Gelderen & Quentin Skinner (Cambridge: Cambridge University Press, 2002), pp. 263-384; C. N. Silva, 'Cidadania e representação política no império', in *Res publica. Cidadania e representação política em Portugal*. Edited by Fernando Catroga & Pedro Tavares de Almeida (Lisbon: Assembleia da República, 2010), pp. 90-111.

44 Pedro Cardim, "As Cortes e a representação política no Antigo Regime", in Pedro Tavares de Almeida ed., *O Parlamento português, vol. 1 – Antigo Regime e Monarquia Constitucional* (Lisbon: Assembleia da República, 2023), pp. 3-48.

45 Pablo Fernández Albaladejo, "Católicos antes que ciudadanos: gestación de una 'Política Española' en los comienzos de la Edad Moderna", in José Ignacio Fortea Pérez ed., *Imágenes de la Diversidad. El mundo urbano en la Corona de Castilla (s. XVI-XVIII)*. (Santander: Universidad de Cantabria, 1997), pp. 103-27; Albaladejo, "Unión de almas, autonomía de cuerpos"; Antonio Feros, *Speaking of Spain. The Evolution of Race and Nation in the Hispanic*

by corporate communities about their own origins and trajectories.[46] They have shown that identities were plural and multi-layered, and have explored both the frequently tense interplay between different forms of corporate belonging and the historical trajectories of entities labelled as 'kingdoms', 'crowns', and 'monarchies'.[47]

The long-lasting persistence of corporate culture is also visible in recent research on eighteenth-century Iberia. Some studies have demonstrated that the growing acceptance of 'self-interest' as a legitimate driving force was not incompatible with a world based on corporate structures.[48] Others have stressed that Enlightenment critiques of corporations coexisted with a strong attachment to corporate notions of social interaction.[49]

Moreover, several surveys have shown that, despite the profound changes unleashed by the French Revolution, many fundamental aspects of corporate structures remained embedded in nineteenth-century liberal constitutions.[50] The same applies to the enduring Catholic overtones of constitutional thinking in nineteenth-century Iberia. As Jean-Frédéric

---

World (Cambridge: Harvard University Press, 2017); I. A. A. Thompson, "Castile, Spain and the Monarchy: the Political Community from 'Patria Natural' to 'Patria Nacional'", in Richard Kagan & Geoffrey Parker eds., Spain, Europe and the Atlantic World. Essays in Honour of John H. Elliott. (Cambridge: Cambridge University Press, 1995), pp. 125-59; I. A. A. Thompson, "La Monarquía de España: la invención de un concepto", in Francisco Javier Guillamón Álvarez et al. eds., Entre Clío y Casandra. Poder y Sociedad en la Monarquía Hispánica durante la Edad Moderna. (Murcia: Universidad de Murcia, 2005), pp. 31-56.

46 Tamar Herzog, Defining Nations. Immigrants and Citizens in Early Modern Spain and Spanish America. (New Haven: Yale University Press, 2003).

47 Albaladejo, 'Católicos antes que ciudadanos: gestación de una "Política Española", pp. 103-27; Albaladejo, "El problema de la 'composite monarchy'"; Xavier Gil Pujol, "Un rey, una fe, muchas naciones. Patria y nación en la España de los siglos XVI y XVII", in La Monarquía de las Naciones. Patria, nación y naturaleza en la Monarquía de España. Edited by Bernardo José García García y Antonio Álvarez-Ossorio Alvariño (Madrid: Fundación Carlos de Amberes & Madrid: Universidad Autónoma de Madrid, 2004), pp. 39-76.

48 Julen Viejo Yharrassarry, Amor Propio y Sociedad Comercial en el Siglo XVIII Hispano. (Bilbao: Universidad del País Vasco, 2018).

49 Edward Jones Corredera, The Diplomatic Enlightenment: Spain, Europe, and the Age of Speculation (Leiden: Brill, 2021).

50 Maurizio Fioravanti, Appunti di Storia delle Costituzioni moderne. Le libertà fondamentali (Turin: G. Giappichelli Editore, 1995); Maurizio Fioravanti, 'Stato e costituzione'. In Maurizio Fioravanti ed., Lo Stato Moderno in Europa. Istituzioni e diritto (Bari: Laterza, 2002), pp. 3-36; Bartolomé Clavero, Happy Constitution. Cultura y lengua Constitucionales (Madrid: Trotta, 1997); José María Portillo, 'El poder constituyente en el primer constitucionalismo hispano', Jahrbuch für Geschichte Lateinamerikas – Anuario de Historia de América Latina 55 (2018), pp. 1-26; Carlos Garriga & Marta Lorente, "Prólogo. Nuestro Cádiz, diez años después", in Carlos Garriga & Marta Lorente eds., Cádiz, 1812. La Constitución jurisdiccional. (Madrid: Centro de Estudios Constitucionales, 2007), pp. 15-40; José María Portillo & António Manuel Hespanha, "Portugal and Spain under the Newly Established Liberal Regimes", in The Iberian World, 1450-1820. Edited by Fernando Bouza, Pedro Cardim & Antonio Feros (London: Routledge, 2019), pp. 656-71.

Schaub observed, in many respects the Ancien Régime survived the Liberal revolutions, a fact that highlights the persistence of traditional institutions within so-called modern societies based on liberal constitutionalism.[51]

In addition to illuminating many aspects of European territorial conglomerates, studies on the varieties of early modern corporate structures also enabled a deeper understanding of the various dimensions of the Iberian seaborne empires.

Several studies have shown that the corporate framework was also extended to the colonial context. Spanish authorities implemented the same corporate and pluralist legal and political frameworks across their colonial societies, notably in the Americas. One major consequence was a form of domination characterised by the incorporation of Indigenous peoples into the colonial enterprise. It thus became necessary to create a space for the Indigenous peoples within the political and legal structures of the new colonial society. Jurisdictional frameworks were essential for constructing the status of Indigenous subjects, establishing the structures within which they manoeuvred. The Christianised 'Indians' were undoubtedly included, but in a corporate fashion, with their legal-political autonomy often curtailed, for instance through the tutelage system. In this sense, Spanish colonization of the Americas was an 'eminently legal operation', in the words of Carlos Garriga.[52]

Similarly, António Hespanha's work on the Portuguese colonial empire in Asia, and François-Xavier Guerra's studies on late colonial Spanish America highlight the heuristic potential of this understanding of the transfer of Iberian corporate logic to colonial settings. Although often forcibly imposed and significantly transformed – first and foremost, by the local populations themselves – the corporate matrix remained a powerful framework for shaping collective life.[53]

---

51 Jean Frédéric Schaub, 'Le Temps et l'État: vers un nouveau régime historiographique de l'Ancien Régime Français', *Quaderni Fiorentini per la Storia del Pensiero Giuridico* 25 (1966), pp. 127-81.

52 Carlos Garriga, "¿Cómo escribir una historia descolonizada del derecho en América Latina?", in Jesús Vallejo Fernández de la Reguera and Sebastián Martín Martín eds., *En Antidora. Homenaje a Bartolomé Clavero* (Cizur: Thomson Reuters Aranzadi, 2019); Luigi Nuzzo, 'Law, Religion and Power: texts and discourse of conquest', in Ignacio de la Rasilla & Ayesha Shahid eds., *International Law and Islam. Historical Explorations* (Leiden: Brill, 2019), pp. 199-227.

53 António Manuel Hespanha, "A constituição do Império português. Revisão de alguns enviesamentos correntes", in João Fragoso, Maria Fernanda Bicalho & Maria de Fátima Gouvêa eds., *O Antigo Regime nos Trópicos. A dinâmica Imperial Portuguesa (séculos XVI-XVIII)* (Rio de Janeiro: Civilização Brasileira, 2001), pp. 163-88; António Manuel Hespanha, *Imbecillitas. As bem-aventuranças da inferioridade nas sociedades do Antigo Regime* (São Paulo: Annablume, 2010); François-Xavier Guerra, 'Identidad y soberanía: una relación compleja', in *Las Revoluciones Hispánicas: Independencias Americanas y Liberalismo*

The contribution of legal history to reshaping the way early modern Iberian empires were understood was not limited to the research stream described so far. Another strand of legal history also played a prominent role in this re-evaluation: the work of Lauren Benton, which, significantly enough, likewise emphasised the central role of jurisdiction in political dynamics.[54] Since the late 1980s, Benton became increasingly interested in examining jurisdictional exchanges, in particular their place in the process of imperial formation. Benton's interpretation centred on the contact of multiple legal frameworks, viewing jurisdictional interactions as the stage for vital power struggles between those seeking to enforce a particular vision of rule and those expected to adhere to it. It was precisely in this context that Benton coined the term 'jurisdictional politics'.

While the term 'jurisdiction' is widely present in her work, Benton's concept clearly represents a distinct approach. The primary distinction lies in the fact that, for Benton, pluralism primarily refers to the contact, interaction, and conflict between different legalities. In contrast, the legal historians discussed above regarded pluralism as an intrinsic feature of a single legal system: that which prevailed in early modern Iberia.

When studying European empires, Benton gave priority to contacts between disparate legalities. In so doing, she decentred not only the study of top-down processes of rule, but also the analysis of how rule was established, thus highlighting the ability of all social actors to engage in jurisdictional interactions, particularly those of Amerindian, African, or Asian descent. As a result, Benton's studies made more visible not just individual and group agency, but also the hybrid character of colonial rule.[55]

Influenced by Benton's work, an increasing number of legal historical studies have examined Western European colonial empires, highlighting the often conflictual process through which actors from diverse backgrounds brought their normative regimes into contact. Because it foregrounded encounters at the ground level, this research strand incorporated an element of cross-cultural analysis that was usually absent from most of

---

Español. Edited by François-Xavier Guerra (Madrid: Editorial Complutense, 1995), pp. 207-39; François-Xavier Guerra, 'L'État et les communautés: comment inventer un empire?', *Nuevo Mundo Mundos Nuevos* (2005) (Online); Teresa Vergara, "Piedad e interés económico: la cofradía de Crispín y Crispiniano de los zapateros indígenas de Lima (1632-1637)", in Alicia Mayer & José de la Puente eds., *Iglesia y Sociedad en la Nueva España y el Perú* (Lima: Pontificia Universidad Católica del Perú-Instituto Riva-Agüero, 2015), pp. 151-71.

54 Lauren Benton, 'Colonial Law and Cultural Difference: Jurisdictional Politics and the Formation of the Colonial State', *Comparative Studies in Society and History* 41:3 (1999), pp. 563-88; Lauren Benton, *Law and Colonial Cultures. Legal Regimes in World History, 1400-1900* (Cambridge: Cambridge University Press, 2002).

55 Benton, 'Colonial Law'.

the previously discussed studies on Iberian corporations, normative plurality, and jurisdictions. The ability of historical actors of all ethnicities to
engage in jurisdictional interaction was placed at the centre, thus making
individual and group agency increasingly visible. Similarly, the conflictual
nature of rule and resistance was also brought to the forefront.

Apart from the groundbreaking studies by Lauren Benton, the collective volume *Legal Pluralism and Empires, 1500-1850* (2013), edited by
Benton along with Richard Ross, is a good showcase for this approach.[56]
The collective volume, *Justice in a New World. Negotiating Legal Intelligibility in British, Iberian, and Indigenous America*, edited by Brian Owensby
and Richard Ross, features a series of studies that explore the dimensions
mentioned above, with a strong cross-cultural component.[57]

One thing is certain: these studies deal with an understanding of 'jurisdiction' that refers to the space where actors from various backgrounds
brought their disparate normative cultures into contact. It therefore has
little to do with the aforementioned notions of *iurisdictio* explored, above
all, by the Italian legal historian Pietro Costa.[58] Moreover, corporate logic
is largely absent from these works. As mentioned earlier, while for legal
historians studying early modern Iberia pluralism was an intrinsic part
of the corporate culture and operated within a single legal system, for
this research strand, pluralism was fundamentally based on the interaction
between different legalities.[59]

Despite their distinct emphases, both research streams have been pivotal in shaping the scholarly agenda in the years that followed. Studies on
the two Iberian empires have explored many of the approaches mentioned,
frequently integrating aspects from both streams. A good example is Karen
Graubart's research on the legal, ethnic, and confessional diversity of early
modern Spain and Spanish America. Graubart's work engages deeply with
the complexities of pluralistic societies, highlighting how legal frameworks
and religious practices intersected in ways that shaped cultural and social
dynamics.[60]

The same could be said of Jorge Díaz Ceballos' recent studies on the
importance of urban corporations in shaping colonial society in Spanish
America.[61] Or the very recent book by Max Deardorff on the political and

---

56 Lauren Benton and Richard Ross eds., *Legal Pluralism and Empires, 1500-1850* (New York:
    New York University Press, 2013).
57 Brian P. Owensby and Richard Ross, *Justice in a New World. Negotiating Legal Intelligibility in
    British, Iberian, and Indigenous America* (New York: New York University Press, 2018).
58 Costa, *Iurisdictio*; Costa, *Lo Stato Immaginario*.
59 Herzog, 'The Uses and Abuses of Legal Pluralism'.
60 Karen Graubart, *Republics of Difference: Religious and Racial Self-Governance in the Spanish
    Atlantic World* (Oxford: Oxford University Press, 2022).
61 Jorge Díaz Ceballos, *Poder compartido. Repúblicas urbanas, monarquía y conversación en
    Castilla del Oro, 1508-1573* (Madrid: Marcial Pons, 2020).

social structure of Granada (in Spain) and the New Kingdom of Granada (in South America). In addition to emphasizing the corporate nature of this social and political order, Deardorff even speaks of a 'Catholic Citizenship' to convey the weight of religion in the mechanisms of inclusion and exclusion, both in Spain and in Colonial Spanish America.[62]

These and other studies have examined a range of fundamental characteristics of the Spanish and Portuguese empires. First, that colonial society was based on normative plurality, including the coexistence (and articulation) of European and Asian, Amerindian, and African normative orders.[63] Second, the belief that inequality was determined by nature.[64] This element decisively contributed to the naturalization of asymmetrical power relations, a feature that was particularly striking (and violent) in colonial societies. Third, the obsession with family order. Both Portuguese and Spanish authorities regarded the Catholic domestic unit as the foundation of colonial society, and thus displayed a constant eagerness to (forcibly) impose this family model in the Asian and American contexts they colonized.[65]

Significantly, over the past decade, corporate frameworks and pluralism have become common currency not only in studies dealing with Spanish and Portuguese empires but also with other early modern European imperial formations. An increasing number of studies have stressed that, parallel to the Iberian conglomerates, the early modern British and French empires also rested upon a corporate structure.

Jack P. Greene has underscored that late colonial British North America was based on a corporate structure.[66] Greene explored the corporate foundations of colonial society and argued that they endured until independence. According to him, corporate identities '... were so deeply rooted in the economic practices, social customs, and legal cultures [of British America] that people developed to enable themselves to live and function in a specific political space that we ought to think of shared corporate iden-

---

62 Max Deardorff, *A Tale of Two Granadas. Custom, Community, and Citizenship in the Spanish Empire, 1568-1668* (Cambridge: Cambridge University Press, 2023).

63 Tamar Herzog, 'Colonial Law and "Native Customs": Indigenous Land Rights in Colonial Spanish America', *The Americas* 69:3 (2013), 303-21.

64 Thomas Duve, "La condición jurídica del indio y su consideración como persona miserabilis en el Derecho indiano", in Mariano G. Losano ed., *Un giudice e due leggi. Pluralismo normativo e conflitti agrari in Sud America* (Milan: Giuffrè, 2004), pp. 3-33; Thomas Duve, "Derecho canónico y la alteridad indígena: los indios como neófitos", in Wulf Oesterreicher and Roland Schmidt-Riese eds., *Esplendores y miserias de la evangelización de América. Antecedentes europeos y alteridad indígena* (Berlin: De Gruyter, 2010), pp. 73-94.

65 Charlotte de Castelnau-L'Estoile, *Un catholicisme colonial. Le mariage des Indiens et des esclaves au Brésil, XVIᵉ-XVIIIᵉ siècle* (Paris: PUF, 2019).

66 Jack P. Greene, 'Atlantic History and Other Approaches to Early Modern Empires', *Ler História* 75 (2019), pp. 231-50.

tities as socially constituted and reinforced-lived and learned: experienced and by no means only imagined'.[67]

Another compelling example of the prominent role corporations played in the political – and not just economic – life of northern European empires is Philip J. Stern's study on the East India Company.[68] Stern gave centre stage to the corporate system of governance and stressed its influence in large political formations, such as England and its imperial territories. According to Stern, political fragmentation undoubtedly characterised early modern England, since its political landscape was populated 'not by singular, sovereign monocracies but by intersecting empires, pluralistic legal cultures, and a variety of shapes and forms of hybrid and competing jurisdictions'.[69]

As for the English overseas empire, Stern argued that 'with some notable exceptions, like Jamaica and Tangier, this was an empire [the English] founded and often administered by corporations, companies, and proprietors, each built on a variety of contrasting ideological, religious, political, and legal foundations. Though theoretically dependent upon the Crown, in both principle and practice, these corporate colonies exercised a great deal of autonomy; some were even literally self-constituting, such as the Mayflower "compact," which set the foundation for colonial government in New England and its relative independence from the English state at least through the 1680s'.[70]

William Pettigrew's research on 'corporate constitutionalism' also illustrates the increasing focus on corporate structures and pluralism in studies on the British Empire (Pettigrew, 2015). This interest is further reflected in Pettigrew and Veevers' edited volume *The Corporation as a Protagonist in Global History, c. 1550-1750*, which effectively highlights the political and quasi-state character of commercial corporations.[71]

Interest in the corporate framework and its relationship with jurisdiction has also attracted the attention of scholars of the history of the Common Law. Bradin Cormack's *A Power to Do Justice: Jurisdiction, English Literature, and The Rise of Common Law* offers a compelling example.[72] Building on the earlier work of Christopher Tomlins, Cormack shows how renewed scholarly engagement with jurisdictions and corporate frame-

---

67 Greene, 'Atlantic History'.
68 Philip Stern, *The Company-State. Corporate Sovereignty and the Early Modern Foundations of the British Empire in India* (Oxford: Oxford University Press, 2011).
69 Stern, *Company State*, p. 10.
70 Stern, *Company State*, p. 10.
71 William Pettigrew and David Veevers eds., *The Corporation as a Protagonist in Global History, c. 1550-1750* (Leiden: Brill, 2019).
72 Bradin Cormack, *A Power to Do Justice. Jurisdiction, English Literature, and the rise of Common Law* (Chicago: University of Chicago Press, 2008).

works is reshaping our understanding of their role in structuring social and political life.

What is evident is that the term "corporation" has a wide range of meanings, and the studies just mentioned referred to rather different realities. Historians like Paolo Grossi, Bartolomé Clavero, and António Hespanha were interested in assessing the deep impact of corporations on social and political life. In contrast, Stern, Pettigrew, and others, when discussing corporations, tend to focus more on the mercantile context and its inherent ability for self-organisation and adaptation.

One thing seems certain: with regard to corporate logic, the contrast between Northern and Southern Europe has been increasingly nuanced. Recent work has even argued that Iberian thinking on social and political order influenced the Anglophone view of corporations.[73] Other studies have shown that the Iberians themselves expressed their admiration for Northern European polities and their ability to overcome the blockages inherent in the corporate matrix of political and social order. They questioned certain aspects of the corporate structure and saw it as partly responsible for economic, political, and social backwardness. At the same time, Spanish Enlightenment reformists even reimagined corporations, reinventing them with a view to meeting the financial, economic, and political challenges of their time. They did so in an attempt to halt the economic decline of the Iberian Peninsula and the decay of the Spanish empire.[74]

The Interpretive Model and its Critics

The examples presented so far suffice to demonstrate that the interpretive framework centred on the role of corporations in early modern politics continues to be widely studied. However, at the same time, it has become the subject of numerous critiques. The final pages of this essay are devoted to examining these in some detail.

Part of these critiques has resulted from changes undergone by research on early modern imperial formations and colonial rule. Over the past two decades, scholarship on early modern European empires has paid significantly more attention to the so-called "non-elite groups". As a result, the understanding of the political role played by individuals from "lower" sections of society has advanced considerably. Attention shifted to the individual agency of the members of these groups, and the main priority became the study of politics at the ground level. Such studies

---

73 Andrew Fitzmaurice, *Sovereignty, Property and Empire 1500-2000* (Cambridge: Cambridge University Press, 2014).
74 Corredera, *Diplomatic Enlightenment*.

demonstrated that no power or dominion was ever imposed, in a uniform and uncontested way, over any kind of social formation. Many of these studies also included a critique of categories – such as corporations – that, due to their Eurocentric connotations, prevented scholars from encompassing the wide diversity of practices and social actors participating in colonial exchanges.

Studies focused on dominant groups became less popular among scholars of early modern empires.[75] In the past decade or more, elites, along with ruling institutions, have been increasingly regarded by many as an outdated object of study, seen as perpetuating Eurocentric views of the past. The same could be said of the corporate structures developed by these elites, including Western European law. Top-down perspectives on power relations were deemed simplistic and were seen as contributing to the elision of the contested character of domination.

Not surprisingly, the explanatory potential of corporations was seriously questioned. As stated, for most historians who highlighted the importance of corporate bodies, the choices of individual actors were largely shaped by corporate culture. As a result, individuals and individual agency became less visible within this interpretive framework. In striking contrast, scholarship from the past decades foregrounded the agency of individuals and groups of all backgrounds and ethnicities, drawing attention to their capacity – including that of women and men from the "non-elite groups" – to contest and subvert the designs of those in power. Studies that underscored individual agency challenged the capacity of corporate bodies to shape social interactions. Many scholars shifted their attention from jurists, magistrates, and members of elite landowning families to peasant, artisanal, and enslaved individuals, including both women and men.

The focus on pluralism and polycentrism has also come under criticism. On the one hand, these concepts were questioned by historians who were accustomed to conceiving early modern monarchies as centralised assemblages of corporate bodies ruled by royal dynasties. The polycentric character of these conglomerates was rejected by those who regarded the Spanish or Portuguese monarchies as forerunners of the modern state and as the basis for the development of strong royal authority. Such scholarship contested the idea that these monarchies lacked a strong governing centre. Last but not least, they also doubted the governability of polities made up of a large number of disparate corporate bodies often making uncoordinated decisions. On the opposite extreme, the insistence on normative plurality, polycentrism, and interdependent power relations was regarded

---

75 Ralph Bauer and José Antonio Mazzotti, "Introduction: Creole Subjects in the Colonial Americas", in Ralph Bauer and José Antonio Mazzotti eds., *Creole Subjects in the Colonial Americas. Empires, Texts, Identities.* (Chapel Hill: University of North Carolina Press, 2009), pp. 1-58.

by many as failing to account for the violent and coercive component of rule in the early modern world, especially in colonial settings.

Studies on litigation have also questioned the explanatory power of the corporate model. They have drawn attention to the pervasiveness of litigation arising from the corporate structure of early modern society, thus highlighting the contested character of corporate structures – for instance, regarding inheritance practices. Studies on family history have challenged the corporate character of the family itself. Instead of being regarded as the basis for stability, the domestic sphere was increasingly seen as a stage for major struggles between its members.[76] Many historians questioned the capacity of corporate frameworks to shape individual and collective agency not just within the domestic sphere, but across society at large.

Likewise, research on early modern economic history, particularly studies on merchants and trade networks (including the transatlantic slave trade), has fully demonstrated that despite corporate insistence on the 'common good', a de facto 'commercial society' based on individualist self-interest and competition was developing from the late medieval period onwards, including across Catholic lands.[77] The image of early modern Iberia as a world fundamentally based on strongly group-oriented (and anti-individualistic) Catholic morals has been seriously questioned.[78]

The idea that the corporate model was transferred to colonial settings also proved controversial. Many scholars disputed that colonial societies were based on a corporate structure and rejected the idea that there had ever been an "Ancien Régime in the tropics".[79] Studies that underscored the corporate character of colonial societies in the Americas have been deemed Eurocentric by various experts in the history of the colonial Americas. Many argued that the enslavement of Amerindians and Africans was the fundamental dimension of colonial societies across the Americas, not their allegedly corporate structure. They thus contended that insisting on the corporate structure of colonial society failed to account for the structural role played by slavery and slave labour. The debate generated by António Hespanha's work on colonial Brazil, by Annick Lempérière's stud- ies on New Spain, and more recently by Alejandro Agüero's research on the

76 Bianca Premo, *Children of the Father King: Youth, Authority, and Legal Minority in Colonial Lima* (Chapel Hill: University of North Carolina Press, 2005); Bianca Premo, *The Enlightenment on Trial: Ordinary Litigants and Colonialism in the Spanish Empire* (Oxford: Oxford University Press, 2017); Víctor Uribe-Urán, *Fatal Love: Spousal Killers, Law, and Punishment in the Late Colonial Spanish Atlantic* (Palo Alto: Stanford University Press, 2015).

77 Luiz Felipe de Alencastro, *The Trade in the Living. The Formation of Brazil in the South Atlantic, 16th to 17th Centuries* (Albany: State University of New York Press, 2018).

78 Bartolomé Yun-Casalilla, *Iberian World Empires and the Globalization of Europe 1415 -1668* (London: Palgrave, 2018).

79 Laura de Mello e Souza, *O Sol e a Sombra: política e administração na América portuguesa do século XVIII* (São Paulo: Companhia das Letras, 2006).

Río de la Plata region before and after independence, are good examples of the current debates surrounding the alleged corporate character of colonial societies across the Americas.[80]

The set of critiques presented here arguably does not diminish the research strand on corporate culture or its capacity to illuminate the underlying structures that governed early modern Iberia. Instead, they highlight opportunities for theoretical and methodological refinement. In these concluding pages, several pathways will be proposed to address the previously mentioned limitations, with the goal of contributing to the further advancement of this research strand.

Firstly, it is important to acknowledge that the legal history studies that stressed the long-lasting persistence of corporations in Iberia have evolved in a somewhat insular way. More comparative, transnational, and inter-imperial approaches, and a greater engagement with broader debates – on topics such as state and empire formation, early modern political thought, and colonial rule – would certainly enrich their scope. Such approaches would allow for the development of a more nuanced understanding of a fundamental aspect of corporations: political pluralism. While it is essential to critically interrogate concepts like the 'early modern state' and the centralisation process, this should not result in the complete erasure of the centre, particularly the prince as the pivotal figure of political authority and recognition.

A more dynamic and nuanced understanding of religion and its role would also be important. A critique often made of Iberian legal history is that it has been based on a somewhat ahistorical notion of Catholicism. The understanding of religion should, therefore, be approached in a more dynamic manner, taking into account diverse historical contexts and conflicts within Catholicism. Numerous studies on the early modern period have shown that Catholicism was a significant field of struggle.

A deeper and more nuanced understanding of the Catholic–Protestant divide and its impact on corporate culture would also be advantageous. Recent research on northern European polities reveals that the Reformation did not result in a complete break from the *ius commune*. Reformed England continued to apply a canon law shared with continental Europe. Similarly, in the Dutch regions and other parts of Protestant Europe, the *ius commune* remained in use, with ongoing legal exchanges between Protestants and Catholics. This prompts questions about another recurrent topic of legal history studies on Spain and Portugal: the longevity of the corporate structure as a specific feature of Catholic Europe.

---

80 Souza, *O Sol e a Sombra*; Annick Lempérière, *Entre Dieu et le Roi, la République. Mexico, XVIe-XIXe siècles* (Paris: Les Belles Lettres, 2004); Alejandro Agüero, 'Sobre el concepto de Antigua Constitución y su aplicación a la historia política rioplatense de la primera mitad del siglo XIX – Respuesta al Prof. Chiaramonte', *Nuevo Mundo, Mundos Nuevos* (2021).

A more refined perspective on the role of corporate culture in promoting social stability would also be highly advantageous. The scholarship devoted to Black brotherhoods across the Iberian world, for instance, has demonstrated that corporate structures were highly contested and involved considerable conflict and litigation.[81] In any case, while it is crucial to recognise that corporations did not necessarily lead to pacification, it remains important to highlight that they played a key role in structuring social interactions, including conflict. Even when individuals contested corporate belonging or rules, corporations still shaped the way these challenges were expressed and confronted. Corporate culture determined how people reached agreements or expressed disagreements.

The legal history of Iberia would also benefit from a deeper theorization of how individual subjects have been constituted and shaped over time. Such an inquiry would allow for a richer understanding of how individuals interacted with collective structures across different chronological and social contexts. Integrating a stronger social history perspective would reveal that individual behaviour did not simply reflect corporate norms, but exhibited complex dynamics shaped by the interplay between personal agency and collective frameworks.

A particularly recent strand of scholarly renewal lies in the emphasis on the historicity of legal culture. Advocating for the use of 'normativity' instead of 'law', legal historian Thomas Duve has contended that early modern laws should not be regarded as legislation in the contemporary sense, but rather as part of a wide ensemble of normative material that regulated early modern collective life. According to Duve, norms were artifacts that reflected various underlying assumptions, deeply held beliefs, and cultural paradigms that shaped governance, religious practices, and collective life.[82]

Studies of the past two decades by legal historians such as Thomas Duve, Tamar Herzog, Heikki Pihlajamäki, and Angela de Benedictis, among others, are advancing these approaches. Also worthy of mention is the recent collective volume edited by Manuel Bastias Saavedra on multi-normativity in the Iberian empires.[83] Following the work of Thomas Duve, Bastias's work is based on the idea that early modern laws were a complex amalgamation of norms, habits, conventions, customs, values, and moral instructions – not imposed on social reality but 'derived' from

81   Erin K. Rowe, *Black Saints in Early Modern Global Catholicism* (Cambridge: Cambridge University Press, 2019); Miguel A. Valerio, *Sovereign Joy: Afro-Mexican Kings and Queens, 1539–1640* (New York: Cambridge University Press, 2022).

82   Thomas Duve, 'What is global legal history?', *Comparative Legal History* 8:2 (2020), pp. 73-115; Thomas Duve & Tamar Herzog eds., *The Cambridge History of Latin American Law in Global Perspective* (Cambridge: Cambridge University Press, 2024).

83   Manuel Bastias Saavedra, *Norms beyond Empire. Law-Making and Local Normativities in Iberian Asia 1500-1800* (Leiden: Brill, 2021).

it.[84] This reevaluation of law challenges the notion that Iberian empires were fundamentally centralised. Two key features of their political and legal frameworks were: a fragmented power structure that prevented the establishment of a unified political order, and the equally fragmented nature of their laws, from their creation to their dissemination.[85]

Research on Iberia's corporate structure has already greatly advanced through engagement with this nuanced understanding of normativity. Mariana Candido's recent book offers an excellent example of the pluralistic character of the early modern Portuguese empire.[86] Focusing on Angola under Portuguese colonial rule, Candido examines a multi-normative system of local and colonial laws that persisted from the early 1500s onwards and involved some recognition, by Portuguese authorities, of West Central African norms and usages. This system was only eventually dismantled in the nineteenth century, as the colonial enterprise increasingly aligned with liberal notions of progress, civilisation, and property rights. Mariana Paes's work is another excellent example of this long-lasting persistence of pluralistic normative structures in African lands colonised by the Portuguese.[87]

Finally, it is important to highlight studies that move beyond mere comparative approaches to situate the Iberian case – and its corporate and legal pluralistic culture – within the broader framework of early modern European polities. Although this article's focus has been on early modern Iberia, it becomes evident that many of the arguments put forward by Iberian scholars have broader, pan-European relevance. This raises the important question of whether such perspectives provide insights that extend beyond the Iberian context. This aligns with works such as that being prepared by Tamar Herzog and Heikki Pihlajamäki. Herzog and Pihlajamäki are currently editing a collective volume on the history of early modern European law and its role in shaping colonial empires. The volume's ambition lies not in covering all Western European empires and legal systems, but in its approach: each chapter is thematic and problem-oriented, transcending national analytical frameworks.

Approaches like these will certainly enhance our ability to critically assess the commonalities and the specificities of each case under study. They will also allow for a more nuanced evaluation of the extent to which corporatism, pluralism, and jurisdictional culture were truly specific to early modern Spain and Portugal.

---

84 Thomas Duve, 'Was ist "Multinormativität"? – Einführende Bemerkungen', *Rechtsgeschichte-Legal History* 25 (2017), pp. 88–101.
85 Bastias Saavedra, *Norms beyond Empire*.
86 Mariana Candido, *Wealth, Land, and Property in Angola: A History of Dispossession, Slavery, and Inequality* (Cambridge: Cambridge University Press, 2022).
87 Mariana Dias Paes, "What Is Global Legal History and How Can It Be Done?", in Duve and Herzog eds., *The Cambridge History of Latin American Law*, pp. 73-94.

BETHANY ARAM _____

Comparative Approaches to Gender and Ethnicity

Early Modern Iberian & British Empires[*]

The *History of Caledonia or, The Scots Colony in Darién* authored by "a gentleman lately arrived" and published in Dublin in 1699 described a treaty the Scots had signed with the Cuna, whose priests assured them that the bearded newcomers would not involve themselves 'in matters of religion'. The Cuna chief received and entertained the Scottish delegation, offering its members food, wine, and, finally, female companionship, 'which was modestly refused'. Rather than women, the Scots returned to the Fort of Saint Andrews with a group of young boys who, in spite of their mothers' protests, were sent to learn their language and secure the treaty.[1]

In contrast to the Scots, the Spanish, who had reached the Isthmus of Panama almost two centuries earlier, had sought female company upon arrival. An early leader, Vasco Núñez de Balboa, had established alliances with the area's chiefs, receiving their food, slaves, and 'sisters and daughters to take in order to marry them or use them at will, so that the peace grew'.[2] Female knowledge regarding local foods, which proved crucial to Spanish survival on the Isthmus, may have eluded the short-lived Scottish settlement. Spanish and Scottish imperial strategies envisioned the Isthmus of Panama as a privileged conduit for trade between Europe and

---

[*] I am grateful to Jorge Díaz Ceballos for suggestions on this text, which has been written with support from the Fondo Europeo de Desarrollo Regional (FEDER) (80%) and the Consejería de Economía, Conocimiento, Empresas y Universidad de la Junta de Andalucía, in the framework of the FEDER Andalucía 2014-02 operative program, FEDER-UPO-1380997, as well as the research group HUM 1000, Historia de la Globalización, directed by Igor Pérez Tostado.

1 *The History of Caledonia, or, The Scots Colony in Darien in the West Indies* (Dublin, 1699), pp. 25-26.

2 'hermanas e hijas que llevasen consigo para que las casase o usase dellas a su voluntad, de que iba creciendo la paz'. Archivo General de Indias, Seville, Patronato 174, R.8, fotograma 26, Licenciado Alonso Zuazo to Monsieur de Chièvres.

Bethany Aram • Universidad Pablo de Olavide

Supplicant Empires, ed. by Edward Jones Corredera, Habsburg Worlds, 8 (Turnhout: Brepols, 2025), pp. 63–75
BREPOLS ❦ PUBLISHERS   10.1484/M.HW-EB.5.145064

Asia. Nevertheless, they recorded very different attitudes toward gender, religion, ethnicity or nation. During the early modern period, Catholic and Protestant doctrines informed the use of shared or separate burial spaces for peoples of different origins.[3] They also shaped attitudes toward inter-group sexual and spiritual relations, as exemplified in Spanish and Scottish responses toward indigenous overtures on the Isthmus of Panama.

Intersectional analyses of gender and ethnicity have proven fruitful in recent studies of British and French America, as well as in the Iberian world. Recent scholarship on Virginia, Barbados, New Orleans and Mexico, among other cities, invites attention to the interaction of religious, cultural and demographic factors shaping practices that included marriage, prostitution and witchcraft. In an extended comparison of the Spanish and British Atlantic Empires, the late John Elliott explained that the fact that Iberian overseas ventures preceded those of the British, French and Dutch by at least one century belies the possibility of synchronic comparisons.[4] The Crown of Castile drew upon Portuguese skills and knowledge, just as subsequent ventures preyed upon Iberian precedents. The same processes informed shifting ideas of gender and ethnicity. The comparative analysis of empire, which rarely features gender or ethnicity, may benefit from cross-cultural and comparative attention to matters of 'intense intersectionality',[5] including marriage, prostitution, and witchcraft.

Marriage

Marriage policies reflected and attempted to assert religious and state authority by regulating sexuality, reproduction, and inheritance. At the same time, marriage practices provided means for ignoring, contesting, or subverting official attempts to define belonging and exclusion. In colonial settings, marriages expressed evolving attitudes toward gender and inter-ethnic relations.

---

3 T. Douglas Price, James H. Burton, Robert Frei, Andrea Cucina, Pilar Zabala, Robert H. Tykot, and Vera Tiesler, 'Isotopic studies of human skeletal remains from a sixteenth to seventeenth-century AD churchyard in Campeche, Mexico', *Current Anthropology* 53:4 (2012), pp. 396-433. Bethany Aram, Juan Guillermo Martín, and Iosvany Hernández Mora, 'Aproximaciones a la población de Panamá Viejo a partir de la arqueología funeraria y la documentación histórica, 1519-1671', *Anuario de Estudios Americanos* 77:2 (2020), pp. 485-512. Carter Clinton K., and Fatimah L.C. Jackson, 'Historical overview, current research, and emerging bioethical guidelines in researching the New York African Burial Ground', *American Journal of Physical Anthropology* 175:2 (2021), pp, 339-49.
4 John Elliott, *Empires of the Atlantic World: Britain and Spain in America, 1492-1830* (New Haven: Yale University Press, 2006).
5 Sara McDougall and Sarah M.S. Pearsall, 'Introduction: Marriage's Global Past', *Gender & History* 29:3 (2017), pp. 505-28.

Iberian policies toward mixed marriage reflected pressure for religious conversion and cultural assimilation. From the early sixteenth century, Lusitanian officials favoured marriages with local women at outposts along the coasts of Africa and India. Marriage ties, and the ensuing offspring, often facilitated trade with the interior.[6] Intermarriage formed part of a Portuguese strategy, with the mixed population considered free by royal decree and permitted full access to paternal property when legitimate or legitimized.[7] With some ambivalence, the Crown of Castile also encouraged Spanish intermarriage with Amerindian elites.[8] At the same time, the Catholic Church sought to impose baptism and monogamous marriage or celibacy among all peoples, free and enslaved.[9] With or without religious sanction, marriage alliances extended trade and kinship networks. Of course, colonial powers' assimilationist aspirations, through marriage or otherwise, did not preclude misunderstanding, resistance and conflict,[10] or the migration of European women.[11] When the number of European men outnumbered that of European women, social insertion by marriage into the colonial elite appeared easier for women than men of mixed, Indigenous American or African ancestry.[12] On the other hand, men enjoyed other avenues for manumission and social ascent, including military service.[13]

---

6 António Manuel Hespanha, *Filhos da terra: Identidades mestiças nos confins da expansão portuguesa* (Lisbon: Tinta-da-china, 2019).

7 Arlindo Manuel Caldeira, *Mulheres, sexualidade e casamento em São Tomé e Príncipe (séculos XV-XVIII)* (Lisbon: Cosmos, 1999), p. 43.

8 Alejandro E. Gómez, "De los Engleiz de la Terre a los Anglo-Indians. Representaciones de alteridad e identidades propias de sectores mezclados en los mundos coloniales", in *Tratas, Esclavitudes y Mestizajes. Una Historia Conectada, Siglos XV-XVIII*. Edited by Manuel Francisco Fernández Chaves, Eduardo França Paiva, Rafael M. Pérez García (Sevilla: Universidad de Sevilla, 2021), pp. 329-48, p. 334.

9 Magnus Mörner, *Race Mixture in the History of Latin America* (Boston: Little, Brown and Company, 1967).

10 Patricia Seed, *To Love, Honor, and Obey in Colonial Mexico: Conflicts over Marriage Choice, 1572-1821* (Stanford: Stanford University Press, 1988).

11 Amelia Almorza Hidalgo, *'No se hace pueblo sin ellas'. Mujeres españolas en el Virreinato de Perú: emigración y movilidad social (siglos XVI-XVII)* (Madrid: CSIC, 2018); Jane E. Mangan, *Transatlantic Obligations. Creating the Bonds of Family in Conquest-Era Peru and Spain* (Oxford: Oxford University Press, 2016); and Allyson M. Poska, *Gendered Crossings: Women and Migration in the Spanish Empire* (Albuquerque: Albuquerque: University of New Mexico Press, 2016).

12 Joanne Rappaport, *El Mestizo Evanescente: Configuración de la diferencia en el Nuevo Reino de Granada*. Translated by Santiago Paredes Cisneros (Bogotá: Editorial Universidad del Rosario, 2018).

13 Alex Borucki, *From Shipmates to Soldiers: Emerging Black Identities in the Río de la Plata* (New Mexico: University of New Mexico Press, 2015) and Ben Vinson, *Bearing Arms for His Majesty: The Free-Colored Militia in Colonial Mexico* (Stanford: Stanford University Press, 2001).

Historians cannot elude the impact of slavery on the demographics shaping and, in turn, shaped by, marriage policies. From the late fifteenth century through 1820, David Eltis has shown that enslaved Africans constituted four out of five women and three out of four men who crossed the Atlantic.[14] In sixteenth- and seventeenth-century Mexico City Herman Bennett has demonstrated that marriage choice enabled Africans to seek freedom from bondage for themselves and their descendants.[15] In sixteenth- and seventeenth-century Lima, Michelle McKinley has examined the attainment of 'fractional freedoms' through intimacy, baptismal manumission, self-purchase, and adept use of the courts.[16] In Spanish-occupied territories, the Catholic Church insisted on the right of all people to baptism, religious instruction and marriage choice. After initially accepting settlers' official as well as informal alliances with Native American and African women on different frontiers,[17] during the seventeenth century English and French authorities began to oppose and, indeed, to legislate against mixed relations.[18]

Religious conversion and Christian marriage, which Iberian authorities considered imperative for royal subjects, often proved less accessible for Indigenous Americas, Africans and Afro-descendants in the British colonies.[19] In this sense, the conversion and marriage of a mediator like Pocahontas entailed more of an early exception than a subsequent norm.[20] Soldiers deserted and entered into Indian communities more easily than native women converted to the Protestant faith.[21]

---

14 David Eltis, 'A brief overview of the Trans-Atlantic Slave Trade', *SlaveVoyages* (2007) (Online) [Consulted 31 August 2022].

15 Herman Bennett, *Africans in Colonial Mexico. Absolutism, Christianity, and Afro-Creole Consciousness, 1570-1640* (Indiana: Indiana University Press, 2003).

16 Michelle A. McKinley, *Libertades Fraccionadas. Esclavitud, intimidad y movilización jurídica en la Lima Colonial, 1600-1700*. Translated by Guillermina Cuevas Mesa and Marta Lozano (Valencia: Tirant, 2021).

17 The relevant bibliography has proliferated following two influential works: Richard White, *The Middle Ground: Indians, Empires, and Republics in the Great Lakes Region, 1650-1815* (Cambridge: Cambridge University Press, 1991) and Susan Sleeper-Smith, *Indian Women and French Men: Rethinking Cultural Encounter in the Western Great Lakes* (Amherst: University of Massachusetts Press, 2001).

18 For examples from colonial Virginia and the French Caribbean, see Kathleen Brown, *Good Wives, Nasty Wenches, and Anxious Patriarchs: Gender, Race, and Power in Colonial Virginia* (Chapel Hill: University of North Carolina Press, 1996) and Dorris Garraway, *The Libertine Colony: Creolization in the Early French Caribbean* (Durham: Duke University Press, 2005).

19 Saliha Belmessous, *Assimilation and Empire: Uniformity in French and British Colonies, 1541-1954* (Oxford: Oxford University Press, 2013).

20 Karen Ordahl Kupperman, *Pocahontas and the English Boys. Caught between Cultures in Early Virginia* (New York: New York University Press, 2019).

21 Nicholas P. Canny, "The Permissive Frontier: The Problem of Social Control in English Settlements in Ireland and Virginia, 1550-1650", in *The Westward Enterprise. English Activities in Ireland, the Atlantic, and America 1480-1650*. Edited by Kenneth R. Andrews, Nicholas

Among enslaved subjects in urban Hispanic territories, Michelle McKinley has argued that the ecclesiastical defence of marriage rights marked the single most important distinguishing factor with respect to the subsequent United States. As McKinley has shown, marriage choice enabled women and couples to pool resources in order to pursue and purchase their own as well as their offsprings' freedom.[22] On the other hand, Virginia's planter elite increasingly considered enslaved persons in a category apart from 'Christians', and, after 1662, practically condemned the children of enslaved women to bondage.[23] In comparison to Iberoamerica, the more frequent use of African names among enslaved men and women in the British colonies reflected lower rates of baptism and religious indoctrination.[24]

In British America, growing restrictions upon enslaved persons often accompanied laws to discourage mixed marriages.[25] Such constraints even reached French New Orleans in the 1724 Code Noir.[26] Updating Herbert S. Klein's path-breaking comparison of Cuba and Virginia, Alejando de la Fuente and Ariela J. Gross have added Louisiana into the comparison as an 'intermediate case'. In contrast to Virginia and Louisiana, they emphasize the legal validity of inter-racial relations in Cuba over time, alongside the endurance of the practice of purchasing freedom (*coartación*).[27] As Jessica Marie Johnson points out, more slaves attained (or purchased) manumission in New Orleans during four years of Spanish rule than decades of French government.[28] Although in 1778, Spain prohibited "unequal marriage" in its dominions, including the Viceroyalties of Peru and New Spain, estimations of status remained flexible and based on specific interests and concerns, including legitimacy and occupation, with

---

P. Canny and Paul Edward Hedley Hair (Detroit: Wayne State University Press, 1979), pp. 24-38.

22 McKinley, *Libertades fraccionadas*, p. 109.

23 Brown, *Good wives, nasty wenches*, pp. 107-96.

24 Philip D. Morgan, *Slave Counterpoint: Black Culture in the Eighteenth-Century Chesapeake and Lowcountry* (Chapel Hill: University of North Carolina Press, 1998). Gwendolyn Midlo Hall, *Slavery and African Ethnicities in the Americas: Restoring the Links* (Chapel Hill: University of North Carolina Press, 2005), p. 54.

25 Jennifer Morgan, *Laboring Women: Reproduction and Gender in New World slavery* (Philadelphia: University of Pennsylvania Press, 2004), pp. 71-72.

26 Jessica Marie Johnson, *Wicked Flesh. Black Women, Intimacy, and Freedom in the Atlantic World* (Philadelphia: University of Pennsylvania Press, 2020), p. 134.

27 Herbert S. Klein, *Slavery in the Americas: A comparative Study of Virginia and Cuba* (Chicago: University of Chicago Press, 1967); Alejandro de la Fuente and Ariela J. Gross, *Becoming Free, Becoming Black: Race, Freedom, and Law in Cuba, Virginia, and Louisiana* (Cambridge: Cambridge University Press, 2020).

28 Johnson, *Wicked Flesh*, pp. 190-91.

the "quality" of grooms questioned more frequently than that of brides.[29] Marriage persisted as a vehicle for female social mobility, which could include increased degrees of freedom.

Without presenting slavery in Iberoamerica as more benign than under British rule, the evolution of marriage law and practice does provide some basis for comparison.[30] For centuries, Iberian evangelical and socio-political interests encouraged the religious conversion and autonomous incorporation or assimilation of 'others'. In an attempt to restrict the social integration and promotion of recent converts to Catholicism, many Iberian institutions adopted 'purity of blood' statues intended to limit access to offices and honors to the descendants of Christians.[31] Puritan theologians, in general, did not confront numerous converts or face such concerns. Many of their early congregations, with the exception of the Quakers, had less universal, inclusive, or even expansionist, aims. On the other hand, after 1563, the Council of Trent affirmed the importance of marriage as a sacrament. Such differences impacted marriage law as well as opportunities for manumission and other forms of social mobility. Of course, the correlation between marriage choice and manumission, while visible in different societies, does not imply that most colonial subjects opted to marry.

Concubinage and prostitution

Notwithstanding official efforts to promote sacramental marriage, the practice proved unpopular in some settings. According to Arlindo Manuel Caldeira, inhabitants of Portuguese São Tomé commonly chose cohabitation over matrimony for a variety of reasons, including African precedents, previous marriage ties, membership in the clergy, and greater personal freedom. At the same time, Caldeira notes the difficulty of establishing

---

29 María del Carmen Olague Méndez, 'Género, calidad y sociabilidad de las categorías jurídicas en Colima, 1765-1821', Seminario Pespectivas de Género para la Investigación actual, Universidad Pablo de Olavide de Sevilla, 30 June 2022. Michelle McKinley notes that couples of enslaved, Afro, or mixed persons were exempted from the obligation of parental approval in the 1776 pragmatic, extended to Spanish America in 1778: Michelle McKinley, Libertades fraccionadas. Esclavitud, intimidad y movilización jurídica en Lima colonial, 1600-1700 (Ciudad de México: Tirant Lo Blanch, 2020), p. 132.

30 On the formation of these views of slavery in Iberoamerica, Tannenbaum's argument remains influential. Frank Tannenbaum, Slave & Citizen. The Negro in the Americas (New York: Alfred A. Knopf, 1946). Marcelo Santos Matheus, 'Frank Tannenbaum e os direitos dos escravos: religião e escravidão nas Américas', Afro-Ásia 51 (2015), pp. 215-52.

31 María Elena Martínez, Genealogical Fictions (Stanford: Stanford University Press, 2008). See also De Sangre y Leche. Raza y religión en el mundo ibérico moderno. Edited by Mercedes García Arenal y Felipe Pereda (Madrid: Marcial Pons, 2021).

clear frontiers between prostitution and concubinage.[32] In São Tomé, the overlapping prevalence of both types of informal unions sustained high levels of illegitimate births.[33]

Prostitution enabled some women to earn money for food and clothing, or even to purchase their liberty, as a significant presence of free Black women alongside others of European ancestry in the profession on São Tomé might suggest. At times of high demand for accommodations in port cities like São Tomé or Havana, centrally-located brothels rented rooms to provide complementary hospitality services.[34] They also attracted women seeking relief and profits from the price of lodgings and foodstuffs, which rose with the number of seagoing vessels stationed at the port. In the sixteenth century, prostitutes arrested in Lisbon were even sent to São Tomé, where their services may have been considered more essential.[35] Similarly, English 'wenches' were shipped to Virginia and Barbados in the seventeenth century, and two hundred French 'women of ill repute' were sent from Paris to Martinique in 1680-1682.[36] Whether they migrated as prostitutes, captives, indentured labourers or prospective brides, women entered colonial settings as potential sex providers. Frontier settings and tropical transport hubs with high mobility and mortality demanded their services.

In cases of need or opportunity, prostitution entailed 'a reliable form of capital accumulation' and could coincide with support for a family or marriage as well as with unmarried cohabitation.[37] A recent study of sex work on a long-term global scale has found migrants, including women enslaved and sold or otherwise forced into prostitution, were over-represented among prostitute populations. At the same time, from the standpoint of labor history, the comparative study of prostitution emphasizes an overriding motivation for the occasional or ongoing provision of sexual services: profits exceeding those available in other sectors of the economy.[38]

Few early colonial regimes attempted to forbid sexual relations, and especially prostitution, between members of different ethnic groups. In fourteenth-century Aragon, however, David Nirenberg encountered the

---

32 Arlindo Manuel Caldeira, *Mulheres, Sexualidade e Casamento em São Tomé e Príncipe (Séculos XV-XVIII)* (Lisbon: Cosmos, 1999), pp. 107-13.

33 Maria Emma Mannarelli, *Private Passions and Public Sins: Men and Women in Seventeenth-Century Lima* (Albuquerque: University of New Mexico Press, 2007).

34 Amelia L. Cabezas, "Prostitution in Havana", in *Selling Sex in the City: A Global History of Prostitution, 1600s-2000s*. Edited by Magaly Rodriguez Garcia, Lex Heerma van Voss, and Elise van Nederveen-Meerkerk (Leiden: Brill, 2017), pp. 414-40.

35 Caldeira, *Mulheres*, pp. 112-13.

36 Brown, *Good wives, nasty wenches*, pp. 9, pp. 81-104, and Morgan, *Laboring women*, pp. 74-75.

37 Luise White, *The Comforts of Home: Prostitution in Colonial Nairobi* (Chicago: University of Chicago, 2009), p. 2.

38 Maja Mechant, "The Social Profiles of Prostitutes", in *Selling Sex in the City*, pp. 833-58.

prohibition of sexual relations across religious lines applied to Christian prostitutes fined for accepting Jewish or Muslim clients.[39] In this case, sex entailed a boundary for the definition and separation of communities whose members interacted in many other ways, in addition to a prerogative of Christian masculinity. In most global cities, however, attempts to limit prostitutes' sexual encounters (as well as the spread of disease) to members of their own ethnic or racial groups only arose in the second half of the nineteenth century.[40]

While challenging sexual boundaries, early colonial demographics and power relations commodified women in general, and particularly those enslaved or free without other sources of income. Marissa Fuentes explored the case of Rachel Pringle Polgreen, a former slave abused by her father and master in Bridgetown, Barbados, who subsequently earned considerable wealth as the owner of a brothel frequented by British navy officials. While exploiting and beating the enslaved women she owned, Polgreen attained sufficient status and social connections in order to be buried in Bridgetown's Anglican Church of Saint Michael.[41] Through a close analysis of Polgreen's relationship with an enslaved and subsequently indentured woman, Marisa Fuentes depicted the brutality and lack of consent involved in enslaved women's prostitution. Even after obtaining or purchasing their freedom, in practice, Afro women's sexualization and commodification could reflect a lack of choice.[42]

In contrast, Jessica Johnson has depicted sexuality as a source of female agency. She has linked hospitality services and common-law marriage from the coast of Senegambia to eighteenth-century New Orleans. Without denying sexual exploitation, Johnson points to Afro women's use of intimate relations to exercise a measure of freedom and pursue their own interests.[43] Port cities like Bridgeport, Gorée, and New Orleans faced periods of intense demand for room and board, as well as foodstuffs. Women's provision of accommodations, washing of clothes, or sale of food in the public plaza, could provide pretexts and contacts to arrange sexual services. While officials in the Iberian Peninsula regulated prostitution as a

39 David Nirenberg, *Communities of Violence. Persecution of Minorities in the Middle Ages* (Princeton: Princeton University Press, 1996), pp. 127-65.

40 Elise van Nederveen-Meerkerk, Magaly Rodríguez García and Lex Heerma van Voss, "Sex sold in World Cities, 1600s-2000s. Some conclusions", in *Selling Sex in the City*, pp. 871-80.

41 Marisa J. Fuentes, "Power and Historical Figuring. Rachael Pringle Polgreen's Troubled Archive", in *Connexions: Histories of Race and Sex in North America*. Edited by Jennifer Brier, Jim Downs, and Jennifer L. Morgan (Champaign: University of Illinois Press, 2016), pp. 143-68, p. 125.

42 Marisa J. Fuentes, *Dispossessed Lives. Enslaved Women, Violence, and the Archive* (Philadelphia: University of Pennsylvania Press, 2016), pp. 46-69. See also Fuentes, 'Power and Historical Figuring', pp. 120-36.

43 Johnson, *Wicked Flesh*, pp. 12-51.

profession, those in the colonies often tolerated it as an option for women in times of need.[44]

In Panama, testimony gathered to oppose the exaction of tribute from free Blacks in 1576 reported that some Afro-descendants had sold their own clothing and hired themselves out to serve Spaniards in order to pay the tax. One tailor even declared that, with the imposition of the new tax, 'some Black or mixed women would offend God in order to earn it with their bodies, lacking goods in order to pay'.[45] Witnesses emphasized the social and moral price of the new fiscal demands to argue that the Crown should avoid placing such an onerous burden on the poor.

In general, however, the Crown of Spain, and of Portugal in 1580-1640, appeared more concerned about concubinage, repeatedly prohibited by law, than prostitution, often considered a necessary evil. Concubinage undermined Christian marriage, which prostitution arguably upheld by providing an outlet for men's pre- (and extra-) marital sexual desires. While tolerating prostitution, the Crown also supported the claims of abandoned wives whose husbands had taken up residence with other women in America, ordering them to send for or return to their spouses.[46] Prostitution, on the other hand, met clear economic demands, in addition to a perceived social function.

While often implicit in historical sources, prostitution became more visible in literary works, including *La Tragicomedia de Calisto y Melibea* by Fernando de Rojas (1499) and *Measure for Measure* by William Shakespeare (1604). In Shakespeare's drama, the Duke of Vienna's deputy orders the brothels razed and condemns men to death for extra-marital relations. Rather than eradicating a widespread practice, however, the deputy finds himself drawn to the same sin, so that the brothel and the convent both survive his attacks.[47] In the novel by Fernando de Rojas, the Celestina, like Shakespeare's 'Mistress Overdone', attends to vital social needs and manages extensive information. As the regent of a brothel trafficking in intimate knowledge, she forged love magic through witchcraft.[48]

---

44 On these regulations see María Teresa López Beltrán, *La prostitución en el Reino de Granada a finales de la Edad Media* (Málaga: Centro de Ediciones de la Diputación de Málaga, 2003); Francisco Vázquez García and Andrés Moreno Mengíbar, *Historia de la prostitución en Andalucía* (Sevilla: Fundación José Manuel Lara, 2004).

45 'algunas negras o mulatas ofenderían a Dios para lo ganar con sus personas por no tener bienes con que lo pagar'. Archivo General de Indias, Seville, Panamá 42, N.1, f. 100-98, 'Interrogatorio presentado por parte de los negros y negras mulatos y mulatas libres', August 21, 1576. ArtEmpire. Documents. Number 4308.

46 María José de la Pascua Sánchez, *Mujeres solas. Historias de amor y de abandono en el mundo hispánico* (Málaga: Servicio de Publicaciones, Centro de Ediciones de la Diputación de Málaga, 1998).

47 William Shakespeare, 'Measure for Measure', *The Folger Shakespeare Library* (Online).

48 Fernando de Rojas, *La Celestina*, ed. by Julio Cejador y Frauca, in Biblioteca Virtual Miguel de Cervantes (Online).

The devil's allies

Demonic interference appeared as pervasive as extramarital sex, which it frequently accompanied, in the early modern world. Satan loomed large as a source of power that Protestants and Catholics alike considered opposed to their own.[49] Beyond religious denominations, contrasting trends emerge in different regions' witchcraft persecutions. Comparative research into witchcraft in Europe and America reveals a differential impact of gender, with witchcraft or sorcery normally aimed at men in Mediterranean and Iberian societies, where few executions took place.[50] In contrast, authorities from Augsburg, Germany to Salem, Massachusetts accused witches of killing babies, animals and crops, and ordered them executed as an intolerable threat to social order.[51] Along such lines, neither Puritan New Englanders nor Iroquois Indians would 'suffer a witch to live' among them.[52] In episodes of persecution, authorities often targeted and convicted older, marginalized women, without excluding their husbands.[53]

The Salem trials (1692-1693) famously erupted after a century of less-virulent persecutions in colonial Massachusetts, and with witch hysteria in Europe on the wane. In Spain, the rise of official scepticism regarding such phenomena began with judge Alonso de Salazar's review of testimony from the Basque village of Zugarramurdi, 1609-1614.[54] Salazar's doubts about demonic intervention in local disputes marked the Spanish Inquisition's last executions for witchcraft.[55] The tribunals, nevertheless, continued to record and investigate accusations of witchcraft and sorcery, which they normally classified as a more individual, urban phenomena.

---

49 Jorge Cañizares-Esguerra, *Puritan Conquistadors: Iberianizing the Atlantic, 1550-1700* (Stanford: Stanford University Press, 2006).

50 Ana María Díaz Burgos, *Tráfico de Saberes: Agencia femenina, hechicería e Inquisición en Cartagena de Indias (1610-1614)* (Madrid: Iberoamericana/Vervuert, 2020); Emma Maria Mannarelli, *Inquisición y Mujeres: Las Hechiceras en el Peru* (Lima: Ediciones del Congreso del Perú, 1998, 1987).

51 Lyndal Roper, *Witch Craze: Terror and Fantasy in Baroque Germany* (New Haven: Yale University Press, 2004).

52 Matthew Dennis and Elizabeth Reis, 'Women as Witches, Witches as Women', *Women in Early America* (New York: New York University Press, 2016), pp. 66-94; Alison Games, *Witchcraft in Early North America* (Lanham: Rowman and Littlefield, 2010).

53 Paul B. Moyer, 'Diabolical Duos: Witch Spouses in Early New England', *Early American Studies: An Interdisciplinary Journal* 20:3 (2022), pp. 371-406.

54 These cases inspired a prize-winning film directed by Pablo Aguero, *Akelarre* (Avalon, 2020).

55 Gustav Henningsen, *El Abogado de Las Brujas: Brujería Vasca e Inquisición Española*. Translated by Marisa Rey-Henningsen (Madrid: Alianza Editorial, 1983).

In the Iberian world, sorcery and witchcraft often involved a sexual component and drew upon erotic filters common in the Mediterranean.[56] In the Americas, such practices incorporated diverse Catholic, Indigenous, and African traditions of amatory and culinary magic. The Spanish Inquisition, which extended to America and the Philippines, investigated such practices and recorded abundant testimony about them. At the same time, however, Native Americans' exemption from inquisitorial scrutiny, as neophytes in the Catholic faith, facilitated the survival of traditional knowledge alongside an important degree of religious syncretism. Rather than social misfits, the women, and occasionally men, accused of witchcraft included well-connected and respected members of their communities.[57]

Native Americans from the Inca to the Iroquois identified outsiders' practices, yet never their own, with witchcraft and demonically-driven destruction.[58] Roughly the same could be said for Africans and Europeans. Inquisitorial trials in Lisbon record cases of sorcery and witchcraft practiced with *bolsas de mandinga* or bags containing charms and amulets associated with the Mandinga of Upper Guinea.[59] Among the Congo, witches harnessed other-worldly forces for good or evil purposes, and could be powerful women or men, including selfish and greedy rulers or slave traders believed to consume shiploads of captives. Catholic priests in the Congo identified ritual specialists with charms and amulets as speaking with the devil, on the one hand, while seeking to appropriate their sacred power on the other.[60]

In seventeenth-century Panama, sorcery and witchcraft, often employed as synonyms, moved between urban and rural areas. While sheltered from Inquisitorial action, indigenous traditions of shamanic medicine and religion offered local communities reservoirs of knowledge about their world. Recourse to indigenous healers led Europeans, Africans and creoles to access or, alternatively, to fear, such power. A seventeenth-century divorce case preserved in the episcopal archive of Lima recorded the accusations of an enslaved man, Baltasar de Biafra, that his wife, Francisca Ponce de Villareal, a free Black cattle-owner who resided near Panama's Mercedarian monastery, had attempted to kill him. When Biafra fell ill and began to vomit blood at the Cruces warehouse between Portobello and Panama, he and his owner, Blas Rico, attributed the malady to herbs that his wife had sent in order to poison Biafra's wine. Francisca

56 Romain Bertrand, 'Where the Devil Stands: A Microhistorical Reading of Empires as Multiple Moral Worlds (Manila-Mexico, 1577-1580)', *Past and Present* 242 (2019), pp. 83-109.

57 Mannarelli, *Inquisición y Mujeres*.

58 Dennis and Reis, 'Women as Witches', 83-84.

59 Caldiera, *Mulheres*, 94.

60 Games, *Witchcraft in Early North America*, pp. 27-28.

Ponce resented their accusations of sorcery and witchcraft, retorting that, although she had cared for Biafra, he had never provided the sustenance he owed her as his wife, a matter that implicated Rico as well. The religious tribunal upheld Francisca's request for a divorce, even when Biafra and Rico appealed the case. Rather than evidence of a pact with the devil, Biafra's accusations against Francisca demonstrated the impossibility of their marital relation.[61]

Culturally-mixed communities drew upon and exchanged diverse ancestral knowledge regarding herbs, healing, birth and death, facilitating survival and adaptation to new environs. Other societies rejected and even persecuted unfamiliar customs as a threat to colonial power. The history of witchcraft, famously equated with 'the history of women' in New England,[62] becomes more complex in Cartagena, Panama or São Tomé, where it involved men and women, inter-culturality and religious syncretism. If intersectionality or hybridity defined the witch,[63] it also facilitated a measure of tolerant scepticism regarding witchcraft itself.

Conclusion

With respect to exogamous marriage, extra-marital sex and magic, tolerance bred tolerance in the early modern world. It also stemmed from necessity in frontier societies hungry for settlers and labor. In 1978, Nicholas Canny compared the early British experience in Ireland and Virginia, using material from one frontier to illuminate the other. Contrary to official aspirations, widespread desertion to the 'natives', the exploitation of indentured servants, and solidarities among indentured and enslaved laborers marked the first century of English overseas ventures.[64] The practical inability to enforce official ideals, which Canny traced from sixteenth-century Ireland to Virginia, also characterized other imperial endeavors. Jean-Frédéric Schaub has suggested that the European takeover of new territories, whether in Mexico or Minas Gerais, featured a period of relative openness, social interaction and possible promotion for the local offspring of parents of different ancestries. Following this initial acceptance, according to Schaub and Silvia Sebatiani, western societies increasingly insisted

---

61 Archivo Arzobispal de Lima, Apelaciones de Panamá, leg. 1, exp. 10, 'Interrogatorio en el pleito de divorcio contra Baltasar Biafra', July 3, 1625, ArtEmpire. Documents. Number 3804.

62 Carol F. Karlsen, *The Devil in the Shape of a Woman: Witchcraft in Colonial New England* (New York: Vintage Books, 1998). See also John Demos, *Entertaining Satan: Witchcraft and the Culture of Early New England* (Oxford: Oxford University Press, 1982).

63 Dennis and Reis, 'Women as witches', p. 69.

64 Canny, "The Permissive Frontier", pp. 17-43.

upon religious and even racial 'purity' for full membership.[65] Yet the rise of racism appears neither linear nor inevitable from the viewpoint of gender and ethnicity. Boundary-crossing practices, including intermarriage, extra-marital sex, and witchcraft, not to mention food preparation or wet nursing, could reinforce social order or spark unrest, depending on the context. Genders, ethnicities and local realities often defied attempts to impose stable categories.

One such attempt, the eighteenth-century *casta* paintings aimed to classify a variegated population, the inhabitants of New Spain and their offspring, after two centuries of mixture. These illustrations, which typified different couples and their descendants, arguably reflected more of an effort to influence than to record social realities. In the absence of laws to enforce distinctions among groups, and amidst extensive admixture, these images appear designed to promote certain unions as increasing status, while discouraging others. After generations of social and sexual relations among groups, the *casta* paintings labelled and caricatured certain partnerships.[66] Societies that had prohibited inter-group relations, on the other hand, did not depict them.

Colonial settlements did not necessarily become less inclusive over time. None of the most influential comparative studies of empires to date, however, focus on gender or ethnicity. Although much empirical work to facilitate such comparisons remains underway, the extant scholarship points to key points of comparison and variables affecting them. Factors including necessity, opportunity and the amount of traffic through a given site appear to have influenced marriage, extra-marital sex, and witchcraft more than religious or 'national' affiliations. Within and across imperial and confessional frameworks, commercial relations and human migrations continually refashioned social norms. Gender and ethnicity informed – and defied – internal and external frontiers. As points of comparison, marriage, prostitution and witchcraft sustained and challenged empires.

---

65 Jean-Frédéric Schaub and Silvia Sebatiani, *Race et histoire dans les sociétés occidentales (XV-XVIIIᵉ siècle)* (Paris: Albin Michel, 2021), pp. 95, pp. 293-94, pp. 484-85.

66 See Carolyn Dean and Dana Leibsohn, 'Hybridity and Its Discontents: Considering Visual Culture in Colonial Spanish America', *Colonial Latin American Review* 12:1 (June 2003), pp. 5-35; Susan Deans-Smith, 'Creating the Colonial Subject: Casta Paintings, Collectors, and Critics in Eighteenth-Century Mexico and Spain', *Colonial Latin American Review* 14:2 (2005), pp. 169-204; and Jean-Paul Zuñiga, 'Muchos Negros, Mulatos y Otros Colores'. Culture Visuelle et Savoirs Coloniaux au XVIIIᵉ siècle', *Annales. Histoire, Sciences Sociales* 68:1 (January 2013), pp. 45-76.

DAVID MARTÍN MARCOS _____

Rustics and Barbarians

Otherness and Counter-hegemony in the Early Modern Iberian World

Introduction

In the early modern age, ideas of barbarism and rusticity were frequently invoked to furnish the construction of otherness. Historians have long demonstrated how barbarism shaped European descriptions of Indigenous Americans from the early fifteenth century onwards. Barbarism informed the classification of Amerindians as a group who supposedly needed to be civilized and Christianized by its "discoverers". On the other hand, during this period the idea of rusticity was frequently used by the European urban elites to describe rural communities, who lived in conditions of isolation and poverty. Both these categories were concerned with the identification of otherness. Both groups – barbarians and rustics – were assigned a clear status of inferiority in contrast to their elite and European observers.

The cultural impact of European, and in particular, ancient concepts of alterity on the representation of American regions and their inhabitants has been widely discussed by historians. Equally, scholars have shown how pejorative concepts of the "Indies" were invoked in the early modern age to denigrate the supposedly uncivilized social traits of European rural populations. However, despite the clear links between these two representations of otherness, a comprehensive study of them has yet to be undertaken. The aim of this chapter is to redress this oversight by exploring how ideas of rusticity and barbarism fed into one another. The discussion that follows sheds light on how ancient and modern ideas of territoriality, alterity, and backwardness shaped the early modern transatlantic circulation of stereotypes and led to a reformulation of the legal definition of the *miserabile persona*. This reformulation of *miserabile persona* reinforced the subjection of those deemed 'different' under the tutelage and moral control of specific forms of authority.

David Martín Marcos • Universidad Nacional de Educación a Distancia

Supplicant Empires, ed. by Edward Jones Corredera, Habsburg Worlds, 8 (Turnhout: Brepols, 2025), pp. 77–100
BREPOLS ❧ PUBLISHERS   10.1484/M.HW-EB.5.145065

This chapter shows how the superposition of these two categories, rustics and barbarians, did not result in a positive understanding of rustics or American Indians akin to the myth of the natural man and the noble savage. Instead, this analysis explores how the myth of an internal European "Indies" – as invoked by European intellectuals to describe isolated rural areas – is a prescient example of the powerful interplay between the conceptual categories that elites applied to both European peasants and the Amerindians. This chapter explores the sources of information, including the plays of Lope de Vega, that fostered these views. In its concluding sections, this chapter proposes a new reading of the widespread use of notions of barbarism and rusticity in the Iberian world, one that suggests that the uses of these terms exhibit some of the counter-hegemonic practices deployed by liminal communities in both Europe and America.

Rusticity: mirror and analogy

Early modern concepts of the rural sphere were conditioned by antithetical views of the characteristics of urban societies, on the one hand, and the countryside on the other. According to Fray Antonio de Guevara, the renowned Franciscan author who was born in the Cantabrian Mountains and who, for many years, pursued a celebrated career at the court of Charles V, men who lived in the countryside were the embodiment of candour. In his view, the rural hamlets they inhabited offered the utmost tranquillity in contrast to the turbulent activity of the court. These men lived lives that were to be envied for their carefree simplicity. In 1539, following his appointment as bishop of the small Galician diocese of Mondoñedo, Guevara wrote his celebrated work *Menosprecio de corte y alabanza de aldea*, in which he declared: 'O how happy is he that hath wherwithal to liue in the village without troubling both of himself and many sondry places, without séeking of so many lodginges'. He lamented the way that '*ciudadanos*', city dwellers, ignored the wonders of rural life and saw those who lived in the countryside as fools. These men were a source of fear and suspicion and, in the minds of city dwellers, they ought to emulate urban models of behaviour, even if these were completely alien to the peasant mindset.[1]

---

1 The research for this chapter was undertaken as part of the project *Contrahegemonías: comunidad, alteridad y resistencia en los márgenes del mundo ibérico* (PGC: PID2021-127293NA-I00), which is funded by the Spanish Ministry of Science and Innovation. "*Quan bienaventurado es aquel a quien cupo en suerte de tener que comer en la aldea, porque el tal no andará por tierras extrañas, no mudará posadas todos los días*". Antonio de Guevara, *Menosprecio de corte y alabanza de aldea* (Madrid: Viuda de Melchor Alegre, 1673 [first edition: 1539]), pp. 28 and 60. The above translation is taken from the contemporary English edition of this work: *A looking glasse for the court. Composed in the Castilian tongue by*

The yearning for a primitive world akin to a bucolic Arcadian land-scape, a recurring trope encountered in compositions like *Menospore-cio*, gained popularity over the course of Guevara's lifetime. The Italian-inspired eclogues that writers such as Garcilaso de la Vega were introduc-ing into Iberian literature at that time fostered the popularity of the *locus amoenus* in educated circles, as well as the stereotype of the figure of the kindly peasant. The poet declared that the shepherds' sweet lament should be sung like a gentle lyric verse that could inspire its readers. Nevertheless, these remarks were made at a time when recent plays devoted to pastoral themes, a different genre, and a seemingly more realistic and specific liter-ary mode, had fostered an impression, among the bulk of the population, of the figure of the rustic as a simple individual devoid of any malice. In this reading, this was a person who lived beyond the vicissitudes of the world, a world with codes that were unknown to him, and which existed beyond the physical limits of the valley or rural regions in which he lived out his life.

Within this tradition, the region of Sayago represented – akin to a Castilian Boeotia – the site par excellence where the rustic was deemed to possess the most archaic customs. From the end of the fifteenth century, the inhabitants of Sayago, who tended to be presented as a people possess-ing few social skills, were represented in the plays of Juan del Encina and his disciples. This was a radical statement in favour of the vernacular. As a result, these characters gave rise to a set of human types, whose garments and idiosyncratic manner of speaking – an example of the *sermo humilis* encountered in Virgil, whose work Encina had translated into Castilian – went against the grain whenever they travelled beyond their own lands. Indeed, as Encina commented in his *Egloga representada en requesta de unos amores*, the rural people could be brutes and lack refinement, but that did not always mean they did not know how to defend themselves in the face of mockery and insult from outsiders: 'Do you think us villagers / do not know how to defend ourselves? You city folk, do not even think / about mocking us, /as we too have hands /and a tongue for giving out nicknames'.[2]

The heterodox positioning of the rustic established a generic counter-point to the milieu of the court. On the basis of this binary representation, rural people were increasingly presented as coarse types. On occasion they

---

the Lorde Anthony of Gueuarra Bishop of Mondouent, and chronicler to the Emperour Charles. And out of Castilian drawne into Frenche by Anthony Alaygre. And out of the French tongue into Englishe by Sir Fraunces Briant Knight one of the priuy Chamber, in the raygne of K. Henry the eyght, (London: William Norton, 1575), p. 23.

2 '¡Cuidáis que los aldeanos / no sabemos quebrajarnos? / No penséis de sobajarnos /esos que sois ciudadanos, /que también tenemos manos / y lengua para dar motes'. Juan del Encina, *Teatro Completo* (Madrid: Real Academia de la Historia, 1893), p. 94.

were presented as burlesque figures in plays; at times authors ridiculed them by caricaturing the ways in which their customs broke with established models of behaviour. At first glance, these literary representations undermined the cultural status of the rural population. However, rural characters also granted authors considerable freedom to criticize social structures deemed to be set in stone, thereby ensuring the survival of a significant form of critique that extended beyond the theatres of Castile. In Portugal, representations of peasants inspired by the inhabitants of Sayago were integrated into the literary construction of the inhabitants of the Beira region.[3] Numerous *autos* by the playwright Gil Vicente developed the topos of the peasant who has lost his way in an educated urban milieu. On both sides of the frontier, this argument became a constant feature of theatrical works, and it lucidly illustrated the distance between the two antagonistic worlds of *civitas* and *rusticitas*. Indeed, this went on to become an enduring staple of Iberian literature.

Gil Vicente's *Auto da Fé*, drafted in 1510, was an inaugural example of this literary trend in Portugal. In this play, Gil Vicente coined his recurring representation of two shepherds astonished by the magnificence of a chapel and its elaborate paraphernalia. While absorbed in their state of wonderment, they were equally taken aback by the presence of countless tonsured men in the church. 'How many of these dimwits there are', declared one of the peasants, in an unequivocal and biting critique of the excessively high number of friars that were found in early modern societies. Since it was uttered by a rustic character, however, this statement appeared as a simple and innocent observation.[4]

The subsequent trajectory of this literary development, which was not immune to external influence, can be easily traced across an extensive chronological period. Over a century and a half later, in *O saloio cidadão*, a late Portuguese adaptation of Molière's *Le Bourgeois gentilhomme*, and published in Lisbon in 1773, a parvenu character celebrates – in a deformation of the earlier topos – how once he became wealthy he set his sights on changing his residence in the countryside for one in the city. This was, he thought, the way to progress in the eyes of society: 'The village is far from here and nobody knows me, which is no small matter, as I have always heard it said that nobility consists in living fifty leagues away from your birthplace'.[5] Among the most pressing needs of this upstart who had only

---

3 Fidelino de Figueiredo, *História literária de Portugal (ss. XII-XX)* (Coimbra: Nobel, 1944), pp. 113-14.

4 '*Cuantos que estos zotes son*'. Gil Vicente, *Obras completas de Gil Vicente*. "Re-impressão fac-similada" da edição de 1562 (Lisbon: Biblioteca Nacional, 1928), f. 14v.

5 '*a terra está longe, e ninguem me conhece que não faz pouco ao caso, porque sempre ouvi dizer, que consiste a nobreza em viver sincoenta legoas for a do natural*'. *O saloio cidadão* (Lisbon: Na Offic. De Simão Thadeo Ferreira, 1773), pp. 1-2.

just arrived in the city, was knowing how to dress appropriately, and taking lessons in the 'Court's customs and refinement' for which he had to call on 'a Master, great Philosopher' capable of helping him.[6]

However, other authors used the idea of the rustic for more radical ends. For Diego de Torres Villarroel, a professor at the University of Salamanca, and another author who addressed the moralizing dichotomy between rural and city dwellers in the early eighteenth century, the limitations of educated urbanites needed to be underscored.[7] He did so in a fictional dialogue with a villager that forms part of the opening pages of his treatise *Cartilla rustica*, published in 1727. He stated: 'You, in your Hamlets, should be aware [...] that these men you consider to be wise, are those who are most lacking in truth'. For Torres Villarroel, many of the allegedly educated individuals formed a clique of idlers who, once they became literate, lapsed into vice and bad habits. By contrast, argued the professor, in the countryside children, barely weaned on this culture, ensured their sustenance by 'the sweat of their brow', or '*el pan sudando*'.[8]

Rustics, Indians and barbarians: overlapping categories

The idealization of the honest peasant, whether that be as a dedicated and willing manual labourer, or a contemplative individual rapt in thought and in constant communion with nature, provided a discursive focus that was partly linked to the topos of the natural man. This stereotype was best known after it was transformed and popularized by Jean-Jacques Rousseau during the eighteenth century, who depicted an individual characterized in terms of innocence, neither good nor bad, and prone neither to vice nor to virtue. However, the tradition of the noble savage also formed part of a prelude to the early modern period and it was drawn from the Europeans' responses to their initial contact with the Indigenous American peoples. One example of this is the naked philosopher who, according to the historian Peter Martyr d'Anghiera, conversed with Christopher Colombus on the island of Cuba. Likewise, the explorer Pero Vaz de Caminha described the innate candour of the Indians encountered in 1500 along the coast of modern-day Brazil by the fleet captained by Pedro Alvares Cabral. In the

---

6 '*politicas, e filagranas da Corte*', '*hum Mestre, grande Filosofo*'. *O saloio cidadão*, pp. 1-2.

7 On Villarroel's life see Ivy Lilian McClelland, *Diego de Torres Villarroel* (Boston: Twayne Publishers, 1976).

8 '*Has de saber* [...] *que estos hombres, que tenéis por sabios en vuestras Aldeas, son los que más en ayunas están de las verdades*'. Diego de Torres Villarroel, *Cartilla rustica, phisica visible, y astrología innegable: lecciones de agricultura y juizios pastoriles, para hacer docto al rustico* (Madrid: Antonio Marin, 1727), p. 3.

second half of the sixteenth century, authors such as Michel de Montaigne declared that the practices of the Indians of Brazil were no more barbaric than some forms of European behaviour.

The seventeenth-century accounts of Paul Le Jeune and other French Jesuits about the North American peoples who had settled along the banks of the St Lawrence River were also used – far more explicitly – by the *philosophes*, who drew on these chronicles as raw material to develop their ideas.[9] While it is true that the convergence of the mental images elaborated from descriptions of the Indigenous communities encountered in the American continent, and those of the European rustic population, combined to reinforce the positive characterizations of both topoi, it was nevertheless clear that the attribution of these specific traits had also fostered unkind representations of these groups. Eighteenth-century writers also drew on the idiosyncratic legacy of the barbarian found in the biblical and Graeco-Latin traditions, a heritage which had originally shaped the discriminatory visions of Native Americans of many colonizers.

Modern historians and anthropologists have been all too aware of the joint legacy of the rustics and the barbarians, as it concerns the rudiments of comparative ethnography and, above all, the transposition of the model of the noble savage from Europe to America.[10] Its development follows a classic Eurocentric conceptual trajectory over the course of which European cultural elements were used to form responses to the new experiences witnessed in America, while also assimilating them within an intellectually recognizable context. As a result, references to the ancient Iberians recurred in Spaniards' accounts and narratives of the so-called New World, despite the fact that their knowledge of this pre-Roman era was grounded in myth. In one of these writings, the *Tratado único y singular del origen de los indios*, Diego Andrés Rocha argued that it was wholly credible that the American peoples were descendants of the biblical ancestors of the Spanish. He explained how, after the Great Flood, the Indies had been populated by the descendants of Japheth; these peoples were related to Tubal, who had colonized Spain. As a result, the Indians had 'fierce customs and [were] slow witted' just like the primitive Spaniards. However, the fundamental distinction was that in America 'barbarity' had endured 'because the customs of Rome and Greece have not reached them'. Furthermore, Rocha argued that there were parallels between the clothing worn by Iberian peasants and indigenous Americans, and likewise

---

9 Charles W. Colby, 'The Jesuits Relations', *The American Historical Review*, 7:1 (1901), pp. 36-55; and Carole Blackburn, *Harvest of Souls. The Jesuit Missions and Colonialism in North America, 1632-1650* (Montreal: McGill-Queen's University Press, 2000), p. 7.

10 Joan-Pau Rubiés, 'Ethnography and Cultural Translation in the Early Modern Missions', *Studies in Church History* 53 (2017), pp. 272-310; Anthony Pagden, *The Fall of Natural Man: the Origins of Comparative Ethnology* (New York: Cambridge University Press, 1982).

there was a proximity between the languages spoken on both sides of the Atlantic. He went on to declare that, out of all those who travelled to America from Iberia, it was the Basques who found it easier to learn the Quechua language, given its proximity to the Basque tongue.[11]

Naturally, parallels were also invoked between the two continents: there were 'barbarians' on Iberian shores. In the wake of the Council of Trent, missionaries travelled to rural zones of Catholic Europe and reported their 'discovery' of genuine local Indies.[12] As was the case in America and elsewhere, it befell these missionaries to redeem the sins and ignorance of those who inhabited these European 'Indies', individuals who were essentially described as examples of a European form of savagery. As a result, the descriptions of the rusticity encountered by European missionaries became interwoven with the accounts of the peoples of the geographical zones that lay beyond Europe, whereby the constructions of otherness that emerged could not avoid being shaped by a bidirectional discourse, shifting back and forth across the Atlantic. As a result, mental images from one side of the ocean fed into those on the other side, and these in turn were used to reformulate what was taken to be the point of departure for any comparison, which thereby blurred any certainty about where the model underpinning this epistemic order was truly located.

'I believe that Your Excellency will have been informed in other [letters] how useful our [confreres] are in Galicia, which some rightly call the Indies': in the mid-sixteenth century, a member of a Jesuit college from Galicia wrote these words to the General of the Society of Jesus.[13] His was just one of a long list of testimonies that reported the existence of 'Indians' across a range of regions in Western Christendom. These 'Indians' were identified in Corsica and Calabria, in Brittany and Ireland, in Andalusia and in the heart of Castile. The idea of an 'internal' exotic subject, which shaped this outlook, was fomented on a daily basis by those letters and accounts that reached Europe recounting the conversions performed by the Jesuits, as well as their sacrifices, in America and the East Indies.[14] In these documents, the Jesuits and their peers in the religious orders exaggerated their devotional activities, the dangers they faced, and their selfless commitment to preaching. As a result, besides stoking a '*deseo de*

---

11 '*costumbres fieras y de torpe entendimiento...*', '*...por no haber llegado la política de Roma y Grecia*' Diego Andrés Rocha, *Tratado único y singular del origen de los indios del Perú, Méjico, Santa Fé y Chile* (Lima: Manuel de los Olivos, 1891 [1681]), vol. 2, pp. 47-77.

12 Adriano Prosperi, *Tribunali della coscienza: inquisitori, confessori, missionari* (Turin: Einaudi, 1996), pp. 551-99.

13 '*Creo que tendrá Vuestra Excelencia por entendido de otras [cartas] la utilidad de los nuestros en Galicia que con razón la llaman algunos Yndias*'. (Padre Arias to Diego Laínez. Monterrey, 1 May 1562. ARSI, *Hisp.* 99, fols. 179-80.

14 Paolo Broggio, *Evangelizzare il mondo. Le missioni della Compagnia di Gesù tra Europa e America (secoli XVI-XVII)* (Rome: Carocci, 2004).

Indias (desire for the Indies)' among those young men who aspired to follow in their footsteps, urban residents received a plethora of arguments and references with which to reformulate perceptions of the outlying regions of these European urban centres.

Over time these meta-narratives merged with the elite's vision of the world inhabited by rustics and lower strata groups, a process that continued well into the modern age. Italian historians have come to realize how this trend fostered the rise of the *questione meridionale* (the southern question). Alongside engrained views underscoring the idea of deep cultural and economic differences between northern and southern Italy, which continued after Italian unification, these ideas became rooted in the myth of an internal Indies. Southern Italy was deemed a place untouched by the word of God, as was metaphorically described in the celebrated novel *Cristo si è fermato a Eboli* written in the 1940s by the intellectual Carlo Levi, and which was set in Lucania. 'A paradise inhabited by devils', reads the saying that is still applied to Naples, and which embodies the discrimination and stereotype of the South as a backward region.[15]

However, these discriminatory views were not just applied to these regions. In Portugal and Spain, the idea of an '*Indias de acá*' (Indies over here) was often linked to remote hinterlands, and those mountainous regions and frontier zones that formed the *Raya*, the dividing line between Spain and Portugal. These spaces were frequently presented as an uninhabited wasteland, awaiting their transition towards 'civilization'. The tones with which these landscapes were depicted were not wholly distinct from those used to portray the *sertões* (hinterlands) and the Pampas in the Americas. In broad terms, the same conceptual palette underpinned perceptions of the wilderness encountered in the British Isles, which were identified with equally inhospitable regions of North America during the early phase of English colonization. This gave rise to the idea that frontiers – both external and internal – formed a barrier between civilization and barbarity. This, in turn, became a key factor that shaped representations of outlying rural regions.

Eighteenth-century examples abounded. One was provided by the Scottish author James Boswell, who said that being in the Highlands was like finding oneself amidst a tribe of Indians. The highlanders were 'as black and wild in their appearance as any American savages'.[16] Other commentators on the state of highland regions were even more precise with their comparisons. With regard to the inhabitants of the mountain regions of the *Raya seca* (the non-fluvial frontier zone) between Portugal and Galicia, the Archbishop of Braga, Fray Caetano Brandão, stated that

---

15 '*paradiso abitato da diavoli*'. Jennifer D. Selwyn, *A Paradise Inhabited by Devils: The Jesuits' Civilizing Mission in Early Modern Naples* (Aldershot: Routledge, 2004).

16 Peter Burke, *Popular Culture in Early Modern Europe* (Farnham: Ashgate, 2009), p. 30.

they had the faces of '*tapuyas tostadas* (toasted Tapuia)'. The prelate was referring to the *castrexos*, the inhabitants of the Portuguese *vila* of Castro Laboreiro, and he made recourse to the term '*tapuya*', which was then generically used to refer to the Indigenous people of inland Brazil. The Tapuia had been considered to be an especially barbarous community, in contrast to the Tupi, who inhabited Brazil's coastal regions and spoke a form of *lingua geral*. The Tupi, unlike the Tapuia, embodied the idea of the docile Indian who could be civilized.[17] Prior to taking up the crozier in the Diocese of Braga, he had served in Brazil as Bishop of Pará. It was there that the Bishop had seen the Tapuis, whom he would later recall – thousands of kilometres away – when visiting Castro Laboreiro. The fact that these eighteenth-century authors, Boswell and Brandão, continued to use racial categories derived from America to refer to both Scottish high-landers and frontier communities living on the Spanish-Portuguese *Raya* illustrates how the persistence of such perceptions of these communities was based on a shared transatlantic alterity that circulated among educated groups. These ideas, in other words, had taken root in European discourse.

Profiles such as Brandão's are – as a point of departure – especially relevant for the task of charting the ideological itineraries that gave rise to savagery and rusticity becoming entwined as concepts during the early modern period. They demonstrate how these concepts were shaped by the accumulation of these conceptual layers. However, this perception of the rural population and the American natives was rarely based on direct expe-rience. Instead, despite the distances involved, it should be noted that the cultural fabric from which analogies linking American Indigenous peoples and European peasants (and vice versa) was woven from numerous inter-connected threads, which extended far beyond their immediate authors. Two centuries before Brandão spoke of the Tapuia and the *Castrexos*, in New Spain the Dominican Diego Durán stated that the American peoples were neither less refined, nor simpler than the inhabitants of certain regions of Castile, including Sayago and Las Batuecas, whereby the topos of the savage Indian underwent a dramatic alteration. Durán had travelled to New Spain as a child. He then entered the Dominican Order, and thanks to this religious community's channels of information, he learnt about the contrasting realities encountered in Iberia. It may therefore be argued that his American knowledge was completed by reading treatises and accounts of distant European places, along with those European reports that were received about those who inhabited other continents. It was by no means a coincidence that Mancio del Corpus Christi, another Dominican, deliv-ered a series of lectures at the University of Salamanca between 1565 and 1567 on the issue of the illegitimacy of the usurpation of the property

---

17 Pedro Puntoni, *A Guerra dos Bárbaros. Povos indígenas e a colonização do Sertão Nordeste do Brasil, 1650-1720* (São Paulo: Hucitec-Edusp, 2002).

of the Indians on the grounds they were barbarians.[18] He declared that in Las Batuecas – and elsewhere in Castile – there were coarser men than the barbarians themselves. His views signalled the fluid circulation of reports and experiences of this kind, and how they emerged in response to the debates, which the Dominicans had contributed to, on indigenous property rights and the American conquest.

But another source of ideas of barbarity of the early missionaries in the Americas was their own gaze of the barbarians in Iberia. The *indipetae*, letters of application to undertake extra-European missions, submitted by Jesuits reveal the genealogy of these prejudices. In 1623, for example, the Jesuit Juan de Llano wrote to the General of the Society expressing his wish to take part in the missions in the Americas. But he also acknowledged that there was a need for people like him to work with the rural peasants of his native land. 'Asturias and the mountains were considered to be another Indies', he argued, and given that he was acquainted with those who lived there 'and they with me', perhaps he could provide a beneficial service to them.[19]

At the heart of this issue was the fact that the European rustics and the Indigenous Americans were linked by a common perception of their social isolation. According to Father José de Acosta's famous treatise, *De Procuranda Indorum salute*, written in Lima in 1576, isolation was a common factor for both the European rural communities and American Indians, and it was the result of geographical determinism: the environment, combined with the lack of education and customs it gave rise to, as opposed to any innate natural traits, was considered to be the determining factor for the genesis of barbarity. Acosta argued: 'Even in our native Spain we see men born in the heart of Cantabria or Asturias, who are deemed inept and boors when amongst their countrymen', although in school, at court, or in the market these same individuals rapidly 'excel thanks to their admirable ingenuity and skill, unsurpassed by none.'[20]

Strategies and discourses of domination

In theory, missionary work was intended to redress the sinful state and ignorance of the barbarians of Europe and America. This view was used

---

18 Augusto Sarmiento, 'Textos inéditos de la Escuela de Salamanca. Mancio (cont.): "De dominio"', *Persona y Derecho* 12 (1985), pp. 262-63.

19 'Eran tenidas por otras Yndias las Asturias y montañas'. Juan de Llano to the General of the Society of Jesus. Salamanca, 16 May 1623. ARSI, *Hisp.* 88, f. 2.

20 'Vemos incluso en nuestra misma España hombres nacidos en plena Cantabria o en Asturias, a quienes se tiene por ineptos y paletos cuando se quedan entre sus paisanos', 'sobresalen por su admirable ingenio y destreza sin que nadie les aventaje'. José de Acosta, *De Procuranda indorum salute* (Madrid: CSIC, 1984), vol. I, p. 151.

to justify the evangelization of the Indies both in Europe and across the Atlantic. Pastoral interventions, supported by the elite, ensured their success. Elites had to tackle the problem of the reserved and uncommunicative nature of the social groups that existed on the margins of society. With regard to inland Galicia, for example, the fact that the population was dispersed in small parishes and hamlets hindered efforts to impose the social discipline exercised by the Inquisition. It prevented agents such as bishops from exercising effective control over the people. In the later sixteenth century, the solution was 'to subjugate the villages [...] so that these barbarian people would adhere to more domesticated customs, and be taught Christian doctrine, because living as they do it is impossible [to achieve]'.[21] Subjugating rural villages, and founding new enclaves, whether these were new settlements in the Iberian Peninsula or Indian villages in America, was deemed to be the best approach to redressing the rustics' savagery. A campaign of subjugation was trialled and implemented in both the Old and New Worlds over a long period of time. A key tenet of this programme was the authorities' firm view that the rustics' own belief that they did not belong to any local community, one structured in accordance with the precepts of religion and monarchy, was a constant source of danger.[22]

In Extremadura, Antonio Ortiz Jarero was all too aware of the need to impose this policy. In 1734, he proposed to the Bishop of Coria that the people of Las Hurdes should give up living in this isolated region, and instead form communities alongside other headwaters in the region, where life, as he understood it, would be easier.[23] Throughout the eighteenth century, Las Hurdes, which was frequently confused with Las Batuecas, came to be associated with a legend that identified it as the quintessential Iberian inland Indies. The playwright Lope de Vega played a part in popularising this association. In his play, *Las Batuecas del duque de Alba*, written in the late sixteenth century, he devoted considerable space to the issue of the isolated lives lived by rustics, and considered ways to redress this matter. Lope recounted the story of a group of individuals, descendants of the Visigoths, who had for centuries lived in isolation in a deep valley in the midst of Castile. There they underwent a regression similar to what the American Indians were thought to have undergone. The Batuecos, having forgotten their Christian faith, worshipped the stars, and in their

---

21 'reducirlos a poblaciones [...] para que esta gente bárbara fuese política doméstica, y enseñada en la doctrina cristiana, que viviendo como viven es imposible'. Jaime Contreras, *El Santo Oficio de la Inquisición de Galicia (poder, sociedad y cultura)* (Madrid: Akal, 1982), p. 94.

22 Tamar Herzog, 'Indigenous *Reducciones* and Spanish Resettlement: Placing Colonial and European History in Dialogue', *Ler História* 72 (2018), pp. 9-30.

23 José Pablo Blanco Carrasco, 'Una visión inédita de Las Hurdes en el siglo XVIII. El auto de Ortiz Jarero de 1734', *Alcántara* 31-32 (1994), pp. 161-92.

little Arcadia they remained unaware of the existence of any other people on the face of the earth. Then, during the era of the Catholic Monarchs, they were 'discovered' by two lovers fleeing the court of the Duke of Alba. Following this chance meeting, the rustic savages were taught by those who discovered them about Christianity, educated, and informed about everything they did not know. When the Duke of Alba appeared on stage, they were converted into his vassals and even undertook a thanksgiving pilgrimage to the sanctuary of Peña de Francia.

Lope's account of this 'discovery' gained renown during the early modern age. It was mistakenly considered to be historically accurate by a great many of the educated elite. *Las Batuecas* was not the only work in which the playwright addressed the issue of savagery. Lope turned to this subject in *Los guanches de Tenerife y conquista de Canaria* and in theatrical works that directly addressed America, most notably *El Nuevo Mundo descubierto por Cristóbal Colón*. In the first of these two plays the writer – drawing on an epic poem by Antonio Hernández de Viana – proposed a domestication of alterity that was not wholly distinct to that reserved for Iberian rustics. However, the play devoted to Columbus's undertaking stands out because it is the first play in which an American-Indian character features as one with a dramatic role. 'These [Spaniards], desiring gold / from your Indies, declare themselves saints, / feigning Christian decorum', explained the figure of the devil, dressed as an Indian, to the Native American Dulcanquellín. Wholly contrary intentions are declared by the Spanish soldier, Castillo, to the Guanche, Siley, in the play about the capture of Tenerife; here Castillo observed that: 'I come solely to obey / what my Monarchs order, / they wish that you should be subject to the law of the holy Christ'.[24]

What these plays reveal is how the barbarity and idolatry ascribed to the "Indians" of these new lands, in conjunction with their exoticism and inferiority in contrast to the Spaniards, were in fact transversal features of the configuration of the generic savage, whether imagined within Europe or America – or in Macaronesia, located between the two continents. During the dialogue between the rustic, Triso, and Brianda, the fugitive lover and newcomer to the valley of Las Batuecas, the former asks who Columbus was. She responds by saying he was nothing more than a man who thought he had found another world, and this is perhaps the clearest proof of how malleable theatre could be when it came to identifying the fluid nature of such a widely projected issue. As a result, during the early modern period, literature represented the space of the barbarian.

---

24 'Estos [españoles], codiciando oro / de tus Indias, se hacen santos, / fingen cristiano decoro', 'Vengo a obedecer no más / lo que mis Reyes me mandan, / que reduciros desean a la ley de Cristo santa'. Lope de Vega, *Los guanches de Tenerife y Conquista de Canaria* (Santa Cruz de Tenerife: Museo de Historia de Tenerife, 1996), p. 41.

Literature, and it could not have been otherwise, served as a catalyst for the growth of a profoundly patronizing attitude towards these marginalized groups. The idea of tutelage was one expression of this worldview, and this formulation provided the last resort to achieve a supposed progression, according to which a community would forge its way out of the penumbra of backwardness and ignorance. The subjugation of 'barbaric' communities would lead to their enlightenment.

But the limits of this civilizing endeavour were too evident for some, irrespective of how much trust was placed in religious virtues. Many were also sceptical of the claims that the American and Asian populations were docile, welcoming, and open to receiving the teachings of preachers.[25] An indication of these reservations is provided by the *Historia General y Natural de las Indias* written by the chronicler Gonzalo Fernández de Oviedo: he justified the death of the many Indians who lived on the island of La Española, on the basis that they were a 'nation that had greatly veered away from any wish to understand the faith'. Oviedo considered their numerous customs and rites to be 'abominable', although curiously he noted similarities between their dances and songs and those of European peasants.[26] Rusticity and barbarity were evidently interlinked, whereby the detection of otherness was not so much tied to the identification of extravagant and distant habits, but instead to the discovery of signs of an apparent lack of civility. Hence, Fernández de Oviedo clearly felt compelled to underscore the distance between the peoples he described in his treatise. He also considered himself obliged to highlight, in the opening pages of his work, that the '*extraños y bárbaros*', strange and barbaric, words included in his text were due to novelties encountered in the indigenous world, as opposed to an alleged ignorance of the orthographic rules governing the Castilian language: 'do not question my use of the vernacular, as I was born in Madrid: I grew up in the royal household and I have conversed with noble people'.[27]

Language: the original grammar of barbarity

Language was, after all, a concern that had been closely linked to the notion of barbarity since antiquity. The term *barbarous* was originally a Greek onomatopoeic term that referred to a babbling child scarcely able to

---

25 Adriano Prosperi, *Il Concilio di Trento: una introduzione storica* (Turin: Einaudi, 2001), p. 20.

26 '*nación muy desviada de querer entender la fe*'. Gonzalo Fernández de Oviedo, *Historia General y Natural de las Indias, Primera Parte* (Madrid: Real Academia de la Historia, 1851), pp. 124-25 and 128.

27 '*no se pongan a la cuenta de mi romance, que en Madrid nací y en la casa real me crie y con gente noble he conversado*'. González de Oviedo, *Historia General*, p. 5.

articulate words, and it swiftly became associated with foreigners, and then those who could not master Greek.[28] Their ignorance of the language of the *polis* was seen as an indication of backwardness, a lack of civility, and a sign of their belonging to an inferior group. Barbarian languages went on to be interpreted as a demonstration of the incapacity for rational thought, and the linguistic plurality that these groups somehow represented soon emerged in Augustinian thought as a threat to peace and understanding, as opposed to a universal tongue that ensured uniformity.[29] Therefore, it should come as no surprise that in the early sixteenth century, the Portuguese and Spanish continued linking certain languages to barbarity in many of their descriptions of the Native Americans. The Jesuit accounts of the Tapuia populations in the Amazon basin are just some such texts, and they offer the clearest insight into how their authors wove together narratives of the Indians' savagery and warlike nature. A range of Jesuit testimonies note their incapacity to decipher a variety of languages which, in their view, nobody could understand.[30] Furthermore, these texts provide unequivocal demonstrations of the Jesuits' vision of the American realities encountered in New Spain. There, inaccessible and difficult languages were spoken by human groups, and these languages did not seem to have been established by men, but instead by nature, like uneducated voices of 'birds or wild animals'.[31]

The moral and political dimension of language, which was used to demarcate these communities, define their natures, and impose an order on their relationships with the Spanish, underpinned views of alterity. Despite the claims that language acted as part of an imperial project within which there was a prevailing apology for the domination exerted over the native populations, this issue was not restricted to the colonial context: this posture was also adopted in Iberian regions. In the early modern period, in other words, linguistic concerns were invoked in numerous debates in

---

28 The OED's etymology for the word barbarous states: 'The Greek word had probably a primary reference to speech, and is compared with Latin *balbus* stammering. The sense-development in ancient times was (with the Greeks) "foreign, non-Hellenic", later "outlandish, rude, brutal"; (with the Romans) "not Latin nor Greek", then "pertaining to those outside the Roman empire"; hence "uncivilized, uncultured", and later "non-Christian", whence "Saracen, heathen"; and generally "savage, rude, savagely cruel, inhuman". The later uses occur first in English, the Latin and Greek senses appearing only in translators or historians'. "Barbarous, *Adj.*, Etymology". *Oxford English Dictionary*, Oxford University Press, September 2023 (Online).

29 Edward G. Gray, *New World Babel: Languages and Nations in Early Modern America* (Princeton: Princeton University Press, 1999), pp. 8-9.

30 Andrea Daher, *O Brasil francês. As singularidades da França Equinocial, 1612-1615* (Rio de Janeiro: Civilização Brasileira, 2007), p. 130.

31 '*páxaros o animales brutos*'. José A. Llaguno, *La personalidad jurídica del indio y el III Concilio Provincial Mexicano (1585). Ensayo histórico-jurídico de los documentos originales* (Mexico City: Porrúa, 1963), p. 200.

order to address specific aspects linked to the issues of integration and conflict associated with Iberian communities and identified in terms of alterity.

On the one hand, some authors advocated that the contact between Moriscos and Old Christians in towns and cities prompted the former to learn the Castilian language, as well as its culture, whereby they became more effectively integrated than the Morisco communities who lived in isolation in the mountains. In contrast, other writers argued that the widespread opposition to acculturation – underscored by the paradigmatic revolt of Las Alpujarras in 1567 – demonstrated that the members of any nation would risk their lives before they risked losing their own language.[32] Following the Morisco uprising, it was stated that this revolt highlighted the concerns held by some about converting unbelievers living in remote regions to Christianity: because although this was considered to be, 'a very good and very holy undertaking, it seems that it is akin to having one's house full of vipers and scorpions and making no effort to clean them out of it'.[33]

On the other hand, according to some missionaries, when evangelization and education were rigorously implemented in neighbouring regions it was always possible to identify clear signs of progress. In this regard, some missionaries emphasised that the progress made was visible in zones where missions focused on rustics and simple folk, which indicated that there was an effort to redress the abandonment and neglect that had theoretically spread for decades, and which had engulfed entire communities across the Iberian Peninsula in ignorance. It was believed that these rural populations were thereby slowly but surely being guided back to orthodoxy thanks to this evangelizing activity. However, even those who embraced the periodic triumphalism vaunted by the friars who propagated the Christian faith in the so-called inland Indies could claim to have dispelled the effects of the 'barbaric' tongues these rustic communities were considered to speak.

In this same period, many argued that some of the indelible traits of the supposed incivility of the many communities living along the Iberian borderlands were the result of how their inhabitants communicated. For many observers, their forms of speech constituted a generic barbaric language, and in numerous chronicles and letters this was noted in both the

32 Kathryn A. Woolard, 'Bernardo de Aldrete and the Morisco Problem. A Study in Early Modern Spanish Language Ideology', *Comparative Studies in Society and History* 44:3 (2002), pp. 446-80.

33 '*obra muy buena y muy santa parece que es como si uno que tiene la casa llena de víboras y escorpiones no pusiera cuidado en limpiarla dellos*'. Florencio Janer, *Condición social de los moriscos de España: causas de su expulsión, y consecuencias que esta produjo en el orden económico y político* (Madrid: Real Academia de la Historia, 1857), pp. 267-68.

northern and southern regions of this frontier. The transitional dialects
between Portuguese and Galician or Castilian, as well as the variant forms
of the Asturian-Leonese language spoken in some regions, were thus
not identified as what they really were, dialects and languages, but were
instead used as the foundation for a negative categorization based on a
diffuse idea of barbarity, one that revealed no concern whatsoever for the
particular characteristics of each language. From an exogenous perspective,
the speakers of these languages were reviled for their vulgar and unrefined
character, which was rooted in their differences with educated spheres. The
vernacular linguistic forms used by frontier peoples and other rural communities thereby placed their speakers on the margins of a set of political
structures which sought to impose its rule over them and excluded them
from political consideration on the basis of sociocultural and linguistic differences.[34] In the eighteenth century, these views continued to be held: the
grammarian Jerónimo Contador de Argote declared that the inhabitants of
the frontiers of Trás-os-Montes and Minho spoke local dialects that were
deemed so 'barbaric', that 'they could not be called Portuguese'.[35]

Two hundred years earlier, Bartolomé de las Casas, in his *Apologética
historia*, had argued that whoever spoke a strange language could certainly
be considered a 'barbarian', but that did not suffice to make the Indians,
nor anybody else, 'true barbarians'. 'True barbarians' were imagined to be
closer to beasts than men, living without laws or institutions, without culture or religion, and Las Casas underscored that the American Indigenous
communities lacked none of these elements.[36] Nor for that matter did
the European rustics. The clearly accentuated polysemous classificatory
criteria outlined in Las Casas's apologetic discourse explained why in
America, as well as Europe, the use of the term 'barbarian' was widely used
in inconsistent ways. The ubiquity of these criteria may be read as an indication that this term gave rise to a striking imprecision, were it not for the
fact that these criteria served to demonstrate that the European continent
was no different than the so-called anomalous legal zones, spaces which
are often taken for granted when speaking of the fragility of the imperial
spaces.[37] If, as historians have shown, the latter were territories framed
by porous and irregular, and on occasion, ill-defined, boundaries, then

---

34 David Martín Marcos, 'Hablar en la frontera: lenguas, estereotipos y contactos en la Raya
hispano-portuguesa durante la Edad Moderna', *Hispania* 273 (2023) (Online First).

35 'no se les podía llamar portugués'.Jerónimo Contador de Argote, *Regras da lingua portugueza,
espelho da lingua latina, ou disposiçaõ para facilitar o ensino da lingua latina pelas regras
da portugueza... muyto accrecentada, e correcta. Segunda impressaõ* (Lisbon: na Officina da
Musica, 1725), pp. 295-96.

36 Bartolomé de las Casas, *Apologética historia de las Indias*, ed. by M. Serrano y Sanz (Madrid:
Bailly Bailliére e hijos, 1909), chapters CCLXVI, CCLXVII and epilogue, pp. 690-94.

37 Lauren Benton, *A Search for Sovereignty: Law and Geography in European Empires, 1400-1900*
(New York: Cambridge University Press, 2009), pp. 1-39.

Europe, with its own borders and internal frontiers, should not be invoked as a contrast that configures an ideal place where everything was clearly intelligible and well ordered.

Forms of resistance and appropriations in the identification of contra-hegemonic spaces

Drawing on this assumption it is easy to perceive how an immense diversity of practices and ontologies were concealed behind the idea of barbarity, and they were deployed to classify peoples with contra-hegemonic histories and practices, irrespective of their origin. The confrontation these peoples found themselves exposed to in conjunction with the tendentious disciplinary attitude taken by the religious, political and cultural elites they came into contact with, was, in reality, the factor that imposed a uniformity on them; this was achieved through elite discourses and modes of representation, which were generally employed to mediate descriptions of their practices and customs. 'Not only do they lack culture, but they do not even use or know about writing, nor do they conserve monuments of their history, [and] they lack any written laws, and they possess barbarian institutions and customs'. In his *Demócrates Segundo* Juan Ginés de Sepúlveda declared these views in the wake of the polemic stirred up by Las Casas about the American Indians, as Las Casas argued exactly the opposite.[38] In Scholastic debates, invoking the character of European peasants proved to be the best form of demonstrating how this type of generalization was not exclusive to the Indies. Francisco de Vitoria, in his *Relectio de Indis*, noted that among the European peasantry there were those who were barely distinguishable from animals.[39] However, this did not mean the Indians were animals. Vitoria went on to argue that this did not make the Indians or the rustics innately inferior beings who could be deprived of their *dominium* – in other words, they could not be deprived of their sovereignty over the territories they lived in – unless this action was justified with criteria that were also applicable to Christians. In spite of these debates, the topos of the animal-like aspect of both the Indians and the rustics did not fade from view during that period.

With the intention of not restricting barbarity to America, José de Acosta himself stated in his *Historia Natural y Moral de las Indias* that in

---

38 'No sólo carecen de cultura, sino que ni siquiera usan o conocen las letras ni conservan monumentos de su historia, [y] carecen de leyes escritas y tienen instituciones y costumbres bárbaras'. Juan Ginés de Sepúlveda, *Demócrates Segundo o de las justas causas de la guerra contra los indios*, ed. by Ángel Losada (Madrid: CSIC, 1984 [1951]), p. 35.
39 Francisco de Vitoria, *Relectio "De Indis"* (1539), ed. by L. Pereña y J. M. Pérez Prendes (Madrid, CSIC, 1967), p. 30.

Italy and Spain there were also 'packs of men, who aside from gesture and figure have no other feature of men'.[40] Meanwhile, Antonio de Guevara, the very same who had previously lauded the peasants' bucolic life, presented the figure of the rustic as an '*animal en forma de hombre*', an animal in human form, in a passage of his *Relox de príncipes* (1529). In this work he recalled the story of a rustic called Milenus, who lived on the banks of the Danube but had met Emperor Marcus Aurelius in Rome. According to Guevara, the latter had been pleasantly surprised by the marked acuity of Milenus's discourse,[41] and remarked that perhaps this was a key factor for identifying the rustics' innate capacities, aside from seeking to categorize their tremendously monolithic attitudes. Essentially, when the elite interacted with them on the ground, and sought to transmit a religious message or idea of government to them, their preconceived notions about the rustics' passivity were challenged: they frequently encountered attitudes that indicated the peasants possessed a noteworthy sense of autonomy with regard to their interpretations of religion and politics.

In a late seventeenth-century hagiography of Frei António das Chagas, the author noted that the inhabitants of the village of Provesende had not hesitated in telling this missionary to leave, arguing that they were already Christian, and that he would make better use of his time 'preaching to the Moors'.[42] This was a clear demonstration that the Church's presence was not always welcome. This sentiment was also noted in 1649, in the arguments set out by the residents of Casares de las Hurdes, and in their opposition to the plan to build a church in the village. This scheme had been proposed by a Carmelite friar from the convent in Las Batuecas: '[in response to my] wishing to build another church in Casares, they replied through their mayor that they be left alone, [...] that just as their ancestors had done without one, they would do the same, and that given this situation that I should cease begging for alms'.[43] Still more intriguing is the declaration made by a rural labourer in Viseu in 1701. In response to missionary endeavours, he stated that he thought that Christ had not suffered as much as the friars who visited his village led him to believe,

---

40 '*manadas de hombres, que si no es el gesto y figura no tienen otra cosa de hombres*'. José de Acosta, *Historia natural y moral de las Indias* (Seville: Iuan de Leon, 1590 [1589]), chap. XXIV.

41 Antonio de Guevara, *Obras completas, II. Relox de príncipes*, ed. by Emilio Blanco (Madrid: Biblioteca Castro, 1994), pp. 633-38.

42 '*predicar a los moros*'. Manuel Godinho, *Vida, virtudes, e morte com opinião de Santidade do Veneravel Padre F. António das Chagas* (Lisbon: Miguel Deslandes, 1687), p. 69.

43 '*queriendo hacer otra iglesia en los Casares, ellos respondieron por su alcalde los dejase que no la querían, [...] que así como sus antepasados pasaron sin ella, pasarían ellos y que visto esto yo dejara de pedir limosna*'. Archivo de Batuecas, Fondo "Documentación histórica de la Casa".

and that it was likely that they invented and exaggerated the accounts of his martyrdom in order to 'invoke greater terror' amongst the local communities.[44]

Miserabiles personae

The foregoing examples allude to forms of resistance to social discipline and cultural appropriation, and they also provide a means to assess the true scope of the labels of the rustic and barbarian in the everyday life of rural communities. The inferior status these communities were subjected to was frequently contested, despite the existence of a lengthy tradition going back to Roman Law and medieval ideas which included the definition of *miserabiles personae* (miserable people) that had evolved at the heart of the *ius commune*. It was within that legal framework that the concept of the wretched had been used to define the state of helplessness of certain social groups – characterized as rustic, ignorant or destitute – who were deemed worthy of the king's special protection, or else of judges in the form of guardianship. Over time this concept was also applied to the Native Americans.[45] In *Política indiana*, Juan de Solórzano Pereira stated that the Indians' *son, i deben ser contados entre las personas que el Derecho llama Miserables'* – '[they] are and must be considered amongst the people the Law terms Wretched', and as such they were deemed entitled to the privileges granted to minors, paupers and rustics.[46]

Despite encompassing continual limitations, it is nonetheless obvious that the foregoing generalization served to confirm the links between representations of European peasants and the indigenous Americans.[47] Legal doctrine considered these two European and American groups to be equal, and it did so to the extent of configuring a transatlantic variant of the category *miserabile*, in Iberian lands and in the Indies, and this was to be constantly controlled and disciplined. On the one hand, there can be no doubt that over the course of the early modern age the invention of the American Indian, as a subject of alterity, drew on these same principles, and that this trend gave rise to archetypes akin to savagery and barbarity, and the wider circulation of this racial concept also encompassed

44 'meter más terror'. José Pedro Paiva, 'Pastoral e evangelização', in *História religiosa de Portugal. Volume 2: Humanismos e reformas*, ed. by João Francisco Marques and António Camões Gouveia (Casais de Mem Martins: Círculo de Leitores, 2000), p. 250.

45 Francisco Cuena Boy, 'Especialidades procesales de los indios y su sustrato romanístico', *AFDUDC* 10 (2006), pp. 157-67.

46 Solorzano Pereira, *Política indiana* (Madrid: Diego Díaz de la Carrera, 1648), ch. XXVIII, pp. 230-39.

47 David Martín Marcos, *People of the Iberian Borderlands. Community and Conflict between Spain and Portugal, 1640-1715* (New York: Routledge, 2023), pp. 14-15.

more "evolved" figures – Aztecs or Incas, for example, represented in a Roman garb, or else Indians who had taken on Spanish customs, and who therefore had had culture bestowed upon them.[48] However, on the other hand, adhering to this logic, in Europe a reconfiguration of a rustic type emerged, one that engaged with a parallel evolution that was, on occasion, inspired by encounters with indigenous American communities. Thus, the feather-adorned Indian who was featured, for example, in the first visual representations of the American continent, was nevertheless a bearded figure who offered a glimpse of a pre-American imaginary. However, the subsequent image of the bearded, blood thirsty Indian, who inhabited wild regions and whose irrational violence would become a staple in popular Western culture until well into the twentieth century, was also used to describe those who inhabited rural and theoretically remote areas of Europe at times of war.

The people of Trás-os-Montes, who mutilated the noses and ears of their enemies during the Spanish invasion of Portugal in 1762, could have easily been considered Iroquois braves, on the basis of the report published in the *Courrier d'Avignon* that year.[49] The Portuguese and the Spanish were, as the Spanish author Manuel Martí complained, the only peoples who, along with the Muscovites, still remained to be civilized in eighteenth-century Europe.[50] Yet, to what extent did the lower strata rural communities accept this claim? Although it is not easy to provide an absolute response to this question, it seems that some regional groups internalized a degree of regional specificity, which for some people indicated an exotic tradition. The priest Francisco Gregorio de Salas, who was born in Jaraicejo and served in Cáceres, was an attentive observer of the peasant life he had known in Jaraicejo as a child. He wrote that his fellow people of Extremadura were '*los indios de la Nación*', 'the Indians of the Nation'.[51] Even in the twentieth century the people of Las Hurdes, like foreigners making their way to another country, would say, '*ir a Castilla*', or 'go to Castile' when they made their way to the plains further north in search of employment as reapers, and then they would proclaim to

48 Jesús Bustamante, 'La invención del Indio americano y su imagen: cuatro arquetipos entre la percepción y la acción política', *Nuevo Mundo Mundos Nuevos* 11 December 2017 (Online).

49 Alain Hugon, 'Heterotopía: las manifestaciones de las identidades europeas e hispánicas en tiempos de guerras en las gacetas en francés en Europa (Gazette de Leyde, Courrier d'Avignon, 1749-1762)', in *Nacionalidad e identidad europea en el mundo hispánico*, ed. by David González Cruz and Pilar Gil Tebar (Madrid, Sílex, 2018), 89-110, pp. 102-03.

50 Manuel Martí to Gregorio Mayans, 8 February 1736, in *Epistolario Mayans-Martí*, edited by Antonio Mestre (Valencia: Publicaciones del Ayuntamiento de Oliva, 1972), p. 383.

51 'in tenebris'. Francisco Gregorio de Salas, 'Juicio imparcial, ó definición crítica del carácter de los naturales de los reinos y provincias de España', in *Colección de los epigramas, y otras poesías críticas, satíricas y jocosas de don Francisco Gregorio de Salas; corregidas en esta cuarta edición* (Madrid: Por Repullés, 1827), p. 41.

'*ir a Extremadura*', or 'go to Extremadura' when they headed back south. Clearly, the geographical distinction they established meant that they identified with a distinctive idea of their homeland, albeit one that had originally been constructed outside of it.

The people of Las Hurdes were not the only people who dealt with this sense of alterity. In Portugal, the settlers of the frontier hamlet of Barrancos were viewed as '*jenízaros*', or 'Janissaries' by the residents of other villages of the Alentejo because they spoke a dialect that many identified as a mixture of Portuguese and Castilian. However, the residents of Barrancos referred to the inhabitants of the region, who from time to time made their way to their cluster of houses, as 'Portuguese', thereby countering the *mestizo* reality they encountered on their own doorstep. Up until the last century, the *Vaqueiros de alzada*, literally, 'nomadic cowherds', of the mountains of Asturias and León formed a marginal social group, and the inhabitants of the surrounding villages distinguished them in racial terms as descended from the "moorish" race. Their differences – as Gaspar Melchor de Jovellanos once pointed out – should in fact be traced to their socioeconomic practices. These were characterized by their employment haulage, transhumant livestock farming, and their residence, in accordance with the changing seasons, high up in mountain pastures. However, these factors also made this community an especially cohesive social group that had no problem accepting its marginalization. Indeed, at times they even encouraged this view in order to preserve their means of subsistence and ways of life.[52]

Other communities segregated by this line of social demarcation were the *Pasiegos*, who lived in the Pas Valley, also in the Cantabrian Mountains, the *Agotes* (Cagots) from the valleys of the Pyrenees, and even, and perhaps more surprisingly, some fishing communities close to Lisbon. Regarding the latter, the people who inhabited the sandy regions running south of the mouth of the Tagus also gave rise to a singular classification that persisted into the modern age. During the eighteenth century, sur-rounded by marshes and swamps, the region known as Caparica began to be permanently inhabited by descendants of fishermen from the Algarve region and the Beira Coast. The people of Lisbon swiftly formed an idea of these communities as a paradigmatic example of a 'rustic way of life [...] akin to beasts'. Furthermore, there was no shortage of detailed descriptions of the violent confrontations between the two regional groups who inhab-ited this coastal region, as well as the 'shrieking of their barbaric and rustic languages'.[53] However, over time the fishermen of Caparica developed

---

52 See María Cátedra Tomás, *La vida y el mundo de los vaqueiros de alzada* (Madrid: Centro de Investigaciones Sociológicas-Siglo XXI, 1989).

53 '*rústico modo de viver* (...) *à maneira de féras*', '*alarido daquellas bárbaras, e rústicas lingoas*'. *Nova relação da batalha naval, que tiveram os algaravios com os saveiros nos mares, que confinão*

an awareness of their singularity by emphasising the contrast with the workers in the surrounding urban areas; since they grew up during an incipient phase of industrialization, their upbringing fostered their strong sense of belonging to this specific marine zone, even though, for many people, this area was little more than a sterile stretch of sandbanks.

Conclusion: the other islands of power

Besides revealing the categorization associated with a negative stereotype, the inherent rusticity and isolation of all the communities discussed over the course of this chapter offers an insight into the existence of regions which, from the perspective of the Iberian elites, were not under their control. These were inexorably linked to notions of barbarity and models of savagery frequently transposed from America. It is well known that, in the so-called overseas territories, the Iberian monarchies extended their control thanks to a discontinuous form of territorial settlement, one that was far from constituting a uniform region of sovereignty. It gave rise to 'islands of government' of a colonial nature amidst broad swathes of territory that remained on the margins of civilizing campaigns. Interaction with the native inhabitants of these territories, considered indomitable by some, prompted the classification of the traces left by their communities in untended and theoretically unproductive regions. These traces were interpreted as signs of their communities' incapacity to achieve any type of progress, and this scenario served to support the repression of any ideas that went against colonial norms by imposing a discourse on the exercise of politics, administration and governability. Furthermore, in accordance with this logic, there were those who indicated that within the Iberian Peninsula's metropolitan framework certain locations were demarcated as 'insular' regions within a sea of land.[54] Some historians have justified this structure of occupation by arguing that during the *ancien régime* political space was conditioned by its miniaturization and division into small communities that exercised a patrimonial control over a specific field of action.[55]

According to this theory, in liminal zones and sparsely populated regions, this process of miniaturization led to the existence of stretches

---

com o celebrado paiz da Trafaria (Catalumna: en la imprenta de Francisco Guevarz, 17––); and Paulo Perestrelo da Câmara, *Diccionario geographico, historico, politico e litterario do reino de Portugal e seus domínios* (Lisbon, n.p., 1850), Volume 1, p. 154.

54 Tamar Herzog, *Frontiers of Possession: Spain and Portugal in Europe and the Americas* (Cambridge: Harvard University Press, 2015), pp. 191-242.

55 António Manuel Hespanha, *Vísperas del Leviatán. Instituciones y poder político (Portugal, siglo XVII)* (Madrid: Taurus, 1989), pp. 81-82.

of land in which the exercise of politics – understood as exclusive to the Iberian monarchies – was seen as incomplete, or else was practically absent. As a result, there were numerous regions that seemingly did not belong to anybody and whose jurisdiction was periodically and inconclusively debated, and which contributed to a recurring lack of clarity along the frontiers, for example, between Castile and Portugal, and a lack of awareness about zones with challenging terrains. Clearly, the problem raised by this reading is that it only seems valid for one of the various groups of actors who engaged with these realities, as this historiographical view simultaneously tends to perpetuate a narrative that excludes those individuals labelled as savages or barbarian precisely because they lived on the margins of "civilized" society. But as this chapter has tried to show, both in America and in Europe, subaltern groups that populated these liminal regions were classified on the basis of interconnected images in which they almost always emerged as subjects predestined to savagery, re-education, or harsh punishment, all part of a chain of action imposed by royal officials or missionaries. This was intended to achieve their complete submission. Thus, for example, it was said of the Pas Valleys in northern Spain that thanks to the activities of the Jesuits at long last 'the spirits of those rustics [were seen to be] so broken that they had become pious, when before they had displayed ferocity, and setting aside the accidental features of brutes they lived not only as men, but as well-adjusted Christians'.[56] In truth, the trajectory through the three social states – brutes, men and Christians – proved universal for the erudite conception of innumerable societies interpreted in terms of otherness.

Seen from this perspective, the infallibility granted to this view of social predestination has led to a considerably limited understanding of the Iberian past. The topoi linked to rusticity and barbarity were in reality vital indexes of counter-hegemonies undertaken by highly varied communities. These communities were much more powerful in the specific zones in which they developed than many would think, and they gave rise to relational and subsistence spaces which over the course of centuries did not require any agreement to be reached with those who categorized them as the renowned barbarians of America and the bemused Indians of Europe. Rather than being viewed as victims, or as people who stood in agonistic

---

56 'los ánimos de aquellos rústicos [se veían] tan trocados, que ya era piedad, lo que antes mostraba fiereza, y ya dejando los accidentes de brutos, vivían en la verdad no sólo como hombres, sino ajustados cristianos'. Juan de Villafañe, La limosnera de Dios: relación historica de la vida y virtudes de la excelentissima señora Doña Magdalena de Ulloa Toledo Ossorio y Quiñones, mujer del excelentissimo señor Luis Mendez Quixada Manuel de Figueredo y Mendoza, comendador del Viso, y Santacruz, de Argamasilla, y del Moral, y obrero mayor de la Orden de Calatrava, ayo del ... señor Juan de Austria ... mayordomo mayor del emperador Carlos Quinto ... fundadora de los colegios de Villagarcía, Oviedo y Santander de la Compañía de Jesus (Salamanca: Francisco García Onorato, [1723?]), p. 399.

opposition against those who sought to classify them in negative ways, the moment has come to also consider them as agents who stood firm in the defence of their practices and customs. This, after all, ensured their survival.

FABIEN MONTCHER _____

Imperial Blind Spots

Iberian Rhizomatic Worlds. Indeterminacy, Thickness, and Multispecies Interactions in Early Modern Travel Accounts[*]

What might a centerless, dynamic, and stateless model for multispecies interactions add to the history of the early modern Iberian worlds? This essay proposes a rereading of seventeenth-century narratives produced by people who did not necessarily identify as Iberian subjects–especially Portuguese, Dutch, Spanish and French travelers, exiles, and enslaved peoples–yet who commented upon the social and environmental diversity of territories related to the Iberian monarchies. The social history of this multitude of privileged, displaced, and/or oppressed individuals brings to the

_____

[*] I am grateful for the support of the Newberry Library in Chicago which, through the auspices of a 2023-24 Long-Term Fellowship, allowed me to bring this article to completion. Many thanks to my Newberry colleagues as well as to my colleagues at Saint Louis University who, through the Taylor Geospatial Institute Spatial Humanities Working Group (TGI-SH) and the Center for the Iberian Historical Studies (CIHS), provided me with valuable feedback.

Indeterminacy often results from the human attempt to observe 'nature' and to impose one-sided political, social, and spiritual orders upon it. Because the natural world could potentially contain all orders, indeterminacy allows humans to consider multilayered regimes of normativity as well as the informal logic of their lives. Indeterminacy makes space for the unpredictable dimensions of any form of power. See Lorraine Daston, *Against Nature* (Cambridge: MIT Press, 2019). Although the concept of 'thick description' has most often been defined as the critical study of scholarly interpretations, thickness, as a historical category, operates as one of the results of the multilayered interpretations of what historical actors experienced and questioned as their realities. See Clifford Geertz, 'Thick Description: Toward an Interpretive Theory of Culture', in *The Interpretation of Cultures* (New York: Basic Books, 1973). For anthropologist Anna Lowenhaupt, indeterminacy forced people in situations of survival to collaborate with other beings across multiple environments. What appears as undetermined can also contribute to human experiences and representations of what this article defines as thick environments. See Anna Lowenhaupt Tsing, *The Mushroom at the end of the world. On the possibility of life in Capitalist Ruins* (Princeton: Princeton University Press, 2015).

Fabien Montcher • Saint Louis University

Supplicant Empires, ed. by Edward Jones Corredera, Habsburg Worlds, 8 (Turnhout: Brepols, 2025), pp. 101–133
BREPOLS ❧ PUBLISHERS   10.1484/M.HW-EB.5.145066

fore unexplored and rhizomatic forms of socio-temporal entanglements across the Iberian worlds. The rereading of the narratives that resulted from their experiences sheds light on concepts emerging from the sources themselves, such as the indeterminacy of human, vegetal, geographical, and geological environments. I argue that this indeterminacy fostered the entanglement of social relations and natural environments located in the so-called far reaches, and at the core, of royal Iberian courts. This indeterminacy generated a thickness which emerges in the seventeenth-century narratives.

Thickness resulted as much from imperial dis-connections as from temporary and ever-renewed knots of interaction between a multitude of beings and things. These disconnections and knots exposed irreducible differences tied to the 'right to opacity' that protected diversity among people and communities.[1] They also generated frictions that bolstered information exchanges through fluid and often violent environments.[2] Taking the concepts of indeterminacy and thickness seriously in the contexts of early-modern interactions contributes to our understanding of the contingent dimension of imperial experiences. Reading these experiences through the lens of contingency allows us to reflect on the multilayered, non-exclusive, and open character of sovereignties that composed the Iberian worlds.[3]

The historical analysis of contingent interactions draws attention to the multiplicity of experiences that generated modes of existence made 'of pure intensive difference'.[4] Early modern multiplicities allow for the navigation between the local and the global, the West and the Rest, as

---

1 Édouard Glissant, *Poetics of Relation* (Ann Arbor: University of Michigan, 1997), pp. 189-94.
2 On how human beings 'inhabit a fluid reality in which nothing is ever the same from one moment to the next and in which nothing ever repeats' as well as on how they 'do not aggregate', but 'interpenetrate' and 'interweave to form a boundless and ever-extending meshwork' with 'loose ends' see Tim Ingold, *The Life of Lines* (London: Routledge, 2015), pp. 11-14. On frictions see Anna L. Tsing, *Friction: An Ethnography of Global Connection* (Princeton: Princeton University Press, 2004). On Iberian disconnectedness see Zoltán Biedermann, '(Dis)connected History and the Multiple Narratives of Global Early Modernity', *Modern Philology*, special issue on 'Multiplicities: Recasting the Early Modern Global' 119-1 (2021), pp. 12-32.
3 For an application of these concepts to the historical analysis of Iberian imperial realities see Jorge Flores, *Empire of Contingency. How Portugal Entered the Indo-Persian World* (Philadelphia: University of Pennsylvania Press, 2024).
4 Eduardo Viveiros de Castro, *Cannibal Metaphysics: For a Poststructural Anthropology* (Minneapolis: University of Minnesota Press, 2009), p. 109. Quoted in a special issue of *Modern Philology* entitled 'Multiplicities: Recasting the Early Modern Global' ed. by Carina L. Johnson and Ayesha Ramachandran, 'Introduction–The Jaguar's Beer: Critical Approaches to Multiplicity in the Early Modern World', *Modern Philology* 119-1 (2021), pp. 1-12.

well as between the cultural and the natural.[5] Beyond dualisms inherent to a period traditionally framed as an 'age of encounters', early modern multiplicities fostered webs of relations that were spatially and chronologically disjointed. Such relations are fundamental to our understanding of the history of the asymmetric regimes of commensurability between societies across the world during the early modern period.

By underlining the importance of interactions between things and beings across the Iberian monarchies, this essay combines contemporary scholarship that analyzes the history of the Iberian monarchies through the lens of 'situated knowledges', and 'activist' calls that consider 'objects of knowledge' as 'actors and agents'. The goal here is to merge the study of the 'radical historical contingency for all knowledge claims and knowing subjects', with 'a no-nonsense commitment to faithful accounts of a real world'.[6] This essay also extends earlier historiographical interventions about the composite or polycentric organization of the Iberian monarchies. It posits the value of a rhizomatic approach to the social and environmental relations at play within and outside early modern empires.[7] Notwithstanding the overwhelming historiographical emphasis on Iberian structures of governance and ever-growing state administrations, a rhizomatic approach makes us think about how ground-up collaborations between non-elite human beings as well as plants, animals, and things – traditionally separated and subjectified/objectified by the culture/nature divide – shed light on the blind spots of empires. On one side, these blind spots corresponded to spaces which generated political ideas and social practices meant to secure reforms that were essential to the Iberian monarchies.[8] On the other side, these blind spots fostered the interweaving of spaces of resistance within and beyond these monarchies. The history of such ideas can be accessed through the testimonies of historical actors that

---

5 'Multiplicities', p. 12. Johnson and Ramachandran's groundbreaking special issue brought to the fore the importance of thinking about early modern worlds through webs of relation and 'irreducible inequalities', originally theorized by postcolonial Caribbean humanities. See Glissant, *Poetics of Relation*.

6 Donna Haraway, 'Situated Knowledges: The Science Question in Feminism and the Privilege of Partial Perspective', in *Feminist Studies* 14-3 (1988), pp. 576 and 593.

7 For a first foray into Iberian rhizomatic worlds see the colloquium entitled *On Iberian Rhizomatic Worlds (1400s-1700s)* that took place at the Newberry Library on March 13th, 2024, and the subsequent blog posts published by the Newberry Center for Renaissance Studies.

8 On how, for example, the dearth of knowledge about inland territories reinforced the focus of imperial powers on the control of maritime and coastal spaces see Dale Miquelon, 'Envisioning the French Empire: Utrecht, 1711-1713', *French Historical Studies* 24-4 (2001), pp. 653-77. See also Nuria Valverde and Antonio Furtado, 'Space Production and Spanish Imperial Geographies', in *Science in the Spanish and Portuguese Empires 1500-1800*. Edited by Daniela Bleichmar, Paula de Vos, Kristin Huffine, and Kevin Sheehan (Palo Alto: Stanford University Press, 2009), pp. 198-215.

perceived the history of the Iberian worlds as an assemblage of fortuitous experiences and ambivalent encounters between a wide array of beings circulating within and beyond the Spanish and Portuguese monarchies.

Composite and polycentric monarchies: in the shadow of the state and under the spell of its elites

Departing from the late John Elliott's seminal observations, world historian Sanjay Subrahmanyam defines composite monarchies as entities governed by 'a ruler [who] could separately rule distinct kingdoms without establishing an evident hierarchy between them'.[9] Two decades later, the editors of *Polycentric Monarchies* took a step away from the omniscient figure of a ruler who was supposed to embody some sort of modern federal state.[10] They advocated for a model of state organization which was not fully conditioned by social and political relations from center to periphery, leaving enough space to consider the contributions of Iberian subjects and pro- or anti-Spanish and Portuguese feelings beyond the jurisdictional boundaries of the monarchies.[11] While the polycentric model sheds light on the history of political communication among interlinked political centers located in the different territories of the Iberian monarchies, its contributions may be less useful when it comes to thinking about the political life that existed through a diachronic set of interactions that did not have to be connected through time and space.

Iberian political life is to be found well beyond empires, kingdoms and cities. Political ideas were often expressed, in their most radical and entangled forms, through spaces and temporalities that challenged the categories that imperial authorities relied on when objectifying and subjectifying the forms of life over which they sought to rule. If one considers that 'situated knowledges are about communities' and 'not about an isolated individual',[12] there is an opportunity for historians to recover the very situatedness of early modern imperial narratives. In his seventeenth-century *Relação da ruína dos Palmares*, Antônio da Silvá commented on

---

9 See John H. Elliott, 'A Europe of Composite Monarchies', *Past & Present* 137 (1992), pp. 48-71; and Sanjay Subrahmanyam, 'Holding the World in Balance: The Connected Histories of the Iberian Overseas Empires, 1500-1640', *The American Historical Review* (2007), pp. 112-50 p. 1360; and from the same author, *Connected History. Essays and Arguments* (London/New York: Verso Books, 2022).

10 *Polycentric Monarchies. How Did Early Modern Spain and Portugal Achieve and Maintain a Global Hegemony?*, ed. by Pedro Cardim, Tamar Herzog, José Javier Ruíz Ibáñez, and Gaetano Sabatini (Eastbourne: Sussex Academic Press, 2012).

11 See the review of *Polycentric Monarchies* by Héloise Hermant in *Revista Complutense de Historia de América* 39 (2013), pp. 307-10.

12 Haraway, 'Situated Knowledges', p. 590.

the maroon community of Palmares (Brazil), describing how its members had based their survival tactics on palm trees to produce wine, oil, clothes, and architectural structures.[13] Displaced people formed social threads with trees that helped reshape their immediate environment.[14] Together, they composed a space of 'wildness'.[15] Da Silvá depicted the quilombo as a site which was 'rough' ('*áspero*'), mountainous ('*montuoso*'), and wild ('*agreste*'). The beings living in it formed a mass thickened by what Da Silvá perceived as an endless variety of known and unknown trees 'with such thickness and confusion of branches that in many parts it was impenetrable, even when exposed under full light' ('*com tal espessura e confusão de ramos que em muitas partes é impenetrável a toda a luz*').[16] The trees bore many thorns, and they could either protect or hurt depending on who and from where one was trying to enter the quilombo – physically and symbolically. Within this space, even the observer's most familiar spatio-temporal coordinates were altered. More than just a fully enclosed site, the quilombo functioned as a base to re-elaborate the political and commercial exchanges organized by the maroon community. Such a community relied on its own crops and fruits, creating its own agricultural stocks and trade outputs. Siding with the Portuguese authorities that aimed to reduce this space into imperial control, Da Silvá implied that the quilombo could only be reconquered thanks to the intelligence of local and indigenous dissenters who had broken with the community. What happened between the formation and dissolution of this communal space is often excluded from official narratives which thin the political history of the Iberian monarchies. Nevertheless, spaces such as the maroon republic

---

13 Antônio da Silvá, *Guerra contra Palmares. O manuscrito de 1678*, ed. by Silvia Hunold Lara and Phablo Roberto Marchis Fachin (São Paulo: Chão Editora, 2021). I would like to thank Aldair Rodrigues for drawing my attention this source.

14 On clothes and textile threads, often made from plants and fruits, being used as a departure point to think about the relational dimension of early modern societies, and on how the metaphorical use of 'threads' helps us think about multispecies political collaborations between Africa, Asia, and the Americas see Cécile Fromont, 'Common Threads: Cloth, Colour, and the Slave Trade in Early Modern Kongo and Angola', *Art History* 41-5 (2018), pp. 838-67.

15 I am indebted here to the anthropological work that Alyssa Mendez conducted in the mountainous regions of Greece (i.e. Agrafa), analyzing the importance of 'relatively wild places' in contemporary debates on climate change and renewable energies. I am relying here on her interpretation of Andreas Malm, 'In Wildness is the Liberation of the World: On Maroon Ecology and Partisan Nature', *Historical Materialism* 26-3 (2018), pp. 3-37. On the distinction between 'wilderness' and 'wildness' and on the importance of considering middle-grounds where interactions among a multitude of beings and environments developed, often violently, see William Cronon, 'The Trouble with Wilderness: Or, Getting Back to the Wrong Nature', *Environmental History* 1-1 (1996), pp. 7-28.

16 da Silvá, *Guerra contra Palmares*, pp. 17-19.

of Palmares, formed part of and/or disrupted, at least for a while, the composite structures of the Iberian monarchies.

European composite monarchies did not always get to negotiate loyalty with their parts. Nor did negotiation define all forms of political relations in the Iberian worlds. While it is crucial to consider what the people who belong to communities like Palmares thought about their emancipation from imperial orders, it is also critical to think about communal forms of adscriptions to such composite/rhizomatic ensembles that have little to do with being committed to the 'one faith, one sovereign, and one dynasty' motto of the Iberian monarchies. To do that, more generous considerations need to be granted to spontaneous and creative social organizations that came together across spaces and timelines that had little to do with the sequential narrating of chronicles that offered bird or god-like views of empires. What would such a bird or god see if, after becoming tired of holding up the air, they decided to rest on a tree branch or touch ground amid thick environments? It is only when confronted with these thick environments that one can understand the outrageous volume of violence unleashed by allegedly more civilized powers against multiplicities.

In both the composite and the polycentric models, analysis of the political life of the Iberian monarchies is often limited to places where royal-court delegates, groups of merchants, and local aristocracies lived and established their influence. These models of interpretation restrict the social and political history of the Iberian monarchies to urban spaces, or, in the best-case scenario, to individuals and low-status officials working in the loose structures of bureaucratic states.[17] Historical studies that rely

---

17 On these questions see Richard Kagan, *Urban Images of the Hispanic World, 1493-1793* (New Haven: Yale University Press, 2000) and Guillaume Gaudin, *El imperio de papel de Juan Díez de la Calle. Pensar y gobernar el Nuevo Mundo en el siglo XVII* (Madrid: Fondo de Cultura Económica, 2017). Emphasis on courts and state structures builds on a long tradition of political history while offering salutary new perspectives. When it was first formulated, the polycentric model benefited from new research on Iberian diplomacy as well as on the history of different forms of delegating royal power across monarchies which were not only centered on royal courts. Early 2010s works dedicated, for example, to the vice-kingdoms of the Spanish monarchy favored the analysis of forms of political communication that were not directly tied to the royal court. See Manuel Rivero Rodríguez, *La edad de oro de los virreyes. El virreinato en la Monarquía Hispánica durante los siglos XVI y XVII* (Madrid: Akal, 2011) and *El mundo de los virreyes en las monarquías de España y Portugal*, edited by Pedro Cardim and Joan Lluís Palos (Madrid: Iberoamericana, 2012). These studies have been inspired by the comparative studies dedicated to the history of early-modern political delegates such as the *favorites* and the *validos*. See *El mundo de los validos*, ed. by John Elliott and Laurence Brockliss (Barcelona: Taurus, 2017). For a new take on political delegations and the cultural history of diplomacy of the Iberian monarchies see *À la place du roi: vice-rois, gouverneurs et ambassadeurs dans les monarchies française et espagnole (XVIᵉ-XVIIIᵉ siècles)*, ed. by Daniel Aznar, Guillaume Hanotin, and May F. Niels (Madrid: Casa de Velázquez, 2015); Natividad Planas, 'Diplomacy from Below or Cross-Confessional Loyalty? The "Christians of Algiers" between the Lord of Kuko and the King of Spain in the Early 1600s', *Journal of*

on the polycentric model of analysis have focused on the period of the Iberian Union of the Crowns (1580-1640) to think about social, cultural, linguistic, identity, and ideological convergences between the Spanish and Portuguese empires.[18] Although the monarchy of Portugal remained jurisdictionally separated as a kingdom from the Spanish monarchy, the Iberian Union is usually seen by contemporary historians as an opportunity to think about the blurry political, social, and cultural borders between Spain and Portugal. Although such an approach has yielded important historical discoveries, it also risks presenting the Iberian monarchies as one coherent and all-encompassing empire whose main forms of socio-political and ecological diversity are constrained to different jurisdictional regimes. In fact, as the examples discussed later in this essay will show, global Iberian worlds were often enacted, witnessed, and reified by actors with loose, coerced, or non-existent ties to the centers of Iberian sovereign power or its representatives.[19]

The composite and polycentric models establish an important distinction between a dynastic state that wished to become omniscient, on the one hand, and its reliance, at the practical level, on a heterogeneous conglomeration of informants and wanderers. Such actors were often weakly and non-linearly connected to the Iberian monarchies while maintaining the quest for the ideal of 'full information' alive among administrative elites.[20] Arthur Weststeijn showed how the notion of 'entera noticia' (i.e. 'full information') was challenged by the dynamics of distance and the development of a market for printed news across the Iberian worlds during the seventeenth century. These dynamics proved to have been well

---

Early Modern History 19 (2015), pp. 153-73; *Embajadores culturales, transferencias y lealtades de la diplomacia española de la Edad Moderna*, ed. by Diana Carrió-Invernizzi (Madrid: UNED, 2016); and Paola Volpini, *Ambasciatori nella prima età moderna tra corti italiane ed europee* (Rome: Sapienza University Press, 2022).

18 See for example, Fernando Bouza, *Felipe II y el Portugal Dos Povos* (Valladolid: Cátedra Felipe II, 2010); Tamar Herzog, *Frontiers of Possession. Spain and Portugal in Europe and the Americas* (Cambridge: Harvard University Press, 2015); Pedro Cardim, *Portugal y la Monarquía Hispánica (c. 1550-c. 1715)* (Madrid: Marcial Pons, 2017); Fabien Montcher, *Mercenaries of Knowledge: Vicente Nogueira, the Republic of Letters, and The Making of Late Renaissance Politics* (Cambridge: Cambridge University Press, 2023); and David Martín Marcos, *People of the Iberian Borderlands. Community and Conflict between Spain and Portuguese, 1640-1715* (London: Routledge, 2023).

19 On the roles that Portuguese freelancers played at the service of non-Christian powers in areas such as the Bay of Bengal see George Winius, 'The "Shadow Empire" of Goa in the Bay of Bengal', *Itinerario* 7-2 (2011), pp. 83-101 and Sanjay Subrahmanyam, *Improvising Empire: Portuguese Trade and Settlement in the Bay of Bengal, 1500-1700* (Oxford: Oxford University Press, 1990). For a general take on this question see *Beyond Empires: Global, Self-Organizing, Cross-Imperial Networks, 1500-1800*, ed. by Amelia Polónia and Cátia A.P. Antunes (Leiden: Brill, 2016).

20 See Arndt Brendecke, *The Empirical Empire. Spanish Colonial Rule and the Politics of Knowledge* (Berlin-Boston: De Gruyter, 2016).

adapted to the uncertainties that fomented and fragmented royal authority across what the historian identifies as an early seventeenth-century 'public Atlantic'.[21] Yet, a dualistic model of interpretation of the social life of the kingdoms that composed the monarchies, between the coercive supervision of state institutions and the possibility of resisting such institutions, does not fully capture the range of interactions which made up Iberian sovereignties.[22]

Going back to Pierre Clastres's observation that it is 'not evident [...] that coercion and subordination [or insubordination] constitute the essence of political power at all times in all places', the investigation of social relations and forms of power that exist in a non-exclusive relation to coercion, away from hierarchies (e.g. 'powerless' powers), and 'against the state' is worth considering in the context of the history of the Iberian monarchies.[23] In *Society Against the State*, the French anthropologist suggested that the very tension between culture and nature needs to be pushed aside to successfully analyze how social relations and political ideas emerged in spaces situated at the margin of the coercion-resistance model. Clastres went even further, stating that 'cultures use the ruse of nature against power', showing that in some societies power is venerated in its impotence.[24] Such a ruse generates a set of tactics that prevent coercive power from gaining ground, pushing it away from the realm of society and transforming it into an 'imago of a social dream connected to natural origins'. In the meantime, societies protect themselves from coercive powers by shaping a political sphere within which the nature and culture divide ceases to exist.[25]

Clastres' reflections might be old news for many, but they can still be useful for those planning to give more attention to actors, spaces, and situations that participated in the elaboration of a political sphere outside of a state-centered history of the Iberian monarchies. Legal history and, more particularly, the study of early-modern conflicts of jurisdiction offer avenues to historians of the Iberian monarchies to think about their social and political histories at the margin of modern state politics.[26] Such an

---

21 Arthur Weststeijn, 'Empire in Fragments: Transatlantic News and Print Media in the Iberian World, *c.* 1600-40', *Renaissance Quarterly* 74-2 (2021), pp. 528-70.

22 Rogers Brubaker and Frederick Cooper, 'Beyond Identity', *Theory and Society* 29 (2000), pp. 1-47.

23 Pierre Clastres, *Society against the State. Essays in Political Anthropology* (New York: Zone Books, 1987), p. 13.

24 Clastres, *Society Against the State*, pp. 46-47.

25 Eduardo Viveiros de Castro, *Politique des multiplicités: Pierre Clastres face à l'État* (Paris: Éditions Dehors, 2019).

26 Works by legal historians such as Bartolome Clavero or António Manuel Hespanha have been influential in thinking about how legal pluralism and conflicts of jurisdictions became essential parts of political practices and discourses. See *António Manuel Hespanha entre a*

approach fostered an interpersonal, relational and polycentric understanding of the exercise of power which did not match contemporary historical narratives determined by the belief in the existence of a centralized state based on increasing fiscal and military pressure. Indeed, the editors of the collective volume on *Polycentric monarchies* stated that:

> Rather than portraying the Iberian Monarchies as the accumulation of many bilateral relations arranged in a radial pattern, they argue that these political entities were polycentric, that is, that they allowed for the existence of many different interlinked centers that interacted not only with the king but also among themselves, thus actively participating in forging the polity. Rather than national, proto-national, or colonial, they were multiterritorial [...]. The constant negotiation, contacts, and competition between their different sub-units and the continuous change in the political weight of each territory, guaranteed that, despite permanence, the internal structure was simultaneously both solid and durable on the one hand, malleable, and changing on the other.[27]

This definition highlights how a relational understanding of social and political actions connected the Iberian monarchies as an assemblage of heteroclite places conditioned as much as by interactions of human and other beings amid local and transregional environments and ecologies. Following this line of interpretation, historian Jean-Frédéric Schaub shows how family relations were woven across the Azores archipelago during the Iberian Union of the Crowns and those relations resulted in complex political affiliations that could not be reduced to pro- or anti-Spanish feelings that followed the 1580 conquest of Portugal by King Philip II of Spain.[28] Schaub underlined the spatial importance of the system of islands itself, within which the representation of royal and religious authorities was diluted. Building on the idea of polycentric monarchies, Schaub analyzes the 'complex, versatile, or ambivalent' dimension of past 'acts and discourses of men and women of this time' among themselves.[29] When considering the correspondences between the political affiliations of Schaub's historical actors and their circulations from one island to another, one is tempted to push the analysis further and consider how such men and women engaged

história e o direito, ed. by Ana Cristina Nogueira da Silva, Pedro Cardim, and Ângela Barreto Xavier (Coimbra: Almedina, 2015). As a practical illustration of this kind of history see Jean-Frédéric Schaub, *Le Portugal au temps du comte-duc d'Olivares (1621-1640). Le conflit de jurisdiction comme exercice de la politique* (Madrid: Casa de Velázquez, 2001).

27 Cardim, Herzog, Ibañez, Sabatini *Polycentric Monarchies*, p. 4.

28 Jean-Frédéric Schaub, *L'Île aux mariés: Les Açores entre deux empires, 1583-1642* (Madrid: Casa de Velázquez, 2014). On archipelagos and the 'thought of Relation', see *Poetics of Relation*, pp. 33-34.

29 Schaub, *L'Île aux mariés*, pp. 179-80.

with non-human elements across the islands, including plants and animals, when expressing their ideas about the new or alternative sovereign orders within and beyond the Iberian worlds.[30]

Beyond a jurisdictional understanding of polycentric entities, eco-critical approaches paired with rhizomatic theories could help foster an understanding of Iberian societies from categories which are not usually used by historians today, like indeterminacy and thickness. These concepts, as the following cases indicate, formed part of the conceptual framework used by historical actors who reflected upon their own social and political experiences from spaces and places and with beings that are not traditionally conceived as the main laboratories of political ideas. A rhizomatic approach offers an interpretative model with more permeability between natural and cultural elements, Iberian and non-Iberian actors, as well as territories which were supposed to be well and fully integrated in the empires. Although composite and polycentric models of interpretation of the political history of the Iberian monarchies are not all dedicated to the teleological advent of an elitist modern state, a vast majority of studies on Iberian monarchies concentrate on such elites, leaving rhizomatic multitudes outside of the picture.

While taking some distance with the definition of 'empire' conceived as a series of supranational organisms united under a single logic of rule aspiring to global sovereignty, the concept of multitude, as developed by Michael Hardt and Antonio Negri becomes useful for thinking about an 'alternative political organization of global flows and exchanges' that fostered flexible hierarchies from places that were neither inside nor located on the edges of empires.[31] It may also allow historians to posit the value of porous networks of command interacting with disturbed eco-systems and unreduced environments during the early modern period.

What follows is a series of case studies that illustrate how a rhizomatic conception of the Iberian worlds – derived from testimonies of improvisation and survival – can advance scholarly arguments concerning the diverse forms of socio-political and environmental relations at play within the Iberian monarchies. The rhizomatic model fosters historiographical

---

30 On the importance of the historical and relational analysis of islands, rhizomatic and 'tortured geographies', and archipelago systems see *Poétique de la relation*, p. 190.

31 On the intricacies of new contemporary world orders and multitudinous alternatives to those orders see Michael Hardt and Antonio Negri, *Empire* (Cambridge: Harvard University Press, 2000), pp. xii-xiii; and from the same authors *Multitude: War and Democracy in the Age of Empire* (New York: Penguin Press, 2004).

connections between the history of empires, spatial and eco-critical studies, animal studies, plant humanities, and the history of the Iberian worlds.[32]

Empires 'as queer as a clockwork orange'

The expression 'as queer as a clockwork orange', refers to 'a person who has the appearance of an organism lovely with color and juice but is in fact only a clockwork toy to be wound up by God or the Devil or the Almighty State'. This is the definition that literary critic and novelist, Anthony Burgess, gave when explaining why he chose the expression for the title of his eponymous novel published in 1962. In his 1972 adaptation of Burgess's novel, film director Stanley Kubrick doubled down on this definition by explaining that his movie 'explores the difficulties of reconciling the conflict between individual freedom and social order'.[33] This tension between individual freedom and social order was at play across the Iberian monarchies, especially when mechanistic interpretations of the plants, animals, and human beings living in this world aimed to reduce the doubts generated by the multispecies collaborations fostered by the first Iberian globalization. That tension invites further reflections on the queerness of the many beings that sustained the social, cultural, religious, economic, and political history of the diverse spaces and societies that composed these monarchies.

The tension between individual freedom and social order at play in the expression 'as queer as a clockwork orange', can be conceived as a form of agency for historical actors. Conceived as such, that tension inspires new interpretations of the narratives that Iberian and non-Iberian subjects wrote regarding the communal spaces and places they traveled through. Indeed, the meanings of such narratives went far beyond campaigns of imperial geographical rationalization and movements of resistance against such campaigns.

Such early modern travel narratives cannot be reduced to the mechanics of empire. Places which witnessed diminishing effects of royal politics and the movements of opposition against those politics were often described as more than just empty or weakly populated and weakly socialized spaces. When reviewing terms and expressions such as 'unknown', 'grown

---

32 Although not relying on a rhizomatic approach, see the important point of connections established among these fields and others (i.e. medicine) by Hugh Cagle, *Assembling the Tropics. Science and Medicine in Portugal's Empire, 1450-1700* (Cambridge: Cambridge University Press, 2018).

33 I am relying here on Anthony Perrotta, 'What Does The Title Of "A Clockwork Orange" Mean?', *The Take* (Online).

without human industry', 'espessura', 'lost' and 'refugee', used by the actors who passed through or lived in such spaces, two concepts stand out: 'indeterminacy' and 'thickness'. It is through indeterminacy and thickness that travelers, exiles, and displaced people,[34] among others, found practical and symbolic means to sustain themselves. Beyond integration, amid the unexpected, and sometimes blind to the dense environments before them, such actors transformed and adapted themselves, including the indigenous populations and representatives they engaged with.[35] They often did so outside the margins of official relations of power.[36]

In an attempt 'to explore indeterminacy and the conditions of precarity, that is, life without the promise of stability', in post-industrial and capitalist ruins, Anna Lowenhaupt Tsing argues that:

> Precarity is the condition of being vulnerable to others. Unpredictable encounters transform us; we are not in control, even of ourselves. Unable to rely on a stable structure of community, we are thrown into shifting assemblages, which remake us as well as our others. We can't rely on the status quo; everything is in flux, including our ability to survive. Thinking through precarity changes social analysis. A precarious world is a world without teleology. Indeterminacy, the unplanned nature of time, is frightening, but thinking through precarity makes it evident that indeterminacy also makes life possible.[37]

European historical testimonies connected to the processes of imperial rationalization of space throughout the Iberian worlds gain further meaning by being read through the thickness of social and natural relations which is being produced by visions of indeterminacy. For example, in his post-1610 relation of his voyage to Mozambique and Goa, the apothecary of King Henry IV and the guardian of the *Cabinet des singularités* of Louis XIII of France, Jean Mocquet (1575-1617), commented on the illnesses that he suffered while sailing aboard a Portuguese ship toward India.[38] Mocquet

---

34 Cornel Zwierlien, *The Power of the Dispersed. Early Modern Global Travelers beyond Integration* (Leiden, Brill, 2022), pp. 1-23.

35 For a historiographical reflection on imperial adaptabilities during the early modern period see José Antonio Martínez's work, including his 'Portugal: un imperio global y adaptable', *Revista de Occidente* 512 (2024), pp. 66-76.

36 On the existence of alternative political spaces at the margin of the 'pacified and normed frame of public debates' defined by eighteenth and nineteenth-century states, see the 2022 volume of the *Mélanges de la Casa de Velázquez* (n. 52-1) titled 'Les espaces alternatifs du politique (monde atlantique, XVIIIe-XIXe siècles)', ed. by Alexandre Dupont and Rachel Renault. This volume is a good reminder of the plurality of spaces from which political ideas about empires were elaborated before the eighteenth century.

37 Tsing, *The Mushroom at the end of the world*, pp. 2 and 20.

38 Jean Mocquet, *Voyages en Afrique, Asie, Indes orientales et occidentales, divisés en six livres et enrichis de figures* (Paris: Jean de Heuqueville, 1617).

explains how he fought against the 'illness of Luanda' (e.g. scurvy) by drinking a syrup made of violet flowers. After bringing his readers with him through his trans-oceanic ordeal, Mocquet introduces those same readers to the African coasts and interior lands that he claimed to have interacted with. The more his report advances, the more explicit it becomes that his explorations had been oriented by the need to access natural products necessary to secure his subsistence, rather than by his desire to gather plants and exotic materials on behalf of his king. What was announced from the start as the story of one of the learned subjects of the Catholic King of France, known for his religious sympathies toward Protestantism and his feelings against Iberian Catholic authorities, became the narrative of a more complex world within which travelers and their confessional affiliations became irrelevant when faced with the need to survive via collaborations with unknown actors and environments. Although the end goal of Mocquet's narrative might be the a-posteriori strengthening of confessional affiliations, especially once the text circulated in Europe as a manuscript or a published book, this same narrative says something more about the importance of unexpected collaborations in the practice of empires.

As Mocquet's journey unfolded, it became more self-reflective about the thickness of the social and natural environments he found himself part of, at least temporarily. Following sixteenth-century humanist garden dialogue tropes, Mocquet explained how he reconnected with his original mission (i.e. collecting plants for his king), after gathering with enslaved Africans in the garden of a Portuguese gentleman he met during his Indian Ocean journeys. While the garden was conceived as an extension of Portuguese jurisdiction to an island which was facing the coast of Mozambique, such space gave only an illusion of stability. Between his previous turbulent navigations and the unexpected campaigns of exploration that followed as soon as he left the garden, Mocquet had to rely on the guidance of enslaved men who performed as translators of what appeared to Mocquet as a thick forest where no paths were to be found.

Mocquet's mission thus acquired another meaning when he entered the 'forest' with the 'three or four slaves' that he had met in the Portuguese nobleman's garden. Although the garden operates in his narrative as a serendipitous space, it also speaks volumes about the precarious state of Portuguese sovereignty in the area. As he advanced through the forest, Mocquet focused on collecting roots and plants to cure illnesses contracted during the voyage. He explained that 'one could catch [some of these illnesses] when maintaining relations with black women'. Building on a gendered and racist understanding of social relations beyond the alleged safe space of a Portuguese nobleman's garden, Mocquet commented that his guides brought him 'with them in the woods to look for [the skin of Antac]. Going like that with them, I [he] found a thousand sorts of plants and fruits, all of them unknown to me [him]'.[39] This quote reflects how Mocquet's world had been turned upside down. While looking for a cure for an illness, which he considered to be of immediate necessity, the collecting of new plants and fruit varieties on behalf of the sovereign power he was supposed to represent was facilitated by the men who accompanied him. The gathering of these other plants and fruits depended on what he portrayed as unexpected encounters. At the time, Mocquet's only connection with Europe and the power he served was secured by collaborations with men who acted as geographical brokers at a point when Mocquet himself could not think about anything else except finding immediate cure to illnesses. Such a situation of improvisation, which was so characteristic of early-modern naturalistic explorations and missionary narratives, forces us to ask questions about who during this outing was really in charge of constructing the knowledge that European monarchies would use to make imperialistic claims over indigenous populations and natural resources.

While perceived as a barrier beyond the supervision of the state authority that Mocquet was supposed to incarnate, the forest he was introduced to was filled with social relations that at first escaped his understanding but that ultimately connected him with far-off state authority by facilitating plant and fruit exchanges. Were spaces like these forests closed to foreigners like Mocquet? Of course not. Nevertheless, aware of the alternative knowledge systems operating within the thickness of the forest and their value, Mocquet's narrative reduced the representation of such spaces to a blind spot, when, in fact, the possibility of being exposed to the unexpected opened opportunities for collaborations that could sustain the individual traveler and benefit the state power he represented. These collaborations were mediated through the lives and relations of many travelers. They were ultimately fictionalized and transformed into manuscript or print commodities exchanged on the global marketplace as signs of the territorial coherence of European empires.

During the rest of his journey, Mocquet became less self-aware of his 'identity' as a subject of the French King. While lost in places where even Portuguese supervision reached its limits, and where the multilayered thickness of other environments unfolded, Mocquet described how his official mission was fulfilled by fortuitous encounters. After boarding a new ship to sail from Mozambique to Goa:

---

39 'Je fis marché avec trois ou quatre de ces Noirs pour m'en emplir un petit sac (pau d'antac, plant roots to cure the Antac a sickness to be with Noirs) et [ils] me menèrent avec eux dans les bois pour la chercher. Allant ainsi avec eux, je trouvai mille sortes de plantes et de fruits à moi du tout inconnus'. The translation in English is mine as well as the following ones in this article. See Jean Mocquet, Voyage à Mozambique & Goa. La relation de Jean Mocquet (1607-1610), ed. by Xavier de Castro and presented by Dejanirah Couto (Paris: Chandeigne, 1996), p. 70.

[...] the carrack called Our Lady of Ajuda lost itself on the coast of Ethiopia near the Castle of Mina where most of the people had found refuge due to the untoward illnesses which had spread within this country, and, among others, a certain disease that started on the bottom of someone, like an ulcer, and which enters in the insides and fills itself with worms that make their way up gnawing the belly, and thus this is how we die with great pain and misery. We have not found any remedy to this disease more singular than using lemon juice to clean as often as possible its bottom because this prevents the worms from sticking there. I believe that the bad waters we drunk are causing such disease.[40]

From Portuguese-owned *hortas* located on Indian Ocean islands to the emergency landings of disoriented ships on Eastern African coasts, Mocquet witnessed spaces where what would have been familiar fruits for him, like lemons, acquired new meanings and were used out of necessity rather than luxury. Far from being prized commodities consumed as candies and oils in royal courts or displayed and curated as precious trees in northern European aristocratic green-houses, lemons became life-savers for men and women traveling upon the seas and across tropical forests. When in Goa, the French apothecary commented on the proliferation of small boutiques dedicated to the selling of both pleasant and necessary fruits and other food staples.[41] For Mocquet such boutiques substituted the European taverns which travelers would have relied on to 'restore' themselves, in the most medical and pre-19th century sense of the term. The allusion to the small size of Goa's boutiques reinforced the idea of a society which was ready to move and, if necessary, to follow the rhythm of relocations of the unstable geographies of empire.

Mocquet's narrative participated in the literary mapping of the colonial geographies of the Iberian monarchies. His geographical descriptions, including his encounters with locals, allowed him to make assessments about 'the constraints on the extension of [the monarchies] of authority'.[42] At the same time, Mocquet was trying to make sense of what Lauren Benton has described as the 'anomalous' spaces of empires. His reflections upon

---

40 'Et premièrement la caraque appelée Nossa Senhora d'Ajuda s'alla perdre en la côte d'Ethiopie près du Castelo da Mina où la plupart du peuple s'arrêta pour les fâcheuses maladies qui prennent en ce pays-là, et entre autres un certain mal qui se met au fondement comme un ulcère qui entre dedans et se remplit de vers qui vont rongeant jusque dans le ventre, et l'on meurt ainsi en grande douleur et misère. On n'a trouvé à ce mal d'autre remède plus singulier que le jus de limon en s'en lavant souvent le fondement; car cela empêche les vers de s'y mettre. Je crois que ce sont les mauvaises eaux qu'on boit là qui causent ce mal'. Mocquet, *Voyage à Mozambique & Goa*, p. 77.
41 Mocquet, *Voyage à Mozambique & Goa*, p. 98.
42 I am following here Lauren Benton, *A Search for Sovereignty. Law and Geography in European Empires, 1400-1900* (Cambridge: Cambridge University Press, [2010] 2011), p. 9.

territorial variations and his experiences as a traveler, real or imagined, presented empires made of congeries of repeating but irregular spaces. His relation offered his readers literary tropes to simplify 'the irregular thrust of imperial jurisdiction into extra-European space'.[43]

Mocquet's impressionistic depiction of ephemeral boutiques – especially those dedicated to the selling of fruits and food staples presented as essential to any European interested in adapting and becoming part of new environments – goes beyond the traditionally understood repertoire of empire-building strategies. Mocquet knew that the people who were connected to the aforementioned boutiques – or with the cultivation or gathering of the products that were sold in them – were aware of the ambivalent nature of such spaces and products. As much as these boutiques embodied the promise of survival and self-restoration, they also testified to insecurity. Mocquet explained how enslaved and *métisse* women in Goa suffered the physical violence of their masters and were often buried in their gardens, under the same trees that produced the fruits sold across the city.[44] Mocquet's references to such despicable acts produced a harsh contrast with his depiction of the fruitful gardens of Goa.[45] This account can also be read as an excuse that European travelers used to short-cut any references to the daily forms of gendered labor that, in reality, secured the survival of colonial spaces of privileges. By moving the attention of his readers away from spaces where, in practice, those same women were selling fruits and herbs, Mocquet avoided making references to daily-life practices that might contribute to the formation of a critical sphere of opinion against official institutions.

Goa's gardens – populated by palm trees, coconuts, citrus fruits, and dead bodies – appear as the ambivalent places where European imperial and urbanistic attempts toward geographical stabilization met the local violence generated by the colonial authors of such stabilization strategies. Mocquet's relation unearthed what state structures were ignorant of, while revealing the fact that they wanted to remain so. In this case, the disaffection of a subject of the French king toward alleged Portuguese Catholic colonialists exposes wishful Iberian underground geographies of ignorance.

In the early modern period, gardens were heterotopias; they functioned as places where the otherness was either contained or uprooted. They could perform as spaces that revealed dead bodies superficially

---

43 Benton, *A Search for Sovereignty*, p. 6.
44 Mocquet, *Voyage à Mozambique & Goa*, p. 113. On violence against women across the *Estado da India* see Jorge Flores, "Colonial Societies in Asia", in *The Iberian World 1450-1820*, ed. by Fernando Bouza, Pedro Cardim, and Antonio Feros (London: Routledge, 2019), pp. 393-415, p. 399.
45 Mocquet, *Voyage à Mozambique & Goa*, p. 141.

covered by the roots of majestic trees as well as by the superficial glow of fruits. In narratives such as Mocquet's travel account, such genealogical varnish is not enough to cover those acts of survival and destruction which had escaped from the rationalization and the literary invention of space in and by the Iberian monarchies.

In seventeenth-century Western Europe, citrus fruits were often associated with failed or disturbed patterns of organic and/or social reproductive systems.[46] The tendency in poetry and myths to communicate examples of individuals who were beaten, raped, and even transformed into citrus plants generated useful allegories to speak about an ever-mutating political body forged amid imperial violence and shaped at the margin of imperial jurisdictions. However, the environments described by Mocquet belied the wishful ignorance of these violent bodily mutations outside the imperial body politic. His narrative denounced what consistently escaped from political control of the Iberian monarchies while also underlining the absence of acts of resistance.

Among the diverse plants, trees, and fruits mentioned by Mocquet, citruses – unlike for example spices and precious metals, which justified transoceanic trade and violence – played a discreet but important role as resources that allowed empires to keep moving and searching for those same spices and precious metals.

Citruses were fruits that kept empires moving in all directions. They also helped secure plantation and extractive strategies that led toward environmental exhaustion. For historians today, such movements are a sine-qua-non condition for the writing of a social history of power that does not take state institutions as the departing or end point of their stories, but, instead, reflects on the improvised social relations within and outside of complex imperial ensembles. For example, a Dutch report of the 1607 siege of the Portuguese fort of São Sebastião in the Island of Mozambique tells the story of how Admiral Paul van Caerden ordered his troops to burn everything during their retreat, including coconut trees that he had once used to make wine to greet his troops. After days of scorched-earth policy, the narrator of the relation commented on how, during the last evening before their departure, the Dutch troops 'took all the oranges and lemons' with them.[47] The Dutch needed these fruits to

---

46 See Giovanni Battista Ferrari, *Hesperides sive de malorum aureorum cultura et usu libri quatuor* (Rome: Hermanni Scheus, 1646). For an interpretation of such works in their own intellectual, cultural, and artistic contexts see David Freedberg, 'Ferrari and the Pregnant Lemons of Pietrasanta' in *Il Giardino delle Esperidi. Gli agrumi nella storia, nella letteratura e nell'arte*, ed. by Alessandro Tagliolini and Margherita Azzi Visentini (Florence: Edifir, 1996), pp. 41-58; and Fabrizio Baldassarri, 'A Clockwork Orange: Citrus Fruits in Early Modern Philosophy, Science, and Medicine, 1564-1668', *Nuncius* 37 (2022), pp. 255-83.
47 Mocquet, *Voyage à Mozambique & Goa*, annexe II, p. 169.

allow them to pursue their navigations while minimizing the disastrous effects of illnesses such as scurvy.

The need for citrus was a primary condition for any campaign of long-distance exploration, exploitation, conquest, and trade. The circulations of fruits often took place through transregional exchanges and at the margin of European commercial channels situated within and outside Iberian territories. Cultivars were also a way to get hold of these territories. While competing with other empires, such places and resources became highly disputed since crews needed them to continue their travels. In some situations, Dutch crews negotiated with Portuguese settlers the acquisition of oranges. Such fruits as well as other crops were fundamental since private slave-owners were looking for resources to maintain their precious human cargoes.[48] Considering the imperial reliance on citrus fruits, enslaved people have a lot to say when it comes to the control of food staples and cultivars. Sourcing such resources was often delegated to municipal administrators, colonial and local ones, or even private persons, as part of the royal economy of grace that was always looking for ways to patch the problem of running a wide empire from a place of ignorance. Among other actions fostered by fruits, imperial circulations depended on the taste of such fruits and on how their taste was mediated by encounters and how then these became connected to specific medical practices, moral considerations, and social strategies of distinction based on alimentary practices.

The irony of the episode that involved the troops of Paul van Caerden is that it was the Dutch historian and member of the *vroedschap* (the city council of the Netherlands), Isaac Commelin (1598-1676), who compiled the relation. Isaac Commelin was also the father of Jan Commelin (1629-1692), a botanist, who at the end of the seventeenth century would write a treatise exclusively dedicated to citrus, advocating for the necessity of post-1648 citrus trees' transplantation and acclimatization in the newly recognized (especially by Spain) independent Dutch Republic.[49] Jan Commelin's treatise followed other works that advocated for the control of real and imaginary citrus geographies by Southern European powers.[50] Mocquet's observations as well as those made by the Dutch

---

48 Dora de Lima explored how fruits, and citrus fruits in particular, were used as strategic resources across the Portuguese world to articulate the empire, especially when securing islands that were key for getting resources for travelers. See Dora De Lima, 'Saveurs et savoirs du monde. Circulations et appropriations de fruits tropicaux dans l'empire portugais atlantique (v.1550-v.1650)' (unpublished doctoral thesis, Université Paris 1 Panthéon-Sorbonne and Universidade Nova de Lisboa, 2014).

49 Jan Commelin, *Nederlantze Hesperides, Dat is, Oeffening en Gebruik Van de Limoenen en Oranje-Boomen; Gestelt na den Aardt, en Climaat der Nederlanden* (Amsterdam: Marcus Doornik, 1676).

50 See for example Ferrari, *Hesperides*.

relation showed how improbable connections and the most innocuous details of the violent life of European overseas explorations, including their unexpected situations, became part of natural histories that fueled conflicts of sovereignty and transfers of hegemonies back in Europe.

Although it is difficult to demonstrate direct causation between these elements, it is interesting nonetheless to point out that the interest given to fruits and plants in imperial narratives of conquests did not only serve to map European sovereignties overseas. The interest shown toward citrus fruits, among other products, contributed to a series of actions and practices that took place in spaces where European monarchies seemed to ignore everything about the complex social and natural relations at play. It was in these same spaces that fruits – via unexpected but recurrent situations of improvisation – nuanced the impact of state control claimed by empires and monarchies. Beyond the interventions of individual actors, through their own agency, these plants exposed the socio-political ambivalences of thick environments that could not be reduced to binary spaces of control nor resistance.

On *Espessura*

The indeterminacy of what happened across the Iberian worlds emphasizes the entanglements between diverse beings. Such entanglements secured the trans-oceanic flows of materials exchanges and human circulations across the Iberian monarchies. They also generated literary imagery as well as new forms of knowledge which reveal the ambiguous relations that men, women, plants, animals, and fruits established among themselves across liminal spaces. Such spaces appeared thick due to the unfamiliar ordering of "nature" but also due to the effect of incomprehension felt by Europeans travelers faced with unfamiliar forms of social, religious, and political relations connected to that "nature". These spaces were made up of multilayered forms of sovereignty. Today, historians specializing in the history of the Iberian monarchies focus a good deal of their attention toward these spaces and the meanings of what contemporaries thought of as their thickness, with a special focus on islands, among other spaces.[51]

Early modern islands under the control of the Iberian monarchies were conceived as places of containment. In these spaces, coercion and

---

51 Among the latest studies that show how diverse spaces of sovereignty coexisted within the Iberian Peninsula and across Iberian islands see Marcos, *People of the Iberian Borderlands*; *Convivencia y conflicto en la frontera de la Monarquía Hispánica. Filipinas (siglos XVI-XVIII)* ed. by Marta María Manchado López (Madrid: Sílex, 2022); and Juan Manuel Santa Pérez and Germán, Santana Pérez, *Puertas en el mar. Islas africanas atlánticas en el Antiguo Régimen* (Valencia: Tirant, 2022).

exploitation operated as driving forces. In parallel, islands also offered shelter and became places of refuge. Their spatial fragmentation favored their role as mediation zones between the Iberian monarchies and other powers with which they entered into contact and collaborated. In such islands diverse social models, environmental considerations, and knowledge cultures overlapped, and imperial and non-imperial representatives coexisted, sometimes peacefully and sometimes not.[52]

When analyzing the thickness that resulted from this aggregative process, the history of the island of São Tomé in the west African Gulf of Guinea is telling, especially if one considers the fact that the island was portrayed as unpopulated before the arrival of the Portuguese in 1471. In this case, thickness constitutes a historical category that the people who came to 'populate' the islands, forcibly or not, were aware of and used when positioning themselves with respect to one another. Unlike other islands that passed under Portuguese control during the fifteenth century, including Madeira, the Açores, and Porto Santo, São Tomé's social forms appeared to be as much influenced by black Africans coming from the Christian kingdoms of West Africa as by a diverse group of Portuguese and European-based populations. Despite attempts to consolidate an exploitative order across the island based on the industry of sugar, coming from Madeira, populations of enslaved and freed people as well as religious and political exiles found zones in the islands where they could develop activities that allowed them to relocate, sustain themselves, and engage with commercial exchanges through land and seas of and beyond the island.[53]

In the case of São Tomé, while some freed black women dedicated themselves to the commerce of fruits – as was also the case in Portugal and would become usual across the Portuguese Indies – the island was not reduced to an all-encompassing colonial order based on the societies that emerged around sugar mills.[54] The south-eastern part of São Tomé welcomed populations originally tied to *engenhos* and *aldeias*. Toward the end of the sixteenth century and throughout the seventeenth, the growing industry of sugar in Brazil released part of the pressure which had been put on São Tomé as the first engine of Portugal's sugar enterprise. The cultivations and the relational understanding of space conceived by slaves and freed men and women, as well as Portuguese *degregados* (convicts) formed

---

52 Jean-Marc Besse, "Une autre partie du monde? Le livre des îles de Giovanni Botero", in *Un mondi di Relazioni. Giovanni Botero nella Roma del'500*, ed. by Elisa Andretta, Romain Descendre e Antonella Romano (Roma: Viella, 2021), pp. 349-68. See also the project *Gouverner les îles: Territoires, ressources et savoirs des sociétés insulaires en Méditerranée (XVIᵉ-XXIᵉ siècle)* (Online).

53 I am following here Isabel Castro Henriques *São Tomé e Príncipe. A invenção de uma sociedade* (Lisbon: Vega, 2000), p. 48.

54 Henriques, *São Tomé*, p. 49.

alternative social orders with which Iberian officials had to negotiate when looking to secure old or propose new forms of agricultural exploitation.

The thickness of the social forest that existed behind the Portuguese colonial trees attracted the attention of European travelers beyond the sole desire of transforming São Tomé into imperial land. Looking at this forest also implies looking at what Europeans saw when describing the island during the early modern period. Political and missionary reports, among other sources, added a literary layer of thickness to the real and imaginary spaces associated with the island. Such reports presented São Tomé as a complex space which was supposed to contrast with streamlined, well-organized, flat, and regimented agricultural landscapes. In practice, even agricultural units and the societies which grew organically around them, especially around sugar mills, continued to be considered by these same colonial eyes as 'difficult' spaces. Forests and cultivars of *'limoeiros, laranjeiras, cidreiras'* emerged among other trees such as *'pessegueiros, amendoeiras, videira, figueira'*.[55] The vision of sugar being produced most often near coasts and rivers, where trees were cut and a new *'povação'* established, does not match more complex and resourceful environments that surrounded, or in fact, were part of the sugar-mill landscapes of São Tomé. Beyond the European civilizational scheme that tended to present clear and clean spaces, in islands where sweetness and spiciness were commodified, the forests of fruits mentioned earlier complicate this vision.

Early modern European spatial depictions of São Tomé present peaceful and top-to-bottom views of agricultural exploitations. In some negative cases, such representations allude to the threat of menacing and surrounding tropical forests. Such forests appear as a single organism, the embodiment of one-sided and stereotypical understanding of nature, showed in its most barbaric form, ready to erase all the progress of the human enterprising spirit. In more positive scenarios, such thickness is neutralized when separated from the sugar and spice trade and depicted as a new Eden or a new garden of the Hesperides where old Christians could read through its vertical trees the tell-tale signs of a space ready to be Christianized, again. However, the island's forest, with its thickness and horizontally interconnected nodes, revealed more about space, plants, animals, and people than just what the colonial eye wanted to reduce through one kind of agricultural and literary imagination.

When delving into *espessura* through the imperial gaze and its archives, it becomes easier to trace other forms of exploitations. For example, the work that enslaved women produced in the *hortas* of Portuguese islands emerges from among this thickness that too often leads readers to believe that most forms of coercion and forced labor were limited to men and to

---

55 Henriques, *São Tomé*, pp. 71-72.

sugar mills and farms. Furthermore, looking at the *espessura* itself provides opportunities to appreciate alternative spaces and reconquered territories that in São Tomé were taken by enslaved or formerly enslaved populations from the *mestres do açucar* who left the island to take advantage of the sugar craze in Brazil. Of course, this process was gradual and did not imply the instantaneous disappearance of mechanisms of oppression and exploitation. However, such movements bolstered the importation to the islands of new kinds of cultivars and agricultural practices coming from the diverse West African regions from where enslaved people came from. More attention was given to plants and products that were necessary for the supplying of ships and the redistribution of enslaved workforce to *armazéns* instead of sugar mills. Considering the transformation of markets during the seventeenth century, the production of fruits and vegetables such as yam, corn, and sweet potato, increased in São Tomé amid the contemporary restructuration of markets across the Atlantic. Although tied to colonial dynamics, the islands promoted flows of exchanges which also contributed to the Africanization of the island. Like indeterminacy, *espessura* contributed to subverting known social orders by generating alternative notions of sovereignty attached to products that grew mostly underground. Such hard-to-survey products were there to stay and would continue to grow even though sugar would be replaced by the coercive exploitation of coffee and chocolate and the colonial order would remain throughout centuries.

Through the lens of the history of São Tomé, and beyond the geography of the island, citrus fruits appear all along the coast and interior territories that official representatives of the Portuguese monarchy as well as foreign missionaries, travelers, and exiles travelled on their way to India, Angola, Kongo, or Brazil. Throughout this mega-zone, citrus fruits were as much connected to the campaigns of imperial rationalization of space as to the *espessura*.[56] The ambivalence of fruits like citrus, due to their rarity, but also due to their practical use for ship crews, soldiers, exiles, priests, and travelers, moving from islands to islands, from coast to interior, and vice versa, incarnated the symbol of spatial interconnectivity as well as the promise of a *métisse* (hybrid) society.[57] Citrus formed part of attempts to create perfect and controlled environments (i.e. seventeenth-century

---

56 On the concept of mega-zone, used here to speak about a citrus continuum that implies fruit diversity and opportunities for transplantation and circulations, see Karin Vélez, *The Miraculous Flying House of Loreto: Spreading Catholicism in the Early Modern World* (Princeton: Princeton University Press, 2019).

57 On the distinction between this concept and their overlaps see Juliane Tauchnitz, *La créolité dans le context international et postcolonial du métissage et de l'hybridité. De la mangrove au rhizome* (Paris: L'Harmattan, 2014).

orangeries and *limonaia*) as much as assemblages of thick, creative, and brutal ecologies.

Counterintuitively, disturbed ecologies fueled the survival of imperial agents involved in constructing and deconstructing controlled environments.[58] Spanish and Portuguese "explorers" were pushed to go beyond coastlines and enter interior lands to find food like rice and plants such as citrus for survival. The search for spices, such as the cloves and nutmeg of the Pacific Maluku islands, often came second when facing the need to survive.[59] These basic needs transformed what appeared on the surface to be well-organized crews into horizontal and non-hierarchical bands in the pursuit of hard-to-find and moving products.[60]

In relations and reports, crews transformed into bands, on one side, and grains and fruits sourced through the thickness of what Europeans depicted as forests, on the other side, reveal to their readers the limits of imperial operations as well as the limits of what such narratives were willing to let their readers know about what happened in extreme moments of need. The extreme spaces and practices evoked in such narratives often relied on exaggerations, misunderstandings, and oneiric spatial boundaries. What happened in the forest stayed in the forest or, at most, inspired grim and hallucinated narratives. This mechanism prevented discussion of a reality where Iberian actions of survival might have been mediated by non-imperial agents or non-human beings. It prevented talk about the agency of things and people that, from the perspective of their authors, might have lessened the uniqueness of their own narratives.

These limitations – coupled with the refusal to present acts of survival that were not, in fact, the result of one individual fighting as a 'saint' against all odds, but were rather the result of needs to collaborate to find his or her way through thickness and disorientation – contributed to reinforce the idea of a dualism between nature and culture which divided the world between its civilized and uncivilized parts. When asked about his expedition to Tidore, for example, the Spanish explorer of the Pacific, Ruy López de Villalobos (*c.* 1500-1546), answered the thirty-six

---

58 On the ambiguous status of controlled environments, such as gardens, see Michael Pollan, *Second Nature: A Gardener's Education* (New York: Grove Press, 1991), pp. 3-4.

59 See the documents on the exploration of the *Islas del Poniente*, including Tidore in Maluku Islands, from New Spain (*c.* 1544) by Rui López de Villalobos, Biblioteca da Ajuda, 51-VII-19, Misc., India Portuguesa 1542-1548, f. 63v.

60 On scholarly interest for social formations which did not correspond to the vertical and hierarchical organization of groups in societies, see the renovated interest for the history of bands, represented for example by the podcast series that traced their histories in France from the medieval to contemporary times. See 'Les bandes de jeunes sont éternelles', an eight-episode Radio France Culture podcast by Perrine Kervran, dir. by Séverine Cassar (2021). Similar studies are needed for the Iberian worlds and the transnational dimension of the history of bands needs to be considered.

questions of a questionnaire by saying that in addition to having spent most of his time sourcing food, 'he knew and saw that dogs, cats, rats, snakes, and lizards, among others poisonous things, were eaten, and that many died after eating them'.[61] Such testimony answers to a governmental logic of full information that sought to possess all knowledge acquired by its agents, including about things that existed at the limits of its real or imagined sovereignty. Far from being unique, these testimonies are legion in Portuguese and Spanish archives. They reinforce the idea of the existence of difficult spaces transformed into extreme and menacing ones, giving opportunities for political powers to moralize what they perceived as their geographical boundaries.[62]

The reading of accounts of European explorations that happened in alleged extreme spaces as well as the parallel transformation of crews into bands, informs critical readings of sources that consider alternative meanings of the experiences of indeterminacy and precarity across the Iberian worlds. Between Portugal and the Portuguese *Estado da India*, the preoccupation about regulating how products such as fruits were sold became recurrent during the seventeenth century. From the precarious status of freed slaves selling citruses across the streets of Goa or São Tomé to those enslaved people who in Portugal were authorized to carry on with selling activities, taxed by their owners, the history of this working and oppressed multitude brings to the fore an unexplored and rhizomatic form of spatial continuity across porous and non-exclusive Iberian worlds. For example, in his study dedicated to the history of slaves in sixteenth and seventeenth-century Southern Portugal, Jorge Fonseca describes how some slaves of '*gente de poder*' used the authority of their masters to found taverns and fashion themselves into micro-banks, establishing a subset of hierarchies among coerced populations.[63] Despite the laws that sought to diminish such activities and regulate the aforementioned ambulatory commerce of fruits, fears linked to the alteration of natural products as well as to the fraudulent transportation of consumables pushed many of these subjects to disrupt this subset of hierarchical relations and promote recurrent acts during which olive trees were cut, vines torn up, and fruits stolen from both *hortas* and gardens.[64] More than just speaking about the control of natural resources, these examples shows how sovereignty on local and regional scales was not the exclusive patrimony of an omniscient

---

61 Biblioteca da Ajuda, 51-VII-19, Misc., India Portuguesa 1542-1548, f. 68v.

62 On the use of nature and natural products to justify and moralize religious geographies of knowledge across the Iberian Atlantic during the early modern period see Jorge Cañizares-Esguerra, *Puritan Conquistadors. Iberianizing the Atlantic, 1550-1700* (Palo Alto: Stanford University Press, 2006).

63 Jorge Fonseca, *Escravos no sul de Portugal séculos XVI-XVII* (Lisbon: Vulgata, 2002), p. 83.

64 Fonseca, *Escravos no sul de Portugal*, p. 80.

state and that hierarchical subsets could foster acts of disruption that aimed to preserve parts of territorial sovereignty for subjects who had eluded the normative imperial social game.

The appropriation of spaces such as vineyards, groves, gardens, and open-air markets, by bands and lone individuals, including inquisitorial convicts who were living in or passing through situations of precarity showed how the spatial fragmentation of the Iberian monarchies created independent pockets of sovereignties where legal jurisdictions reached their limits. Like real and mundane Hercules, bands, lone fruit thieves, and improvised root cutters challenged the moralized geographies of empires by infiltrating themselves into gardens and groves, all of which from an imaginary point of view were conceived as safe spaces and repositories of sovereignty.[65] Thick environments, often situated in the interior of hard-to-reach places like islands, also existed at the center of falsely hermetic spaces, such as the gardens and the archives of the Iberian monarchies. Even these gardens and archives were prone to indeterminacy and could be easily subverted.

One response to the challenges created by individuals and bands to the sovereign order of the Iberian monarchies was the classification of the very same natural products and spaces through which such bands and individuals created pathways of indeterminacy to add thickness to those spaces and become part of them. Such classifications reinforced the dehumanization of those human and non-human beings that thrived in what appeared, from an official point of view, as emblematic and disturbed environments. While European gardens were far from being places of full coherence and were certainly themselves impenetrable, coded, and moralized universes, the fictional existence of non-European spaces reinforced the idea of a nature which grew 'without any kind of human industry' away from the boundaries of the civilized world.[66]

---

65 From a novelistic standpoint, see how Italo Calvino in *Il Barone Rampante* (1957) contextualized, in an eighteenth-century fictional Liguria, the actions of a boy raised as a freethinker who found a way to subvert the social hierarchies established through lands, agricultural, and gardening activities around him, while creating vegetal pathways among the constellation of trees on top of which he lived in. By doing so (by living far above or underground), he overcame all kinds of jurisdictions, devised political reforms, invented new ways of socializing, and imagined new worlds. He did so in a similar fashion as humanists, thieves, and skeptic islanders did centuries earlier. On the improbable 'encounters' between these protagonists and their sharing of 'wild fruits, roots, and all sorts of animals' with *dévots* Catholics and indigenous populations in islands such as *La Martinique* around 1635 see Jacques Bouton S.J., *Relation de l'establissement des François depuis l'an 1635 en l'isle de la Martinique, l'une des Antilles de l'Amérique [...]* (Paris: Sébastien Cramoisy, 1640), pp. 36 and 97.

66 Peiresc to the Capuchin priest, Colombino de Nantes, 10 April 1634, in António Brásio, *Monumenta Missionaria Africana, África occidental (1631-1642)*. Volume VIII (Lisbon: Agência Geral do Ultramar, 1960), p. 267.

While the idea of a natural world which was 'growing without human industry' first attracted the attention of European travelers across the world, in their writings this same expression acquired a deeper meaning; one connected to the *espessura* of imperial and colonial territories. The correspondence established by priests and scholars who were not directly involved in the Portuguese imperial machine, such as the Provençal polymath and antiquarian, Nicolas Claude Fabri de Peiresc (1580-1637) or French Capuchin fathers, who from the Atlantic ports of the eastern coast of France launched missionary campaigns, overlapped with Portuguese attempts of imperial governance in West Africa and added layers of meaning to the perceived thickness of places like the coasts of Angola.[67] Peiresc's interest in African cultures and societies was sparked by his antiquarian desire to explore the pre-Christian roots of modern African kingdoms that had converted to Catholicism. Comments on the '*espessura*' of such societies and cultures that transpire in his letters to several Capuchins friars who traveled through the Gulf of Guinea, Kongo, and East Africa, were at first associated with the idea of a lack of 'human industry'. As his correspondence unfolds, such *espessura* adopts different, if not deeper, meanings. Soon enough the idea of a 'sweet nature' emerges from the *espessura*. This sweet nature was perceived, for example, by the friars when visiting the garden of Kilwa in Mozambique. The Capuchins took great care in underlining the inoffensiveness of black slaves charged with cultivating the gardens under the authority of 'white moors'.[68] The idea of the

---

67 On missions, politics of space, and landscape representations in Angola at that time see Cécile Fromont, *Images on a Mission in Early Modern Kongo and Angola* (University Park: Pennsylvania State University Press, 2022), pp. 80-82.

68 'The city and island have 4000 souls, it grows quantities of fruits, it has a great deal of maize like Guinea, butter honey and wax. [...] Many trees, mostly palms, and others are different from those of Portugal and the same on the mainland, and from there to some places on the mainland is 2 leagues to other ones. Here grow very sweet oranges, lemon, radishes, and tiny onions, sweet marjoram, and sweet basil in the gardens which they water from wells. Here they grow betel which has a leaf like the ivy and is grown like peas each with a stick next to it; the Moors of quality eat this leaf with a kind of lime made to look like ointment and with the stamen of the leaf as if they would use it to put on a sore. These leaves turn the mouth and teeth a deep red and it is said to be very refreshing. In this land there are more Negro (*escravos negros*) slaves than white Moors who work in the gardens tilling the maize etc. [...] all the gardens are surrounded by wooden fences and maize canes that look like a cane-brake, the hay is the height of a man'. 'Account of the Voyage of D. Francisco de Almeida, Viceroy of India, along the East Coast of Africa', 22 May 1506, *Documentos sobre os Portugueses em Moçambique e na África central 1497-1840*, vol. 1 (1497-1506), pp. 524-25. Jesuits also wrote about the sweet nature of Africans and their capacity for conversion in a reports they sent from West Africa. Such reports overlapped with others about the *boticarias* located in Jesuit institutions in places such as Luanda in Angola, and within which sweet fruits such as '*laranjas, limōis, sidras*', among other products, were used to cure bodies and spirits. Such lists of products were often juxtaposed with reports that described how Jesuits introduced themselves in forest lands to baptize locals

sweetness of the fruits they produced served as a proxy for the Capuchins to imply that something in the slaves transcended their condition and that this something could be a good departing point for their conversion.[69]

Peiresc wrote to the Capuchin Gil de Loches, on 13 February 1634, asking for materials and news coming from Guinea, including 'diverse particularities and more about these people, as well as about things of nature [...] that we are less familiar with'.[70] After returning from the Levant, Loches had been involved in the composition of a grammar and *mémoires* dedicated to the comparative study of oriental languages. When about to depart for Angola from the port of St. Malo in France, Peiresc relied on his expertise as a linguist to think about a broader antiquarian connection that would allow him to explore further, between the Orient and Africa, the material and social history of pre-Christian forms of revelation.

Peiresc's letter to Loches was followed by another one to another friar named Colombino de Nantes. On 10 April 1634, Peiresc communicated to the Capuchin his curiosity for sacrificial ceremonies, as well as for the uses of products such as millet in Western African societies. Peiresc was also interested in the plates used when processing the grains or using them during religious ceremonies. He wanted to know more about the existence of cults dedicated to trees in those same societies. What appears today as a somehow eclectic ensemble of curiosities was at the time motivated by the will to establish missions and plantations while comparing contemporary material evidence from Western African societies with the ancient archeological remains of 'pagan' societies. Peiresc's comparative project formed part of a broader religiously and intellectually motivated movement that traced the history of early forms of Christian revelation to ancient civilizations across the world, and with a special insistence on Africa. This quest on behalf of the so-called *Prisca Theologia* generated surprises and doubts, especially when appreciating how societies beyond Europe had configured their social relations within, and not outside nor

---

and performed catechism on new converts. Amid what they considered as extreme spaces and delicate moments, these priests asked their co-religionists for images, such as the ones of Saint Luke, that would intercede on their behalf for their protection since they were 'continuously walking through the jungle (*mato*) amid wolfs and infidels...'. See the letter that Gonçalo João sent to Nuno Mascarenhas, 10 February 1632, in *Monumenta Missionaria Africana, África occidental (1631-1642)*. Volume VIII (Lisbon: Agência Geral do Ultramar, 1960), pp. 109-10.

69 On the sweetness associated with citruses, whose taste could oscillate between bitterness and sweetness, and their uses as symbols of religious conversion see Fabien Montcher, 'Bonds of Sweetness: A Political and Intellectual History of Citrus Circulations across the Western Mediterranean during the Late Renaissance', *Pedralbes* 40 (2020), pp. 143-65.

70 Peiresc to Gil de Loches, 13 February 1634, in *Monumenta Missionaria Africana, África occidental (1631-1642)*, vol. VIII (Lisbon: Agência Geral do Ultramar, 1960), p. 251. See also Apollinaire de Valence (ed.), *Correspondance de Peiresc avec plusieurs missionaires et religieux de l'ordre des Capucins 1631-1637* (Paris: Picard, 1891).

against, natural environments. Peiresc explained to Colombino de Nantes that:

> we are also told about the existence of a vast forest of orange and lemon trees located in other parts of Western and Southern Africa. These trees are born and subsist without any kind of human industry. They do so in unhealthy and swampy places, on riverfronts and near streams. A more detailed study of the quality of the spaces where such trees find themselves at ease needs more attention, as well as a more specific analysis of their diversity [i.e. the trees].[71]

In his letter, Peiresc echoed stereotypes about the disordered dimension of non-European societies and natural spaces. However, his curiosity pushed him to look beyond such stereotypes, forcing him to question assumptions about the fact that, for example, lemons and oranges could not thrive without the help of human cultivation and gardening techniques.

Although Peiresc did not go as far as recognizing that a form of human industry was involved in African citrus forests, his questioning connected him with research that he himself and some of his intellectual peers were conducting on the ancient, mythical, archeological, and anthropological history of citrus fruits. Like him, his correspondents were looking for direct samples of trees, seeds, and fruits that grew in different parts of the world.[72] While such projects reinforced projects of confessionalization and moralization of the natural world during the Thirty Years' War (1618-1648), they also exposed models of spatial organization that differed from European assumptions. They forced scholars to question the meaning and value of citrus forests opposed to well-organized batteries of citrus trees that were displayed during spring and summer across European aristocratic gardens and transferred in green houses during the winter. In some cases, these trees or grafts made from them were even transplanted to Jesuit colleges such as the one of Luanda in Angola.

On 20 June 1634, Colombino de Nantes wrote back to Peiresc, passing on information about his trips to Morocco and Guinea. Colombino de Nantes reported that his trip had been cut short due to a shipwreck.

---

71 'On nous parle aussi des grandes forests d'orangers et citronniers, en d'autres contrées de ceste Affrique occidentale et méridionale, qui naissent et subsistent sans auculne culture humaine dans ces lieux palustres et marescageux, et sur le bord des rivieres et ruisseaux, qui meriteroient pareillement une relation plus particuliere de la qualité des lieux où ilz se plaisent, et la difference de leurs especes'. Peiresc to Colombino de Nantes, 10 April 1634, in Monumenta Missionaria Africana, vol. VIII, p. 267.

72 Peiresc helped his Roman correspondents to gather information about citruses while the latter were collecting information on plants from different parts of the Mediterranean by sending questionnaires that would be filled in by third parties. See Notitie diverse del sig. abb. Cassiano dal Pozzo. Originale spettanti a Agrumi et Historia d'essi [...], Biblioteca dell'Accademia Nazionale dei Lincei e Corsiniana, Archivio Dal Pozzo, ms. 39.

Consequently, he had only been able to see the coast of Cabo Lopo Gonçalves near the Congo and the archbishopric of Angola, as well as the coastline near Mina and Benin. Colombino de Nantes told Peiresc that such coasts were made of rivers and large kingdoms. Their landscapes were filled with tall and evergreen trees that bore excellent fruits and flowers. While the Capuchin said that the interiors were plagued by impenetrable forests, the luxuriant image of the African coasts echoed other relations of similar spaces located elsewhere across the world at the time.[73] These descriptions insisted on the luxuriant and autonomous growing of citrus forests, implying their divine origins and by the same token, that the individuals who were living in or around them had been in touch by very ancient forms of Christian revelation. In consequence, from a European point of view, projects of religious conversion were not only promising but legitimized. Colombino de Nantes replied to Peiresc by stating that:

> Regarding orange and lemon trees, they exist in forests that naturally sustain themselves. I could not see if their flowers were doubled. There are also other trees which are red on the inside. Several ships are taking care of extracting this wood. Other trees, once cut, produce aromatic liquors that I brought with me.[74]

More than just insisting on the complex entanglements of missionary, economic, and imperial projects in West Africa, Colombino de Nantes' quote shows how much confusion there was about places and spaces where orange and lemon trees were supposed to grow and prosper. The images and ideas associated with such trees became more complex as well as the spaces, eco-systems, and social environments that surrounded them. These images nuanced the traditional divide between populated and civilized coasts and thick barbarous interiors. The idea of a lack of human industry oscillated between a negative and a virtuous image of human and non-human collaborations.

---

73 In his fictional and humanistic-like dialogue entitled the *Grandezas do Brasil*, Ambrósio Fernandes Brandão refers to the fact that not all citrus fruits growing in Brazil come from a unitary conception of the natural world. Their hybridity, especially that of the sweetest fruits, generated artificial fruits. From a European neo-platonic understanding of the world, the nature of such fruits needed to be reconciled with their single and divine origin. Human intervention could either foster their hybridity and benefit from their sweetness and use such fruits for conversion projects. The latter would help reconnect such fruits with a divine act of creation. Both options were not necessarily contradictory. They fostered the Baroque craze for citruses among Christian Europeans involved in Iberian processes of colonization during the seventeenth century. See Ambrósio Fernandes Brandão, *Diálogos das Grandezas do Brasil* (Brasília: Edições do Senado Federal, 2010), p. 50.

74 Colombino de Nantes to Peiresc, 20 June 1634, in *Monumenta Missionaria Africana*, vol. VIII, p. 280.

The spaces and trees described by Peiresc and his correspondents fostered an unexpected kind of thickness. Their descriptions bolstered the creation of regimes of commensurability between Iberian conquests and other European colonizing enterprises. The tension between the negative and positive depiction of these far-away, but comparable, environments remained. Amid the *espessura* all appeared to be sweeter, taller, tastier. Beyond the depiction of lost paradises, the images of unhealthy environments, unpopulated and governed by broken and swampy eco-systems remained. In both cases however, the idea of self-governance and self-organization by nature should inspire more scholarly curiosity for territories that would remain set apart, at least partially, from rationalized and commensurable geographies of empires that functioned as European repositories of universal ideas for social and political reforms.

Conclusion

The indeterminacy and the thickness of territories associated with the Iberian monarchies, perceived through the lens of actors who transited through such monarchies without being direct subjects of them, revealed the irreducible queerness of spaces that should have been socially, culturally, and symbolically reduced to the all-encompassing visions that the Iberian monarchies pretended to have over the world. However, what emerged from the attempts of reduction of undetermined and thick spaces was a series of bonds between human and other beings that together formed a laboratory for multispecies collaborations.

Instead of taking for granted the straight linearity of early modern connections among composite and/or polycentric entities, the circular perambulations of improvised and displaced pilgrim-like wanderers are important on two levels. First, their perambulations generated asymmetrical regimes of commensurability that conferred on European political authorities a sense of civilizational superiority over the rest of the world. Second, and even though they were often moralized by European Christians visions of the world, these perambulations insufflated an added layer of indeterminacy and thickness to European societies and natural environments. Far from being a stable environment, Western European societies were very much perceived and experienced as missionary and colonial settings within which disenfranchised populations, discreet laborers, exiles, and enslaved people, as much as transplanted plants and displaced animals, experienced the unstable and ever-changing dimension of 'wildened' environments.

The histories of such spaces add more elements to the history of monarchies and empires that operated as 'improvised entities'.[75] More than being passively used to enforce political control and coercion or conceived as spaces of resistance, such ambivalent spaces fostered an imperial practice centered around the activities of a multitude of beings that, together, bolstered a definition of empires as 'mobile political forms'.[76] When defined as such, different forms of sovereignty appear across the Iberian monarchies and their 'imperfect geographies'. Such sovereignties were tied to what Lauren Benton called 'spaces with an uncertain relation to imperial power'.[77]

The goal here is not to minimize the role that violence and coercion played in the governance of early modern empires. Historians Francisco Bethencourt and Diogo Ramada Curto warned their public against attempting 'to dilute the impact of transfer of the institutions and of the forms of European political action throughout the entire empires'. They argue that such a vision is responsible for giving the impression that early modern imperial structures were fragmented and that mechanisms of negotiation prevailed over instruments of coercion.[78] Indeed, the cases presented in this article show disturbed geographies and ecologies of empires that were highly negotiated and violent. However, we should not assume that the collaboration and the violence that resulted from them were connected to a single, immutable, and enclosed imperial structure. Whether violent and/or collaborative, this structure could be at the same time, composite, polycentric, and rhizomatic.

The rhizomatic model of analysis advocates for a further integration of non-state actors and multispecies relations in a non-exclusive history of the Iberian monarchies. Sabina Brevaglieri recently explained that the intellectual and social histories of the politics of knowledge across the distant territories of the Iberian monarchies were highly mediated by their relationships with other polycentric societies and cultures of knowledge, such as the Roman one. She points out that 'when one introduces Spain and its multiple territorial stages through which knowledge is being produced, exchanged, and transformed, one must also realize that such phenomena took place within a Christian world which was also multidimensional and multipolar'.[79] Via the rhizomatic model, and through categories and concepts such as indeterminacy and the thickness of human and natural

---

75 Jane Burbank and Frederick Cooper, *Empires in World History. Power and the Politics of Difference* (Princeton: Princeton University Press, 2011), pp. 5-7.
76 Burbank and Cooper, *Empires in World History*, p. 178.
77 Benton, *A Search for Sovereignty*, p. 2.
78 Francisco Bethencourt and Diogo Ramada Curto, *A expansão marítima portuguesa, 1400-1800* (Lisbon: Ediçoes, 2010), p. 70.
79 Sabina Brevaglieri, *Natural desiderio di sapere. Roma barroca fra vecchi e nuovi mondi* (Rome: Viella, 2019), p. 15.

environments, one realizes what the history of the Iberian monarchies could gain by fully accounting for the fact that their social, religious, and political structures, if any, were not limited to monotheistic visions of the world nor hermetic to others, including other versatile instruments of political, confessional, ecological, and intellectual communication.

Further integration between studies of the Iberian monarchies with those dedicated to the theory of stateless multitudes, as well as broader reflections on empires that operated beyond one-sided or dualistic identarian and genealogical logics, will allow historians to show how improvised trans-imperial actors contributed, notwithstanding state coercion, to the territorial, intellectual, environmental, and social articulation of the Iberian monarchies. These unstudied multiplicities and collaborations between humans and plants often operated through 'indirect negative actions'.[80] Such actions were non-hierarchical, acentered, horizontal, and often happened on a micro and underground scale, beyond the reach of even the most specific kind of local jurisdictions. These actions favored a world of possibilities. Such a world was not passive per se. It directed the attention toward the power of non-human actors in reforming the life of monarchies and empires, as well as the ones of individuals and communities living therein.

As studies dedicated to the composite and polycentric monarchies have showed, communal social ties were often as important if not more so than well-defined political affiliations in the Iberian worlds. The rhizomatic approach widens this assumption by focusing on interspecies ties as well as shedding light on the undetermined nature of such relations in practice. With these tools in hand, historical, visual, and literary tropes such as the many episodes during which imperial actors found themselves lost in spaces like seas, islands, and oceans, acquire even more relevance since it was during these moments that actors established key relations with "others".

The ability to become lost in an empire was a prerequisite for its existence. Amid such tribulations, senses, such as the one of taste, were mobilized. New tastes for things and people were acquired. Senses such as the one of taste fostered alternative ways of communicating, at the margin of the institutional coherence of empires, while, at the same time, emphasizing intermediate and temporary forms of sovereignties produced by new situations and the access to new products or to the ability of using them in an alternative way.[81] Considering imperial unexpectedness and

---

80 A term first coined in 1962 by the anthropologist, ethnobotanist, zoologist, and linguist, André-Georges Haudricourt. See Igor Krtolica, 'Le rhizome deleuzo-guattarien "Entre" philosophie, science, histoire et anthropologie', *Rue Descartes* 99-1 (2021), pp. 39-51.

81 Leonor Freire Costa, *Império e groupos mercantis. Entre o Oriente e o Atlântico (século XVII)* (Lisbon: Horizonte, 2002), p. 22.

the thickness of no-go zones, historian Dora de Lima showed how new taste for fruits like citruses contributed to redefine the malleable political geographies of the Iberian monarchies.[82]

When looking at the list of people who for example embarked to the *Estado da Índia* from Portugal in the first decades of the seventeenth century, it is interesting to note that a large contingent of them were former captives, who had earlier found – or rather lost – themselves in Africa and the West Indies, and that expertise in getting lost was considered a prerequisite for further similar experiences in a distinct but connected environment related to the Iberian monarchies.[83] On his way to Goa, the ambassador of Philip III of Spain, García Silva y Figueroa spoke about how soldiers and sailors in search of refreshments were shipwrecked when 'distracted all while staring at the green and peaceful perspective of the Island, with its many oranges, bananas, and palm trees'.[84] Before such a vision and while developing a taste for such accounts, human beings had little to say about the multifarious lives and experiences in the Iberian monarchies. This explains why Silva y Figueroa became obsessed with the inner life and circulation of pineapples and other fruits between places like Brazil, Peru, the West Indies, and India. For him, what he perceived as the natural world was organizing itself the same way as citrus forests sustained themselves.

The idea of the ingenuity of nature, coupled with solidarities and collaborations between a multitude of beings, would ultimately become part of early modern political and religious discourses which advocated for, for example, plant and tree transplantations between the tropics and northern European latitudes.[85] The loose relations of an interconnected but decentered world inspired a desire to rule but also to change the way Iberian monarchies were governed. Empires ended up being domesticated by the rhizomatic worlds that somehow sustained them, but also, and always, questioned them, whenever and wherever one stood across the world.

---

82 Lima, 'Saveurs et savoirs du monde'.

83 Arquivo Histórico Ultramarino (Lisbon), UC, Índia, Caixa 8, 19 January 1618.

84 *Estudos sobre Don García de Silva y Figueroa e os "Comentários" da embaixada à Pérsia*. Ed. by Rui Manuel Loureiro, Ana Cristina Costa Gomes, and Vasco Pacheco Resende. Book 1 (Lisbon: CHAM, 2011), p. 83.

85 On the idea of the ingenuity of nature see Javier Patiño Loira, Javier, *The Age of Subtlety: Nature and Rhetorical Conceits in Early Modern Europe* (Newark: University of Delaware Press, 2024).

MARCOS REGUERA

From Manifest Destiny to *destino manifiesto*

The Hispanic Reformulation of Manifest Destiny (1820-1920)

Introduction

During the second half of the nineteenth century and the first half of the twentieth century, the concept of Manifest Destiny was one of the main expressions that best articulated American expansionist and imperialist ambitions. As a seemingly organic concept in US nationalist thought, the historiography on the idea of manifest destiny has not sufficiently considered its reception in other languages and political cultures. This chapter aims to correct this bias. This chapter will present significant examples of the reception – and creative re-appropriation – of the concept by politicians and intellectuals from the Hispanic world during the period when the notion of manifest destiny was politically salient. Overall, this study aims to demonstrate that, by the late nineteenth and early twentieth centuries, the concept of manifest destiny had ceased to be an exclusive notion of the American political vocabulary – it had been incorporated into a broader discourse of Anglo-Iberian Atlantic nationalist thought.

By Manifest Destiny, American historiography has understood both the phenomenon of American territorial expansionism in the mid-nineteenth century, and the set of ideas, discourses and justifications that accompanied this process.[1] This article will consider and study Manifest

---

1 I don't pretend to offer an exhaustive bibliographical account of the phenomenon. Albert Weinberg's work *Manifest Destiny: A Study of Nationalist Expansionism in American History* (Baltimore: The John Hopkins University Press, 1935) could be considered representative of the type of studies that have studied Manifest Destiny as an idea or as a set of ideas. On the other hand, works such as Frederick Merck's *Manifest Destiny and Mission in American History: A Reinterpretation* (New York: Alfred A. Knopf, 1963) while considering Manifest Destiny an expansionist ideology, have focused their study on the expansionist phenomenon

Marcos Reguera • Universidad del País Vasco

Supplicant Empires, ed. by Edward Jones Corredera, Habsburg Worlds, 8 (Turnhout: Brepols, 2025), pp. 135–166
BREPOLS ❧ PUBLISHERS   10.1484/M.HW-EB.5.145067

Destiny in a very specific way: as a conceptual syntagma, a political concept composed by two colligated terms (*manifest* and *destiny*) that articulated and conveyed an expansive idea of nationhood that originated in American expansionist and imperialist discourses. This notion was subsequently received and reinterpreted by numerous politicians and intellectuals, including those in the Hispanic world.[2]

The concept was particularly politically significant for a century: from 1845, when it was coined by the Democratic ideologue John L. O'Sullivan, until 1945, when the rise of the decolonisation movements, coupled with the concept's association with the expansionism of fascist powers, saw its popularity dwindle among the public, and transformed it into a historiographical category.[3]

Reinhart Koselleck defined political concepts as the fundamental linguistic units that allow us to study the structures and events of history through the language of the subjects of the past. They are pointers that show us how historical subjects conceived a given phenomenon or

---

itself rather than on the set of justifying ideas. Some contemporary canonical works on the subject such as Anders Stephanson, *Manifest Destiny: American Expansionism and the Empire of Right* (New York: Hill and Wang, 1995) and Amy S. Greenberg, *Manifest Manhood and the Antebellum American Empire* (Cambridge: Cambridge University Press, 2003) have sought to balance intellectual history with a political narrative on the expansionist phenomenon. Reginald Horsman's *Race and Manifest Destiny: The Origins of American Racial Anglo-Saxonism* (Cambridge: Harvard University Press, 1981), on the other hand, recovers the kind of intellectual history initiated by Weinberg written from the vantage point of Anglo-Saxonism. On the other hand, Thomas R. Hietala, *Manifest Design: American Exceptionalism and Empire* (Ithaca: Cornell University Press, 2003) develops, from a critical perspective, the kind of political history of expansionism initiated by Merk.

2 It is important to clarify that by Hispanic politicians and intellectuals in this article I will consider personalities of Spanish and Hispanic American origin. While US Hispanics may fall into the latter category, they will not be the main focus of my study. The Hispanic character of the reception of the concept that I am interested in highlighting is related to the external reception of the concept, and not to the uses it might have had among American racial minorities (this phenomenon should be dealt with in a separate article that critically studies the uses that this racially marked concept had among those who did not fall within the normative definition of civilized races of the time, a racist convention that was implicit in the background of the concept of Manifest Destiny).

3 Julius W. Pratt, 'Origin of Manifest Destiny', *The American Historical Review* 32 (July 1927), pp. 795-98. In the early 21st century historian Linda S. Hudson proposed an alternative explanation on the authorship of Manifest Destiny contrary to the one proposed by Julius W. Pratt. Hudson's hypothesis stands that the unacknowledged author of the concept was the writer, editorialist and filibusterer Cora Montgomery (Jane McManus Storm Cazneau), a thesis defended on the basis of a computational analysis of the *Democratic Review* editorial. 'Annexation' Linda S. Hudson, *Mistress of Manifest Destiny: A Biography of Jane McManus Storm Cazneau, 1807-1878* (Austin: Texas State Historical Association, 2001). pp. 1-6, pp. 45-68, pp. 201-04. The historian Robert D. Sampson has rejected this hypothesis by analysing multiple flaws and inconsistencies in the method of computational analysis used by Hudson, to the point of disqualifying her research conclusions. Robert D. Sampson, *John L. O'Sullivan and his Times* (Kent: Kent State University Press, 2003) pp. XV, 244-45.

problem during their particular historical moment. They are also discursive factors that allow historical subjects to perform linguistic actions in their historical context. Political concepts do not only convey meaning: they also articulate spatial-temporal semantics with which they express their geographical and temporal consciousness.[4]

In short, political concepts – such as Manifest Destiny – are strategic objects of study for historiography, because they are heuristic vehicles that transport us to a particular epochal understanding, in many cases radically different from our own, but which is nonetheless connected to the issues of our historical moment.[5]

The concept of Manifest Destiny was coined by O'Sullivan as a result of a series of publications that appeared between July and December 1845 in the *United States Magazine and Democratic Review* and the *New York Morning News*. However, the gestation of the concept predated these publications: it began in 1837, seven years earlier, as a result of Jacksonian democratic propaganda, and which O'Sullivan endorsed and deployed from 1837 to 1844 in his publications.[6] In 1844, a number of political developments – the debates about the annexation of Texas, the dispute over the delimitation of the Oregon Territory, the rise of abolitionist debates, and the presidential campaign of the Democratic expansionist candidate James K. Polk – encouraged O'Sullivan to shift his focus. O'Sullivan no longer used providentialist ideas to defend Jacksonian democracy; he now used providentialist ideals, and Malthusian concepts, to justify territorial expansionism.[7]

---

4 Reinhart Koselleck, 'Introducción al *Diccionario* histórico de conceptos político-sociales básicos en lengua alemana'. Translated by Luis Fernández Torres. *Revista Anthropos: huellas del conocimiento* 223 (2009), pp. 93-94, p. 103; Reinhart Koselleck, *Futuro pasado: para una semántica de los tiempos históricos*. Traducción de Norberto Smilg (Barcelona: Paidos, 1993), pp. 207-09, pp. 337-56.

5 Javier Fernández Sebastián, *Historia conceptual en el Atlántico ibérico: lenguajes, tiempos, revoluciones* (Madrid: Fondo de Cultura Económica, 2021), pp. 56-115, pp. 155-81. In the case of Manifest Destiny, this was an archetypal expression of nineteenth-century nationalist and romantic thought that was key to the articulation of expansionist, imperialist, racist and providentialist discourses. As such, it is of great interest today for the study and reflection on imperialism, racism, political theology, as well as its political and cultural manifestations.

6 John L. O'Sullivan, 'Introduction. The Democratic Principle: The Importance of its Assertion, and Application to our Political System and Literature', *The United States Magazine and Democratic Review* 1:1 (Oct. 1837 to March 1838), p. 1, pp. 7-15; John L. O'Sullivan, 'The Canada Question', *The United States Magazine and Democratic Review*, 1:2, (January 1838), pp. 217-18; John L. O'Sullivan, 'The Approaching Census', *The United States Magazine and Democratic Review*, 5:13, (Jan., 1839), pp. 77-81; John L. O'Sullivan, 'The Great Nation of Futurity', *The United States Magazine and Democratic Review*, 6:23 (Nov., 1839), pp. 426-30.

7 John L. O'Sullivan, 'The Texas Question', *The United States Magazine and Democratic Review*, XIV:70, (April 1844), pp. 423-29; John L. O'Sullivan, 'The Re-Annexation of Texas: in its Influence on the Duration of Slavery', *The United States Magazine and Democratic Review*,

In the spring and summer of 1845, O'Sullivan became embroiled in a debate over the annexation of Texas with the Whig editor of the *New-York Tribune*, Horace Greeley.[8] This quarrel forced him to synthesize all his earlier expansionist arguments, leading to the publication in the summer of 1845 of the editorial 'Annexation' in the *Democratic Review*, where he coined the concept of Manifest Destiny as a blend of his progressive philosophy of history, his expansionist spatial theory, and his racist-providential ideal of a white American democracy:

> Why, where other reasoning wanting, in favor of now elevating this question of the reception of Texas into the Union, out of the lower region of our past party dissensions, up to its proper level of a high and broad nationality, it surely is to be found, found abundantly, in the manner in which other nations have undertaken to intrude themselves into it, between us and the proper parties to the case, in a spirit of hostile interference against us, for the avowed object of thwarting our policy and hampering our power, limiting our greatness and checking the fulfilment of our *manifest destiny* to overspread the continent allotted by Providence for the free development of our yearly multiplying millions.[9]

In the winter of 1845, after being absent from the United States over autumn for a personal trip to Europe, O'Sullivan intervened again in the

---

Vol. XV, N. 73, (July 1844), pp. 11-16; John L. O'Sullivan, 'Robert J. Walker', *The United States Magazine and Democratic Review*, Vol. XVI, N. 85, (Feb. 1845), pp. 162-64; John L. O'Sullivan, 'Our Relations with Mexico', *New York Morning News* (December 9, 1844); John L. O'Sullivan, 'The Annexation Question', *New York Morning News*, (December 31, 1844); John L. O'Sullivan, 'Mr. Shannon's diplomacy and the *Morning News*', *New York Morning News* (January 7, 1845); John L. O'Sullivan, 'Annexation at this Season', *New York Morning News*, (January 13, 1845); John L. O'Sullivan, 'Anti-Texas and the Evening Post', *New York Morning News*, (January 20, 1845); John L. O'Sullivan, 'Texas in the Senate', *New York Morning News*, (January 28, 1845); John L. O'Sullivan, 'Annexation: its Effects on Slavery', *New York Morning News*, (February 3, 1845); John L. O'Sullivan, 'Annexation in the Senate', *New York Morning News*, (February, 4 1845); John L. O'Sullivan, 'More! More! More!', *New York Morning News*, (February 7, 1845); John L. O'Sullivan, 'The Oregon', *New York Morning News*, (February 10, 1845); John L. O'Sullivan, 'Extension of the Union', *New York Morning News*, (February, 28 1845); John L. O'Sullivan, 'Texas is Ours', *New York Morning News*, (March 1, 1845); John L. O'Sullivan, 'Texas is Ours', *New York Morning News*, (March 1, 1845); John L. O'Sullivan, 'The Popular Movement, *New York Morning News*, (May 24, 1845); John L. O'Sullivan, 'Texas Safe', *New York Morning News*, (July 7, 1845); John L. O'Sullivan, 'The Taste of Blood', *New York Morning News*, (July, 1845); John L. O'Sullivan, 'The Democratic Energy', *New York Morning News*, (July 17, 1845).

8 Horace Greely, 'Free suffrage: The Morning News', *New-York Daily Tribune*, (March 23, 1846); Horace Greeley, 'The Game of Annexation Pocketing the Stakes- What are they?', *New York Daily Tribune*, (July 8, 1845).

9 The underlining is my own. John L. O'Sullivan, 'Annexation', *The United States Magazine and Democratic Review*, vol. 17, N. 85/86, (July-August 1845), p. 5.

debates over the dispute with Great Britain regarding the delimitation of the Oregon Territory. This occasion led him to summarize the theses of the 'Annexation' in another *Morning News* editorial titled 'The True Title' in which he again deployed the concept with all its expansionist rhetoric.[10] Ironically, it was this piece of journalism that popularized the concept: Congressman Robert C. Winthrop's attempt to ridicule it gave the editorial notoriety and spread its ideas to the broader American public.[11]

The concept, in its original formulation, was an ideological amalgam. In the first place, it emerged from a Jeffersonian republican matrix and was then filtered through agrarian thesis of contemporary Jacksonian populism. This provided a justification for the pursuit of the acquisition of new lands: the imperative to create a republic of self-sufficient small landholders would resolve the growing miseries of industrial society.

From a theological point of view, his discourse blended an enlightened natural theology mixed with the emotional faith of the Second Great Awakening. Through this framing, the concept articulated a providentialist discourse of geographical determinism in which divinity had preordained the American continent in such a way that the chosen people could, through their westward migration, occupy its lands. The concept also posited a Hegelian-style progressive philosophy of history, in which the course of empire and civilisation moved westward as the resolution of a logical historical development. On the basis of this historical determinism, the United States was called upon to be the nation of the future.

Malthusian debates were central to the formation of the concept. In particular, the anti-Malthusian idea that prospective population catastrophes, and the depletion of the subsistence means, could be remedied through territorial expansion. The concept also benefited from the fact that exponential population growth was seen as a sign of divine predilection. Closely linked to the biopolitical Malthusian thinking, the concept fostered a racist Anglo-Saxon ideology that justified the expropriation of land – and even advocated the extermination of natives and Latinos on the basis that the whites would make better use of the land[12]. It is worth noting that some saw territorial annexation as a way to end slavery with the annexation of new territories in the nation's tropical fringes; the plantations and their slaves would eventually move southwards until they disappeared from the US.

The concept of Manifest Destiny was widely used as propaganda to justify the invasion of Mexico during the Mexican-American War of 1846-1848. Ever since, Manifest Destiny has been adopted, both favorably

---

10 John L. O'Sullivan, 'The True Title', *New York Morning News* (December 27, 1845).

11 *Congressional Globe, First Season of the 29th Congress*, (Washington: Blair and Rives, 1846), p. 143; Pratt, 'The Origin of "Manifest Destiny"', p. 796, p. 798.

12 Horsman, *Race and Manifest Destiny*, pp. 219-21.

and critically, by politicians and intellectuals in favor and against expansionism and imperialism. Those on opposing sides gave it different meanings. Over time, the concept of Manifest Destiny became a key term in US foreign policy discourse, especially in relation to the defense of US interests in Latin America, which led to the concept to be linked to, and in many cases confused with, the Monroe Doctrine.[13]

The concept was also heavily present in the international press. It was particularly prominent in the British public debate, in the great imperial power at the time, and one which showed great interest in the developments of its geopolitical rivals and potential allies.

As this chapter will show, the concept of Manifest Destiny was also widely discussed in the Hispanic world. Spanish-American politicians and intellectual elites appropriated the term for two ends. On the one hand, some used it to condemn the aggressive nature of the expansionist, and imperialist policies that were bolstered by this concept, and which had Latin America and Spain as their main targets. On the other hand, however, the concept was a suggestive concept, one that served to articulate civilizing and nation-building theories during the second half of the nineteenth century and first half of the twentieth century in Hispanic thought.

By exploring how this ambiguity was created through the rejection and re-appropriation of the concept, this article shows how a term that was fundamental in the development of Anglo-Saxon racist thought, ended up becoming a crucial discursive device in Anglo-Iberian Atlantic civilizing discourses.

Before manifest destiny: escaping medieval fatalism

Before the concept of Manifest Destiny was coined in the anglophone world it appeared as a rhetorical catchphrase in Spanish. It was first used by José Antonio Conde, a Spanish historian and Arabist, a relative of Leandro de Moratín and a member of the Royal Academies of Language and History. Conde used the expression in his three-volume book *History of the domination of the Arabs in Spain, taken from various Arabic manuscripts and memoirs*, published in 1820-1821.[14] In the first volume, he specifically used the term when describing the conversation that allegedly took place in the 11th century between Aben Omar, vizier of the Muslim King Muhamad Almoatemed Aben Abed of the *taifa* of Seville, and the prince Obeidala Arraxid. Omar had been imprisoned by his King on charges

---

13 Frederick Merk, *The Monroe Doctrine and American Expansionism, 1843-1849* (New York: Random House, 1972), pp. 74-104, pp. 288-89.

14 *Historia de la dominación de los árabes en España, sacada de varios manuscritos y memorias arábigas.*

of high treason, and while awaiting Aben Abed's sentence he was visited by some courtiers, including Arraxid, to whom he complained about the King's attitude:

> My Lord, I see that my fate is clear as the end of my *manifest destiny*, the evil wind of envy and enmity carried away the auras of life that Muleyna breathed: yesterday he did not think of taking my life, and today he is extending it to reflect on which torment he will use to end it to the taste of my enemies...[15]

This is the earliest use I have found of the Manifest Destiny syntagma in any language, and it is worth noting that Conde was transcribing original sources. This was not a fictionalized historical dialogue: this usage dated back to 11th century Al-Andalus. Alongside this example was a second use of the syntagma used by the Spanish Romantic playwright and poet José Zorrilla in his 1843 play *The Great Comedy of King Don Sancho's Horse*, or *La gran comedia del caballo del rey don Sancho*. In this play set during the reign of Sancho Garcés III of Pamplona, a character identified as *the queen* – who historically would correspond to Muniadona of Castile – tells King Sancho and his son the infant Ramiro: 'Hold on, hold on: the finger of *manifest destiny* is here, and to innocent the righteous God opens the way'.[16]

Finally, there is a third mention in Spanish that coincided with the time when O'Sullivan coined the concept. This is found in a passage from the work titled *The Two Kings: A Historical Novel* (*Los dos reyes: novela histórica*), written in 1845 by the Spanish Romantic author Juan de Ariza. The novel is about the conflict between Peter "the Cruel" and Henry II, or Henry of Trastamara, over the Crown of Castile. The mention of Manifest Destiny comes when King Pedro receives a missive from an Arab astrologer predicting his defeat by King Enrique II, which leads him to reflect on his fate:

> When Don Pedro had finished the letter, Doña Inés had already disappeared, and the Monarch, with his eyes fixed on the signature of the Arabian astrologer, had not noticed her absence. Immobile, lifeless, thoughtful, he saw his *manifest destiny*, and his own heart read

---

15 José Antonio Conde, *Historia de la dominación de los árabes en España, extraída de varios manuscritos y memorias arábigas. Volume I* (Madrid: Imprenta que fue de García, 1820), p. 348. The emphasis is my own. Original: 'Señor mío, ya veo que mi suerte es clara y el fin de mi destino manifiesto, llevóse el maligno viento de la envidia y enemistad las leyes auras de vida que respiraba Muleyna: ayer no pensaba quitarme la vida, y hoy me la dilata pensando con qué tormento me han de acabar más a sabor de mis enemigos...'.

16 José Zorrilla, *La gran comedia de el caballo del rey Don Sancho* (Madrid: Imprenta de Repullés, 1843), p. 92, underlined by me. Original: 'Tened, tened: el dedo del destino manifiesto está aquí, y á la inocencia el justiciero Dios abre camino'.

in an unknown book more fateful than the stars and clearer than the entrails.[17]

In all three cases, Manifest Destiny appeared as a figure of speech composed of the noun "destiny", and accompanied by the verb "manifest" in the passive form. This introduces a subtle grammatical difference from later English usages where *manifest* will be an adjective that qualifies the noun *destiny*. The reason for this grammatical difference in the conceptual syntagma emerged from the fact that in these three Spanish formulations the syntagma is a rhetorical figure which replaced the concept of '*hado*' (fate). This introduced a dramatic twist to the term which emphasized the fatalism of the concept. In contrast to this rhetorical formula, the English version of Manifest Destiny will be a political concept that will articulate a set of geopolitical hypotheses and bolster a philosophy of history that would justify nineteenth-century American territorial expansionism.

With regard to the literary context in which the Castilian rhetorical formula appeared, it was used by Romantic historicist writers, who deployed it in dramatic episodes set in the medieval Iberian Peninsula. The subjects of the Manifest Destiny are members of royalty or characters close to them. In these episodes, references to Al-Andalus and the Muslim world abound, as the intention was to convey a fatalistic message associated with them. From 1820 to 1850, a fatalistic discursive context emerged in Spanish romantic liberalism, which reached its zenith in 1840, and which was fuelled by the feeling that neither revolutions nor the representative model of liberalism met the expectations which had been placed on them. Nor did they warrant the sacrifices that had been necessary to foster their growth.

However, this fatalistic discourse also served to vindicate the freedom of Catholic Spain against the Muslim world and Protestant countries. From the point of view of the Spanish liberals, Catholicism, with its vision of free will, would be a much more fruitful foundation for freedom than the doctrine of predestination, which Hispanic authors associated with Protestantism.[18] The Muslim imaginary in their texts was a model of fatalism and failure, which represented the heresy of the Spanish historical enemy against whom Catholic Spain had successfully carried out its Re-

---

17 Juan de Ariza, *Los dos reyes: novela histórica* (Madrid: L. González y compañía editores, 1845), p. 175, underlined by me. Original: 'Al terminar la carta don Pedro, había desaparecido doña Inés, y el Monarca, con los ojos fijos en la firma del astrólogo árabe no había reparado en su ausencia. Inmóvil, yerto, pensativo, veía su destino manifiesto, y su propio corazón leía en un libro desconocido más fatídico que los astros y más claro que las entrañas'.
18 They did not differentiate these views on the basis of the various groups within Protestantism.

conquest. From the liberal and Romantic Hispanic worldview, this conflict could be presented as a conflict between liberty and free will against despotism, fatalism, and predestination.[19]

Manifest Destinies

Although the Spanish language developed its own formula before the English concept of Manifest Destiny appeared, there is, it seems, no evidence of its continuity. On the contrary, the irruption of the American concept after the Mexican-American War of 1846-1848 shows a rapid dissemination in the Hispanic world of the new concept coined by O'Sullivan, which quickly replaced Spanish rhetorical formulas.

In the Spanish-speaking world during the second half of the nineteenth century and the first half of the twentieth century, the new concept would generally refer to US expansionism. Hispanic authors emphasized the fact that the US expansionism was particularly focused on Latin America – that US officials formulated the conflict in racial, cultural, religious and civilisational terms – in some cases even posing an existential threat to the region. There was, moreover, some confusion regarding the compatibility between this concept and the Monroe Doctrine, and the two were sometimes seen as one and the same.

However, apart from these standard uses in the press and in political essays, the concept was also the object of a process of appropriation and re-signification by the Spanish-speaking intellectual elites of the period. These authors appropriated the concept for its evocative historical drama and focused on its capacity to convey the temporal semantics of ineluctability. Although these conceptual uses bear some relation to the original formulation proposed by O'Sullivan, they also showed a certain degree of originality. These were genuine re-appropriations and not mere imitations.

Among Spanish intellectuals and politicians, the most outstanding cases of this process of conceptual re-appropriation were found in the abolitionist ideology of the Cuban-Spanish author Rafael María de Labra Cadrana, the democratic socialist politician Fernando Garrido, and the journalist and polymath Ramón Verea.

In the case of Labra, he engaged with the concept through his interest in the American abolitionist movement, specifically with the figure of Lincoln, who he admired. Labra pursued the abolition of slavery in his native Cuba and, in this context, the United States offered a reference

---

19 Pablo Sánchez León, "El bucle fatalista: cultura histórica y opinión pública a mediados del siglo XIX", in *De plebe a pueblo La participación política popular y el imaginario de la democracia en España, 1766-1868* (Barcelona: Bellaterra, 2022), pp. 12-13, pp. 16-23.

and a counterexample. Labra would condemn American expansionism and make use of Manifest Destiny for this purpose.[20] But at the same time, he harnessed the idea to suggest that certain peoples and races, worthy of their own value, would be called upon to have a Manifest Destiny in history. They therefore required vigorous public instruction and the establishment of institutions that served this purpose.[21]

This philosophy of history was to influence his defense of pan-Iberism and Ibero-Americanism. In Labra's view, the Manifest Destiny of Latin America consisted in the confederation of its peoples, an objective to which the best men in the region were committed, but which had been truncated by the endless wars between the different countries of the continent.[22] In his work on *Politics and Colonial Systems: Colonisation in History*, or *Política y sistemas coloniales: La colonización en la historia* (1876), Labra examined the situation of the monarchical Brazilian Empire, and its acquiescence towards slavery, and suggested that the Manifest Destiny of South America was the adoption of republicanism. By Manifest Destiny he understood 'the indispensable condition of liberty and progress in South America'.[23] On the other hand, in a lecture delivered in January 1912 on the centenary of 1812 and the Cádiz Constitution at the Ateneo de Madrid, Labra argued that Portugal's Manifest Destiny would consist of serving the constitutional interests of Spain, and, in his view, this was at the core of the foreign policy of the neighboring nation since 1820.[24]

Fernando Garrido, for his part, used the concept in two very precise contexts linked to an anti-monarchist and European federalist discourse, both linked to his belief in a socialist future. The first formulation of Manifest Destiny appeared in a paragraph that Garrido repeated word by word in several of his works. In this paragraph he explained that monarchies had originally been an element of progress by freeing European societies from

---

20 Rafael M. de Labra, *Estudios biográfico-políticos* (Madrid: Imprenta de 'La Guirinalda', 1887), pp. 123-24; *La Correspondencia de España*, 'Política internacional', Madrid, N. 15.454 (27 May 1900).

21 In his speech he explicitly refers to the University of Havana, which in his opinion was not receiving institutional and financial support from the Spanish Cortes Generales. Rafael M. de Labra, 'La instrucción pública en Cuba: Discurso pronunciado en el congreso de los diputados por Don Rafael María de Labra (continuación)', *La justicia: diario republicano*, Madrid, Year I, N. 159 (11 June, 1888), p. 1.

22 Rafael M. de Labra, 'Las Repúblicas Sud-americanas', *El Correo de España*, Madrid, Year II, N. 16 (28 April, 1871), p. 11.

23 Rafael M. de Labra, *Política y sistemas coloniales: La colonización en la historia. Conferencias del Ateneo político literario de Madrid. Europa en América. Tomo II* (Madrid: Librerías de San Martín, 1876), pp. 334-35.

24 *La Correspondencia de España*, 'Ateneo: Inauguración de las conferencias históricas. Discurso del señor Labra. Tema: Del año 1812 y el centenario de Cádiz', Madrid, N. 19.699 (18 January, 1912), p. 6. Original: 'la condición imprescindible de la libertad y el progreso en la América Meridional'.

of the anarchy of feudalism: 'To constitute the great national unity, to accumulate great elements of strength and to bring civilisation by conquest to distant countries, such has been the providential mission of the monarchy'. However, monarchies accomplished these feats by sacrificing individual freedom, so that their progressive function died as its providential mission unfolded. In his opinion: 'The propagating agents of civilisation today are the arts, science, commerce and, above all, the idea of fraternity, of the fusion of all peoples and all races into one great family, which is the dogma of modern democracy'. The project of pan-European national unity would have failed in its monarchical form under Napoleon I, so this process would have come about as the result of a spontaneous movement of democratic federation.[25]

> The national wars, promoted by the bastard interests of the monarchies, have expired like the interests which produced them. The great national units in Europe are divided; they aspire today to merge into a great federative unity, a prelude to the unity of the species, which will take place in a more distant epoch, which is the *manifest destiny* of mankind.[26]

This paragraph displayed the democratic providentialism that was embedded in the original concept coined by O'Sullivan. It first appeared in point IV of his chapter on monarchy in his pamphlet *Democratic Propaganda. The People and the Throne*, or *Propaganda democrática. El pueblo y el trono*, published in 1855.[27] This text was written during the July Revolution of 1854 to justify the popular uprising. Five years later, and under the rule of Leopoldo O'Donnell and his party, La Unión Liberal, Garrido would again publish, under the pseudonym of Evaristo Ventosa, another pamphlet titled *The Regeneration of Spain*, or *La Regeneración de España*, (1860), in which he criticized O'Donnell's government and Queen Isabella II. There he repeated the same reasoning and the use of the concept of Manifest Destiny. Finally, the aforementioned paragraph about the Manifest

---

25 Fernando Garrido, *Propaganda democrática. El pueblo y el trono* (Tarazona: Imprenta de G. Casañal, 1855), pp. 7-8. In the original: 'Constituir la gran unidad nacional, acumular grandes elementos de fuerza y llevar la civilización por la conquista á lejanos países, tal ha sido la misión providencial de la monarquía' and 'La civilización tiene hoy por agentes propagadores á las artes, las ciencias, el comercio, y sobre todo, las ideas de fraternidad, de fusión de todos los pueblos y de todas las razas en una gran familia que constituye el dogma de la democracia moderna'.

26 Ibid. pp. 8. Emphasis my own. Original: 'Las guerras nacionales, promovidas por los bastardos intereses de las monarquías, caducaron como los intereses que las produjeron. Las grandes unidades nacionales en Europa están divididas, aspiran hoy a fundirse en una gran unidad federativa, preludio de la unidad de la especie, que tendrá lugar en una época más lejana, que es el destino manifiesto de la humanidad'.

27 *Democratic Propaganda. The People and the Throne.*

Destiny of the European democratic federation and the union of mankind appeared again in the first volume of his *The Reign of the Last King of Spain* (*El Reinado del último Borbón de España*), a pamphlet published in 1868 in support of La Gloriosa.[28]

Along with this use of the concept, Garrido would use it again in his pamphlet *Socialism, Democracy and its Enemies*, or *El socialismo y la democracia ante sus adversarios*, a book written in 1862 during his exile in London. Its main concern was to mediate the debates between democratic socialist and non-socialists by expounding his doctrine on the unity of both principles. Chapter XXXV of the book explains that the democratic republic and associationism would be the two pillars that would support the political project to enable the emancipation of workers and end the condition of the proletariat as an exploited class. Its doctrine would empower the individual, in the sense that every individual would have the right to intervene directly in the administration of political life as well as in the production and redistribution of economic wealth. However, this would only be possible thanks to workers' associations, which would facilitate the coordination and harmonization of all individual wills. In this way, Garrido's democratic socialism would be organized on the basis of three principles: a first one proclaiming individual autonomy, rights and liberties; a second one of an associative character which would allow for collective action and redistributive justice; and a third one, a properly political principle, which, through the federal democratic republic, would make possible the establishment of the principles of liberty, equality and fraternity.[29] Garrido concluded his analysis as follows:

> This is my utopia, my programme, my hope. This is the future of humanity; this is its *manifest destiny*, and all the progress it has made so far is but a step along the road leading to the realization of this true social order.[30]

Garrido, like O'Sullivan, would formulate the concept of Manifest Destiny as a utopian temporal notion in which the fusion of the democratic ideal and faith in the march of progress would bring about an ineluctable

---

28 Evaristo Ventosa Fernando Garrido, *La regeneración de España* (Barcelona: Librería de Salvador Manero, 1860), pp. V-VIII, 376; Fernando Garrido, *Historia del reinado del último Borbón de España: de los crímenes, apostasías, opresión, corrupción, inmoralidad, despilfarros, hipocresía, crueldad y fanatismo de los gobiernos que han regido a España durante el reinado de Isabel de Borbón. Volume I* (Barcelona: Salvador Manero Editor, 1868), p. 23.

29 Fernando Garrido, *El socialismo y la democracia ante sus adversarios* (London, 1862), pp. 3-4, pp. 68-69.

30 Ibid., p. 69. Emphasis my own. In the original: 'Esta es mi utopía, mi programa, mi esperanza. Este es el porvenir de la humanidad; su destino manifiesto, y cuántos progresos ha realizado hasta hoy no son más que pasos dados en el camino que conduce a la realización de este verdadero orden social'.

emancipatory future for humanity. The great difference between their philosophies of history rested on the fact that while O'Sullivan approached his thinking from a liberal, nationalist and federalist prism, Garrido based his notion of Manifest Destiny on an internationalist and federalist socialism. O'Sullivan's Manifest Destiny was based on his view that territorial expansionism would allow a state to avoid a Malthusian catastrophe. Garrido's idea was based on the fraternity of populations already constituted and anchored in specific territories: this concept of Manifest Destiny assumed the abolition of borders as a result of class fraternity, and not their displacement as a result of the territorial competition.

The idea of progress was also fundamental for the polymath and publisher Ramón Verea, to the point that he named one of his publications after it, in which the concept of Manifest Destiny appeared three times. Verea had been living in New York since 1865; he was a Spanish émigré who produced his intellectual work in Spanish but wrote in the United States. Verea was therefore strongly influenced by the American political culture of the time, but he was also critical, drawing on his own Hispanic experience, of many of its characteristics. The tension between his culture of origin and that of adoption strongly emerged in his use of the term Manifest Destiny.

Two uses of the concept were made in the eleventh issue of the journal *El Progreso*, published in 1884. The first was titled 'Manifest Destiny: Commercial Treaties', or '*El destino manifiesto. Tratados comerciales*'.[31] The text argued that the English peoples had been the first to understand the true spirit of conquest of modern civilisations. They replaced declarations of war with free trade treaties, deploying armies of diplomats and traders instead of conventional armies, dominating other peoples without firing a shot. Verea considered this a breakthrough in human history. The Americans, through the Monroe Doctrine, had, in this reading, tried to secure their ascendancy over the rest of America in the face of this new form of commercial domination developed by Britain. But the future of American policy was not to be found in wars of aggression, but in the imitation of their old metropole through a new commercial imperialism based on free trade treaties with which to market their manufactured goods. This would be its new Manifest Destiny.[32]

A second article appeared in the same issue, in which Verea used the concept in an ironic reading of a confrontation with the editors of a Catholic and conservative Mexican publication. In the eighth issue of the periodical, Verea published two anti-clerical articles titled 'the Criminal Cult' and the 'True Cult', or '*Culto criminal*' and '*Verdadero culto*',

---

31 Manifest Destiny. Commercial treaties.
32 Ramón Verea, 'El destino manifiesto. Tratados comerciales', *El Progreso*, New York, year 1, N. 11 (November 1884), pp. 193-94.

which caused some controversy in Mexico. The newspaper *La hoja del pueblo* published in Oaxaca accused the magazine *El Progreso* of being a mouthpiece for the interests of the 'Yankees' and Manifest Destiny. Verea responded with irony in an article titled 'The Cults and the Press', or '*Los cultos y la prensa*'. The article read:

> *El Progreso* is neither atheist nor is it written in favour of *manifest destiny*, if this does not include that of those who live off religion [...]
> And if this newspaper were atheist and in favour of *manifest destiny*, who else but a 'Patriotic and Catholic' newspaper should fight us? We forget that these *Catholic patriots* like to burn things, but they do not argue.[33]

However, despite these observations, Verea's position on US foreign policy and Manifest Destiny was somewhat ambiguous. While he declared himself against American expansionism and the principles expressed in the Monroe Doctrine, he nevertheless embraced the philosophy of history underlying Manifest Destiny.

This was evident in another of his articles that appeared in *El Progreso* titled 'Mexico's Manifest Destiny', or '*El destino manifiesto de México*'. In this article Verea criticized the Porfiriato, the fin de siècle administration that grew Mexico's economy and aggravated the nation's socioeconomic inequality. He linked the Porfiriato to the defunct Conservative Party, while defending the progressive policies of extending the telegraph and the railway throughout Mexico. For Verea, Mexico's problem was the country's cultural isolation. The predominance of Catholic obscurantism was to blame for its intellectual narrowmindedness. As a result, Mexico needed to open up to foreign ideas and influences that would allow it to modernize: the new means of communication would allow it to flourish. Verea also argued that the United States had abandoned its territorial ambitions over Mexico and had encouraged Mexicans to open up to the influence of their northern neighbors. Verea identified the Mexican Liberal Party as the political force capable of carrying out this technological and cultural modernisation of Mexico; its policies that would lay the foundations for the Manifest Destiny of the country's future greatness.[34]

Finally, another way the concept of Manifest Destiny was appropriated by Spanish authors was through the idea of Hispano-Americanism. As the

---

33 Ramón Verea, 'Los cultos y la prensa', *El Progreso*, New York, year 1, N. 11 (November 1884), p. 204, emphasis my own. In the original: 'El Progreso ni es ateo ni está escrito en favor del destino manifiesto, si en este no se incluye el de los vividores a costa de la religión ... Y si este periódico fuera ateo y favorable al *destino manifiesto* ¿a quién más que a un periódico "Patriótico y católico" correspondía combatirnos? Nos olvidábamos de que estos *patriotas católicos* queman, pero no discuten'.

34 Ramón Verea, 'El destino manifiesto de México' in *Contra el altar y el trono: Artículos varios publicados en 'El Progreso' de 1884-85* (New York: Imprenta El Políglota, 1890), pp. 94-96.

nineteenth century progressed, it became clear that Spain was not going to recover its former colonial empire in the Americas. Its image as a threat to the Spanish-American republics had softened as numerous US military interventions in Latin America after the Mexican American War of 1846-48 had made the United States the main danger to its southern neighbors. Spain's defeat in the Spanish-American War of 1898 contributed decisively to rethinking the relationship between the ex-metropolis and its former colonies.[35]

Hispano-Americanism was one of the responses of the Spanish politico-cultural elite to rebuild political, commercial and cultural relations with the Spanish-American republics. This was a project that, in its most conservative iteration, sought to exercise a kind of paternalistic cultural hegemony over the Spanish-American republics by highlighting the civilizing mission of the former metropolis, and by pointing to the many 'spiritual' contributions made by Spain to the New World. From a more progressive perspective, Hispano-Americanism offered new framework for the common and joint development for Spain and Latin America. In both conservative and progressive Hispano-Americanism, the cultural and commercial dimensions were key strategies to relaunch Spain's projection in the region; the way these factors were articulated would, however, change depending on the ideological tendency of the author.[36]

Ibero-Americanism, on the other hand, was an alternative formulation of Hispano-Americanism that made it possible to encompass non-Hispanic South American realities, such as the Portuguese-speaking world or indigenous communities. For this reason, the expression was generally more popular among Latin American intellectuals. The Ibero-American Union founded in Madrid in 1885 was the main institution created for the purpose of disseminating Hispano-Americanism in the face of the rise of Pan-Americanism promoted by the United States through the Pan-American conferences. It was also a way to counter French attempts to influence the region with the idea of Latin Americanism, formulated by the communities of South American intellectuals exiled in Paris.[37]

---

35 Cesilda Martin Montalvo, María Rosa Martín de Vega and María Teresa Solano Sobrado, 'El hispanoamericanismo, 1880-1930', *Quinto Centenario* 8 (1895), p. 153; Marina Zuloaga Rada, 'La diplomacia española en la época de Carranza: iberoamericanismo e hispanoamericanismo, 1916-1920', *Historia Mexicana* 45:4. Issue: Una mirada hacia afuera: México y América Latina, siglos XIX y XX (April-June, 1996), pp. 812-14.

36 Martin Montalvo, Martín de Vega and Solano Sobrado, 'El hispanoamericanismo, 1880-1930', pp. 150-52, pp. 156-59.

37 Arturo Ardao, "Panamericanismo y Latinoamericanismo", in Karina Batthyany and Gerardo Caetano eds., *Antología del pensamiento crítico uruguayo contemporáneo* (Buenos Aires: CLACSO, 2018), pp. 180-86; Zuloaga Rada, 'iberoamericanismo e hispanoamericanismo, 1916-1920', pp. 814-26; Martin Montalvo, Martín de Vega and Solano Sobrado, 'El hispanoamericanismo, 1880-1930', pp. 162-65.

Hispano-Americanism and Ibero-Americanism made it possible to deploy a spatial imaginary consigned in civilisational terms that was intended to enable Spain to return as a key player to its former colonial sphere. This geographical imaginary was a fertile space for the use of the concept of Manifest Destiny. Through a neo-imperial discourse, this model posited Spain's historical duty to intervene in Spanish America and within a zone of racial and civilizational influence: militarily to defend the independence of the former colonial possessions from the expansionist aggressions of the United States, and culturally to defend the purity of the Hispanic language and culture from the growing Anglo-Saxon influence.[38]

Ironically, this discourse ended up becoming a Hispanic version of the Monroe Doctrine, in which Spain's manifest destiny was seen as the duty of the former metropolis to defend the integrity of the Latin race from the aggression of the Anglo-Saxon peoples.

Manifest Destiny in Mexico and Argentina

The concept of Manifest Destiny was also widely debated in Latin American countries, especially among the creole political and intellectual elites, who developed an ambivalent relationship with it. The Mexican-American War of 1846-1848 and James K. Polk's transformation of the Monroe Declaration into the imperial Monroe Doctrine, led South American creole elites to experience a certain distancing from the United States, no longer perceived as a sister republic, but as a potential threat to their sovereignty. Despite this change in perception, the cultural and exemplary power of the United States continued to exert a powerful influence on South American elites, who found in the concept of Manifest Destiny a striking expression with which to convey their yearnings for national development.

The writings of the Colombian intellectual José María Torres Caicedo demonstrate the centrality of the concept of Manifest Destiny in the process of self-definition by opposition to the concept. Torres Caicedo was a particularly influential Latin American author since, together with Francisco Bilbao Barquín and Michel Chevalier, he is considered one of the possible authors of the concept of "Latin America", a notion formulated in Paris and which was instrumentalized years later by France to promote

---

38 R. de I. 'Vicisitudes de una guerra entre España y los Estados-Unidos', *La asamblea del ejército: periódico mensual de ciencia, arte e historia militar*. Tomo III (Madrid: Imprenta y estereotipia de M. Rivadeneyra, 1857), p. 376; 'Nuestra situación en América', *Crónica Hispano-Americana*, Madrid, Year II, N. 18 (24 November 1858), p. 9; 'Revista Internacional', *El Globo*, Madrid, Year VIII, N. 2,330 (8 March 1882), p. 1. 9; 'Las simpatías del "standard"', *La época* (17 September 1895); Arturo Llopis, 'Los Estados Unidos: sus expoliaciones pasadas, política presente y futuras ambiciones', *Revista contemporánea* 24:111 (1898), pp. 23-39.

an idea of Latinity different from the Spanish Hispano-Americanism sponsored by Spain. France would then be able to present its cultural past to
South American elites as an alternative civilizing reference point.[39]

The concept of Manifest Destiny played an important role in his work
Latin American Union: Bolívar's thoughts on forming an American league,
or *Unión Latino-Americana: pensamiento de Bolívar para formar una liga
americana* (1865), a work that aimed to revive Bolívar's project to create
a Latin American confederation, one which was frustrated by the failure
of the Congress of Panama in 1826. In this work, the concept of Manifest
Destiny appeared in Chapter XII on the Monroe Doctrine and its true
and false interpretations. According to Torres Caicedo, the Monroe Doctrine was originally the United States' reaction to the attempts of the
Holy Alliance to restore the Spanish colonial empire after overthrowing
Rafael Riego, as well as an assertive move against Great Britain in Western
Hemisphere politics. The Monroe Doctrine was, he reasoned, a statement
against European colonialism, a doctrine of non-intervention in the affairs
of the American republics, and as such, an idea that could be supported by
Latin America.[40]

By contrast, Manifest Destiny was a caricature of the Monroe Doctrine,
an idea that Torres Caicedo attributed to former US president James
Buchanan and that had, in his view, been promoted by expansionist politicians in the 1850s, with the aim of conquering and annexing as many Latin
American territories as possible. Against Manifest Destiny and American
ambitions, Torres Caicedo proposed the creation of a Latin American
confederation, 'a kind of American *Zollverein*, more liberal than the German one'. This would be the only way for Latin American republics to
guarantee their sovereignty in the face of American and European colonial
expansionist ambitions.[41]

His rejection of Manifest Destiny as the means to build the future of a
Latin American union was even more evident in his book *The Anglo-Saxon
America and Latin America*, or *La América Anglosajona y la América Latina*
(1882) where he dedicated the following words of rejection to the first
Pan-American congress:

> Congresses for the [establishment of a] Latin-American Union, have as
> many as you like: the idea of the Continental Union will be a historical
> fact; but these congresses must meet on Latin American territory, to
> seek the means of preserving themselves, of uniting and of confronting
> all those in Europe or America who have the pretension of subjugating

---

39 Ardao, 'Panamericanismo y Latinoamericanismo', pp. 183-86.
40 José María Torres Caicedo, *Unión Latino-Americana: pensamiento de Bolívar para formar una
   liga americana* (Paris: Librería de Rosa y Bouret, 1865), pp. 63-66.
41 Ibid., pp. 64, 67-72, 88-94. Original: 'una especie de Zollwerein americano, más liberal que el
   alemán'.

us. After the theories of *Manifest Destiny* proclaimed most forcefully in 1881, the Congress of the two Americas in Washington would be a political and diplomatic mistake on the part of Latin Americans. And yet we long so much for the close and cordial friendship between the North American Union and those republics that were formerly colonies of Spain; but that union must be in the bosom of equality, reciprocity, loyalty, and after the theories of Brown, Seward, Blaine, and others have been retracted.[42]

In contrast to Torres Caicedo's anti-American attitude, Argentina's President Domingo Faustino Sarmiento was strongly influenced in his thinking by the example of the US, to the point of adopting much of the theoretical background of the concept of Manifest Destiny as part of his political philosophy for Argentina.[43]

The text which evidenced the influence of Manifest Destiny on Sarmiento's thought was his famous letter to Valentín Ansina of November 12th, 1847. In this letter he described his trip to the United States at the time of the US invasion of Mexico, during the height of the use of the concept of Manifest Destiny by the US expansionist press.

In the letter Sarmiento gave an account of the social, political and religious characteristics of the United States, contrasting them with the situation of the Latin American republics. In this comparison, the United States was constantly presented as an example of success and industriousness as opposed to a failed South America. In Sarmiento's narrative, multiple cultural and religious causes were adduced to explain this divergence between North and South America. But one of the main points of divergences between the two continents rested on a geographical providentialism, which would lead Sarmiento to consider that North America might have been singularly favored by God in its physical layout and abundance of natural resources:

---

42 José María Torres Caicedo, *La América Anglosajona y la América Latina* (Paris: Imprimerie Nouvell, 1882), quoted in Ardao, 'Panamericanismo y Latinoamericanismo', p. 186. 'Congresos para la Unión Latino-Americana, cuantos se quieran: la idea de la Unión será un hecho histórico; pero esos congresos deben reunirse en territorio latinoamericano, para buscar los medios de preservarse, de unirse y de hacer frente a cuantos en Europa o América tengan la pretensión de subyugarnos. Después de las teorías del "Destino Manifiesto" proclamadas con más energía en 1881, el Congreso de las dos Américas en Washington sería un error político y diplomático de los latino-americanos. Y sin embargo nada anhelamos tanto como la estrecha y cordial amistad entre la Unión Norteamericana y las repúblicas antes colonias de España; pero esa unión que sea en el seno de la igualdad, de la reciprocidad, de la lealtad, y despeés de haber sido retractadas las teorías de los Brown, Seward, Blaine'.

43 Although, to my knowledge, he never actually used the concept in any of his works. This influence has previously been spotted by Dardo Scavino in 'Sarmiento y la *translatio imperii*', *Estudios de Teoría Literaria* 5:10 (2016), pp. 167-69.

If God were to commission me to create a great republic, our own republic for example, I would not accept such a serious petition, except on the condition that he gave me at least these foundations: A space without limits so that one day two hundred million inhabitants could live in it; [...] Is there no order and premeditation in all these events? Why did the Saxon race stumble upon this piece of the world which also suited their industrial instincts, and why did the Spanish race have the luck of South America, where there were silver and gold mines, and meek and abject Indians, which suited their master's laziness, their backwardness and industrial ineptitude? Is this not Providence? Oh friend, God is the easiest solution to all these difficulties.[44]

This paragraph is unique because it synthesizes many of the ideas that appeared in the editorial 'Annexation' written by O'Sullivan and where the concept of Manifest Destiny first appeared.[45] As in the *Democratic Review*'s editorial, Sarmiento's letter emphasized the need for a large physical space for national development and population growth as the key to a country's progress. The contrast between the industriousness of the Anglo-Saxon as opposed to the laziness of the native and the Hispanic population is another key narrative of the 'Annexation' editorial that justifies the American settlers' right to the land, a trope that is reproduced in its literal form by Sarmiento, who sees in this geographical arrangement the hand of providence.

Of particular relevance is Sarmiento's insistence throughout his work on linking national progress to population growth and the need for new land to enable this development. This is a Malthusian argument that was central to the formation of the concept of Manifest Destiny in O'Sullivan's thought. We can find it clearly repeated several times throughout the missive, where population tables and allusions to the US census appear, comparing the population growth ratios of the United States with those of South America to highlight the progress of the North American republic as opposed to the lethargy of its southern neighbors.[46]

---

44 Domingo F. Sarmiento, *Viajes en Europa, África y América* (Santiago: Imprenta de Julio Belin i Ca., 1851), pp. 335-36. In the original: 'Si Dios me encargara de formar una gran república, nuestra república a nous por ejemplo, no admitiría tan sério encargo, sino a condición que me diese estas bases por lo ménos: Espacio sin límites conocidos para que se huelguen un día en él doscientos millones de habitantes; ... No hai órden i premeditacion en todos estos acasos? ¿Por qué la raza sajona tropezó con este pedazo de mundo que tambien cuadraba con sus instintos industriales, i por qué a la raza española le cupo en suerte la América del Sud, donde habia minas de plata i de oro, e indios mansos i abyectos, que venian de perlas a su pereza de amo, a su atraso e ineptitud industrial? No hai Providencia? Oh! amigo, Dios es la mas fácil solucion de todas estas dificultades'.

45 O'Sullivan, 'Annexation', pp. 5-10.

46 Sarmiento, *Travels in Europe, Africa and America*, pp. 335-41, pp. 349-50, 361, pp. 392-96.

Despite accepting the American providentialist discourse, Sarmiento was not entirely deluded about American territorial ambitions and divine predilection for the US. In another paragraph where Sarmiento faithfully echoed the idea put forward by O'Sullivan that, as a result of expansionism, the United States will one day cover the entire northern part of the western hemisphere, from the North Pole to the Isthmus of Panama, he noted:

> I do not wish to make Providence an accomplice in all the North American usurpations, nor in their bad example, which in a more or less remote period may attract them, unite them politically, or annex them, as they call it Canada, Mexico, etc. The Union of free men will then begin at the North Pole, and end, for lack of land, at the Isthmus of Panama.[47]

Sarmiento would echo this expansionist dream by describing to Ansina in great detail the story of a group of settlers on their way to Oregon. In his account, Sarmiento narrates in epic detail the encounter and adventures of these settlers with different indigenous tribes in what will be one of the fundamental tropes of his work and thought: the dialectic between civilisation and barbarism in the process of nation-building.[48]

This theme would be central to his work *Facundo or Civilisation and Barbarism in the Argentine Pampas*, or *Facundo o civilización y barbarie en las pampas argentinas* (1845), a book published right as the concept of Manifest Destiny was emerging in US debates. In *Facundo* the ideas of Argentinian Unionism can be found in his criticism of the federalist *caudillos* who challenged the political power of Buenos Aires from the provinces. These *caudillos*, described by Sarmiento in orientalised tones, would lead all those considered to be barbarians: the *gaucho* and the native.[49] In Sarmiento's account, the contrast between the urban civilisation of Buenos Aires and the barbarism of the *pampa* and its inhabitants is evocative of the North American dichotomy between civilisation and wilderness, key to the frontier expansionist narrative, later popularized by intellectuals such as the historian Frederick J. Turner.[50]

---

47 Ibid., p. 339. In the original: 'Yo no quiero hacer cómplice a la Providencia de todas las usurpaciones Norte-americanas, ni de su mal ejemplo que en un período mas o ménos remoto puede atraerle, unirle políticamente o anexarle como ellos llaman, el Canadá, Méjico etc. Entónces, la Union de los hombres libres principiará en el Polo del Norte, para venir a terminar por falta de tierra en el Istmo de Panamá'.

48 Ibid., pp. 358, pp. 369-71, pp. 374-82.

49 Felipe Rigna, *Los mitos de la historia argentina: de San Martín a 'El granero del mundo'.* *Five Volumes. Volume 1* (Buenos Aires: Planeta, 2004), pp. 269-70; Scavino, 'Sarmiento y la *translatio imperii'*, pp. 172-76.

50 Frederick J. Turner, *The Frontier in American History* (Tucson: The University of Arizona Press, 1986), pp. 1-38.

However, Sarmiento's *gaucho* was not exactly like the Turnerian pioneer. Both share the idea that contact with the *pampa* and wilderness undermines the character of its inhabitants, generating a particular typology. But while in Turner the pioneer becomes a syncretic unit between civilisation and savagery that acts as the germ of civilisation in the wilderness in Sarmiento's case the *gaucho* as a barbarian will always be antithetical to civilisation. The intervention of the migrant of urbanite and European origin was considered necessary by Sarmiento in order to redeem the *pampa* from barbarism.

This mentality was clearly reflected in his policies when he became President, especially in the sale of land to European migrants and inhabitants of Buenos Aires. This policy was inspired by the idea that the building of the Argentine nation would necessarily consist in the taming and civilizing of the *pampa*, a task which only urbanites and people of European extraction would be qualified to carry out. His initiative to build railways and telegraphs was inspired by the pattern of civilizing expansion implemented by the United States in its westward expansion, and had an important influence on the growth of the nation.[51]

Ultimately, Sarmiento considered that, although separated by their culture and history, the United States and the South American republics constituted a geographical and historical unity that would be destined to merge in the near future. This was expressed in *Conflict and Harmony of the Races in America*, or *Conflicto y armonía de las razas en América* (1883), in which his civilizing theses, inspired by the United States, took the form of a comparative history of the two Americas. In this book, the native would be central in Sarmiento's thesis: a burden that would partly explain the backwardness of South America compared to North America.[52]

During Argentina's Oligarchic Republic (1880-1916), and in the context of Ibero-Americanist thought, the concept of Manifest Destiny received a new reception in the thought of nationalist authors such as Ricardo Rojas and Manuel Gálvez, and the historian Emilio Ravignani.

In the case of Rojas and Gálvez, as representatives of nationalist and neo-Romantic thought, the concept of Manifest Destiny would emerge as a result of a cultural nationalism inspired by the German *Völkisch* movement animated by a Herderian ideal of nationhood, which would contrast with the civic patriotism inherited from the time of independence, predominant during most of the nineteenth century.[53]

---

51 Rigna, *Los mitos de la historia argentina*. Volume 2, pp. 278-83.

52 Domingo F. Sarmiento, *Conflicto y armonía de las razas* (Buenos Aires: Imprenta y litografías "Mariano Moreno", 1900), pp. 7-39, pp. 333-37.

53 Earl T. Glauert, 'Ricardo Rojas and the Emergence of Argentine Cultural Nationalism', *The Hispanic American Historical Review* 43:1 (1963), pp. 1-5; Jean H. Delaney, 'Imagining "El Ser Argentino": Cultural Nationalism and Romantic Concepts of Nationhood in Early

The thought of Ricardo Rojas showed certain parallels with O'Sullivan. Both authors were key to the transformation and development of the literary culture of their period, both promoted a nationalist conception of the literary canon that was coherent with liberal democratic values.[54] To achieve this nationalist and liberal democratic turn in their national cultures, both authors drew inspiration from German Romanticism, adapting its premises to the particularities of their national context. This resulted in a common conception of the people in essentialist and organicist terms, where the nation was understood as a natural reality animated by an immanent and teleological force of development, by virtue of which the national community would be called upon to display essential characteristics latent in itself, and which shaped its identity and its destiny.[55]

In this context, Rojas deployed the concept of Manifest Destiny in an article in the journal *La Nota*, as the eighth part of a collection of meditations on politics and history.[56] The subtitle of the article evoked its content: 'On nationalism in Argentine history: the national epiphany of 1810; the rotundity of its "facts", the hesitation of its "ideas", the origins of the territorial and historical consciousness of the Argentine people'.

According to Rojas, it was not destiny, but "Argentinianness" that manifested itself with the independence of 1810. The revolution fused into a single political consciousness the set of elements that would make up Argentina's essence and which were present, if dispersed, in its indigenous and colonial realities of the previous three hundred years. However, the *Libertadores*, despite their greatness, did not have a clear vision of the Argentine nation, its limits and characteristics: they acted quickly, but reflected little on their act. This meant that:

> ...while our *manifest destiny* is that the native genius should not perish, so that it may flourish in wealth, in art, in science, in freedom; see, on the other hand, the Unitarians of the Triumvirate trying to stifle the regional spirit, and those of 6 April demanding for themselves the "jobs", which – according to their memorial accepted by Saavedra –

Twentieth-Century Argentina', *Journal of Latin American Studies* 34:3 (August 2002), pp. 625-37.

54 Joshua D. Scholnick, 'Democrats Abroad: Continental Literature and the American Bard in the "United States Magazine and Democratic Review"', *American Periodicals*, Volume 3 (1993), pp. 80-88.

55 Meyer H. Abrams, *El espejo y la lámpara: Teoría romántica y tradición crítica* (Barcelona: Barra, 1975), pp. 12-13, pp. 299-311; Glauert, 'Ricardo Rojas and the Emergence of Argentine Cultural Nationalism', pp. 1-3; Delaney, 'Imagining "El Ser Argentino"', pp. 630-32.

56 Definition of nationalism.

should be taken from the *peninsulares,* since that, according to them, was what the revolution had been made for.[57]

Argentina's Manifest Destiny was the preservation and development of a native genius linked to the land and to its dual indigenous and colonizing past. For Rojas, unlike Sarmiento and many other creole intellectuals and politicians, did not abjure the indigenous past, but tried to capitalize on it in order to fuse it with the colonial experience in a kind of nationalist syncretism[58]. But independence-era politicians had failed in their task of national construction. In Rojas' view: 'They were agents of destiny in its titanic performance, leaving to successive generations the "human" task of understanding and explaining what they achieved'.[59]

For Rojas, the patriotism of 1810 would have created a nation that had been forming since before the conquest, but it would be the mission of future generations to shape the destiny of the nation. This would have led the present generations to become aware of their situation: 'That is to say, of their origin, their evolution, their geographical forces, their present problems and their own destinies'.[60]

The Spanish Manifest Destiny

Other authors were more emphatic in their support of the Spanish legacy in the Americas. Manuel Gálvez generated a nationalist-conservative

---

57 Ricardo Rojas, 'Definición del nacionalismo: Del nacionalismo en la Historia Argentina: la epifanía nacional de 1810; rotundidad de sus "hechos", vacilación de sus "ideas", orígenes de la conciencia territorial e histórica del pueblo argentino', *La Nota,* Bueno Aires, N. 14 (13 November 1915), p. 260. Emphasis my own. In the original: 'Y mientras nuestro destino manifiesto es que el genio nativo no perezca, para que llegue a florecer en riqueza en arte en, ciencia, en libertad; véoles, en cambio, a los unitarios del Triunvirato queriendo ahogar el espíritu regional, y a los del 6 de abril pidiendo para sí los "empleos", que -según su memorial aceptado por Saavedra- debían quitarse a los peninsulares, pues para eso, según ellos, se había hecho la revolución'. The historical references made by Rojas refers to the conflict between centralists and federalists that opened up after the Revolution of 5 and 6 April 1811. With the popular petition of 6 April that denied any public employment to people born outside the Provincias Unidas del Río de la Plata'. The Triumvirate was the executive body set up after the Junta Grande was overthrown, which gave power to the centralists of Buenos Aires over the provinces, giving rise to Unitarios and Federales.

58 Daniel Mesa Gancedo, 'Nacionalismo y excepción cultural en el proyecto historiográfico de Ricardo Rojas', *Revista de crítica literaria latinoamericana* 70 (September 2009), pp. 185-89; Delaney, 'Imagining "El Ser Argentino"', pp. 657-58.

59 Ricardo Rojas, 'Definition of Nationalism', p. 260. In the original: 'Ellos fueron agentes del destino en el titánico obrar, dejando a las generaciones sucesivas la tarea "humana" de comprender y explicar lo que ellos realizaron'.

60 Ibid., p. 261. In the original: 'Es decir, de su origen, su evolución, de sus fuerzas geográficas, de sus problemas actuales y sus propios destinos'.

reading of Manifest Destiny that would derive from a conception of His-panism understood through the prism of *translatio imperii*. In his work *The Soil of Race*, or *El solar de la raza* (1913), Gálvez began with a first chapter titled 'Spanish Spiritualism'. The last section focused on the hypothetical decline of the Latin European countries (Spain, Portugal, Italy and France) caused by the loss of international influence of these countries and their values in favor of the Anglo-Saxon powers. This decline would lead to the most dynamic elements of Southern Europe migrating to Latin America, bringing with them the last remnants of the drive and vitality of their countries of origin. These men would be the modern versions of the Spanish *conquistadores* of old, the contemporary Cortés and Pizarro:

> The Latins of Europe, for almost all those men are Latins, would be called vestals of the lineage: they bring the mission, providential and invisible, of preserving the Latin excellences in the mixture of peoples, of consolidating the predominance of the amalgam of so many metals, of the pure gold of Latinity.[61]

This racial providentialism of transporting the cultural excellences of Latin Europe to the American continent contained two distinct discursive tropes: first, a cultural version of *translatio imperii*, which posited that the supposed decline of the empires of Southern Europe, far from being a problem for Latin America, represented an opportunity for the latter to become the new civilizing focus of Latinity. On the other hand, he employed the North American ideas of the promised land, the chosen people, and the "melting pot" –in a very similar way to the theory of the "cosmic race", or *"raza cósmica"* of the Mexican author and statesman José Vasconcelos, who envisioned the Americas as the space for the creation of a new civilisation. Gálvez proposed that Argentina would serve as a meeting place for the population of Southern European origin where Latin greatness could be reborn on the basis of a Spanish mold:

> It is precisely Latin decadence that gives us this unique place among the peoples of today: that of being destined to make the virtues of the race prevail in the world, like a sun among the stars. If Spain were a great power and France and Italy were not already bitten by the microbe of decadence, the future of Argentina would be different. [...] The future of our country is not purely material. It will be the granary of the world, but it must not be that alone. A higher and perennial destiny will magnify it magnificently. But will we have any spiritual

---

61 Manuel Gálvez, *El solar de la raza* (Buenos Aires: Sociedad Coop. 'Nosotros': Libertad 543, 1913), p. 61. In the original: 'Los latinos de Europa, pues latinos son casi todos aquellos hombres, se dirían vestales de la estirpe: traen la misión, providencial e invisible, de conservar las excelencias latinas en la mezcla de pueblos, de afianzar el predominio de la amalgama de tantos metales, del oro puro de la latinidad'.

influence on the world, will we create in the centuries a beautiful and harmonious type of civilisation?[62]

Gálvez found that material abundance was a shared element between the United States and Argentina. But while the United States was animated by a 'barbaric energy' resulting from modernisation without spirit, Argentina would benefit from being an heir to Latin culture, especially from the *'solar de la raza'*, or Spain, whose political decadence and spiritual wealth would offer Argentina the opportunity to inherit the position previously held by the former metropolis, and which would allow it to become a world power in wealth and spirit.[63]

While the concept of Manifest Destiny was not present in its literal form in Gálvez's text, all the semantic components of Manifest Destiny were to be found in its discourse. At times it is almost indistinguishable from that of O'Sullivan's ideas in his article 'The Great Nation of Futurity' (1839).

In the context of Ibero-Americanism, Emilio Ravignani made use of the concept in his essay *'Definición histórica del Iberoamericanismo'* (1929).[64] In this text, Ravignani attempted to sketch the link between Latin America and its former metropolis from a historical perspective. To this end, Ravignani depicted the process of colonization as the encounter and fusion of two realities, a dominant Hispanic one, which through the conquest brought the fundamental elements to the continent by means of institutions, customs and the Spanish language. Secondly, there was a part of an indigenous character which, after the Spanish conquest, had contributed the distinctively American character to the new republics. In this way, Ravignani's narrative would place him somewhere between Rojas's syncretistic nationalism and Gálvez's defense of Hispanism. Finally, Ravignani pointed out that the historical rise of the Anglo-Saxon world, especially the United States, posed a challenge to the Latin peoples. If they wanted their voice to be heard and respected in the concert of nations, these nations should join Spain in the common cause of Ibero-Americanism. Ravignani concluded:

---

62 Ibid., p. 63. In the original: 'Es la decadencia latina, precisamente, lo que nos da este sitio único entre los pueblos actuales: el de ser nosotros los destinados a hacer imperar en el mundo, como un sol entre astros, las virtudes de la raza. Si España fuera una gran potencia y Francia e Italia no estuviesen ya mordidas por el microbio de la decadencia, fuera otro el porvenir de la Argentina. ... El porvenir de nuestra patria no es puramente material. Será ella el granero de orbe, pero no debe ser eso tan solo. Un más alto y perenne destino la engrandecerá magníficamente. Mas ¿tendremos sobre el mundo alguna influencia espiritual? ¿Crearemos en los siglos un bello y armonioso tipo de civilización?'.

63 Ibid., pp. 64-65.

64 Historical Definition of Ibero-Americanism.

History, known better every day with more serenity, with a more
adequate interpretation of events, is a beautiful source to verify
how the past does not contradict future possibilities. And although
contingencies constantly arise in the human future that escape
prediction, nevertheless, life has taught us that there is a "manifest
destiny" linking Hispanic action to the soil of America, and that this
same destiny now unites us towards the future in the elaboration of
new historical values, inspired by the ascending ideal of offering men a
new world, the seat of well-being and the archetype of civilisation.[65]

Just as it was popular in the United States to consider Manifest Destiny
in racial terms as the civilizing mission of the Anglo-Saxon race in the
Americas, Ravignani deployed a Hispanic version of this hypothesis with
"la Hispanidad" as the civilizing framework and the Ibero-Americanism as
the vehicular political project.[66]

However, by the early twentieth century, most Ibero-Americanists
were reluctant to adopt the concept because of its link to US foreign policy.
Manifest Destiny would henceforth be considered in most of their works
as a synonym for American expansionism. This would stop them from
appropriating it as a political concept, in the way that Torres Caicedo
did. The Argentine Manuel Baldomero Ugarte, despite having a markedly
providentialist discourse for a united Latin America, only used the concept
of Manifest Destiny to refer to North American expansionism[67]. The same
pattern was present in the work of Peruvians: Edwin Elmore, and to a
lesser degree in the oeuvre of José Santos Chocano, for whom the doctrine
of Manifest Destiny wielded by the United States was a reason for Latin
Americans to unite.[68]

---

65 Ibid., p. 409. In the original: 'La historia, conocida cada día con más serenidad, con una
   interpretación más adecuada a los sucesos, es una hermosa fuente para comprobar cómo
   el pasado no contradice posibilidades. Y aunque en el porvenir humano se presentan
   constantemente contingencias que escapan a las previsiones, sin embargo, la vida nos ha
   enseñado que existe un "destino manifiesto" vinculador de la acción hispánica al suelo de
   América, y que ese mismo destino ahora nos une hacia el porvenir en la elaboración de
   nuevos valores históricos, inspirados en el ideal ascendente de ofrecer a los hombres un
   mundo nuevo, asiento de bienestar y arquetipo de civilización'.
66 Horsman, Race and Manifest Destiny, pp. 1-6.
67 Manuel Baldomero Ugarte, El Porvenir de la América Latina (Valencia: F. Sempere y
   Compañía, 1909), pp. 179-98, pp. 307-19; Manuel Baldomero Ugarte, El destino de un
   continente (Madrid: Editorial mundo latino, 1923), pp. 1-5, pp. 177-214, pp. 393-424;
   Manuel Baldomero Ugarte, 'El porvenir de la América española', Unión Ibero-Americana,
   (June 1920), pp. 3-4.
68 Andrés Pando, 'Leopoldo Lugones y el hispanoamericanismo', Unión Ibero-Americana,
   (March-April 1925), p. 4; Edwin Elmore, 'El proyecto de un congreso iberoamericano
   de intelectuales', Cuba Contemporánea 60:157-58 (January-February 1926), pp. 47-48;
   José Santos Chocano, El libro de mi proceso (Madrid: Compañía ibero-americana de
   publicaciones, 1931), pp. 539, 566-69. In the case of Santos Chocano, unlike Elmore, a

On the other hand, a curious episode in the use of the concept of Manifest Destiny by Ibero-Americanists occurred during the celebration of the tercentenary of the death of Cervantes, when Alfonso XIII of Spain received a telegram from a group of Ibero-Americanist stating:[69]

> As the Children of the Republics separated from the arms but never from the heart of Spain, we continue to call her by the most beautiful and moving words of our language: Mother and Fatherland. We yearn for a great Spanish homeland, with peoples of the same language and Spain and its great king as our guide, certain that the *manifest destiny* of prosperity and glory will be fulfilled.[70]

The Venezuelan President Antonio Guzmán Blanco made use of the concept in a similar way, on the occasion of the reception of Manuel García Cortés, one envoy of the newly proclaimed Spanish Republic in 1873:

> The government of the United States of Venezuela will correspond frankly and loyally to the wishes which you assure us are cherished by the Spanish Republic, both our peoples being linked as they are by ties of origin and language, strengthened today that Spain has proclaimed for its government the republican-democratic form; the *manifest destiny* of all the nations of the earth by the irresistible action of modern civilisation.[71]

---

certain appropriation of the concept took place. This is clear in the article '*Dos palabras*' (Two words) in which he argues that 'Three great armed movements have opened the path to Mexico's manifest destiny: that of independence, that of reform and this one which will be that of organization' (p. 539), or in the article '*A Propósito de Panamericanismo*' (With regards to Pan-Americanism) in which he states that 'All this leads us to think that the Manifest Destiny of Tropical America, today, is to organize ourselves, not with the intention of subtracting benefits from the United States of North America, but with the intention of avoiding our own prejudices' (p. 568).

69 The signatories of this telegram were José Manuel Pérez Sarmiento (Colombian), José Gallegos del Campo (Ecuadorian), Joaquín García Conde (Mexican), José María Gil Pablos (Cuban), Rodolfo Ramirez (Mexican), Antonio Barba Martín (Cuban), Emilio León (Dominican) and Alfonso García (Mexican).

70 El rey en el centenario', *El imparcial: diario liberal*, Madrid, N. 17.666, 24 April 1916. Emphasis my own. In the original: 'Hijos de Repúblicas separadas de los brazos, pero nunca del corazón de España, seguimos llamándola los más bellos y conmovedores vocablos de nuestro idioma: Madre y Patria. Anhelamos una gran patria española, con pueblos del mismo idioma y España y su gran rey por guía, seguros de que se cumplirá el destino manifiesto de la prosperidad y la gloria'.

71 *La Igualdad*, Madrid, (23 October 1873). Emphasis my own. In the original: 'El gobierno de los Estados Unidos de Venezuela corresponderá franca y lealmente álos deseos que aseguráis abriga el de la República española, enlazados como están ambos pueblos con vínculos de origen é idioma, robustecidos hoy que la España ha proclamado para su gobierno la forma republicano-democrática; destino manifiesto de todas las naciones de la tierra por la acción irresistible de la moderna civilización'.

This combination of republicanism and Hispanism found in the concept deployed by Guzmán Blanco was to be a constant theme in the way Spanish-American leaders understood Manifest Destiny.

This fusion of elements was also present in the writings of the Colombian President Rafael Reyes Prieto. An explorer, military man and politician, he embodied the principles of Manifest Destiny once defended by O'Sullivan, since he was one of the main people responsible for the exploration and colonization of the Colombian Amazon at the end of the 19th century. A few years before assuming the presidency, Reyes Prieto was appointed Colombian representative to the Pan-American Conference held in Mexico City in 1901.

At the conference, Reyes Prieto made a toast in honor of Spain, which he described as a common mother that contributed its language, religion, glories and blood to the Latin American republics. Reyes Prieto urged the other representatives to express their gratitude to Spain, including the representatives of the United States, which he also saluted as the nation that best represented the principles of progress, civilisation and justice. Reyes Prieto's speech adopted an accelerationist message, indicating that in past times the life of nations was counted in centuries, while in the present day it was counted in decades. The march of progress would emerge in the great cities of the continent and expand to the more untamed and remote areas still populated by the natives. For Reyes Prieto, this gradual replacement of the native peoples by the colonisers would be an unmistakable sign of progress, the Manifest Destiny of the American continent, which he felt would be characterized by the principles of progress, truth and justice – the three ideas that in his thought would characterize the United States.[72]

In Reyes Prieto's discourse, Sarmiento's contrast of the city as the focus of civilization with the countryside as a stronghold of indigenous savagery can be observed. In his discourse there was a fusion of the exaltation of Hispanic culture and an idealization of the American future as the two influences that should inspire the Spanish-American republics in their process of national construction, the eradication of the native and in their Manifest Destiny.

However, not all Latin American voices who invoked Manifest Destiny would be so indulgent towards the United States' model of progress. One of the most detailed criticisms of the concept was collected and presented in a pamphlet titled *Refutation to the report of the commission of the senate of New Granada, on the treaty of friendship and limits of this republic with the Empire of Brazil*, or *Refutación al informe de la comisión del senado de Nueva Granada, sobre el tratado de amistad i límites de esta república con el Imperio del Brasil* (1857). This anonymous work, possibly written by the Brazilian

---

72 El general D. Rafael Reyes y su famoso brindis por España', *Unión Ibero-Americana*, N. 190 (30 November 1901), pp. 1-2.

admiral Joaquim Marqués Lisboa,[73] included as a preface an article from the Colombian newspaper *El Tiempo* (N.152. November 24, 1857) titled '*Destino manifiesto – área de la libertad – razas*'.

The preface contained an extensive critique of the concept of Manifest Destiny – the most detailed critique I have found – in which the main hypotheses of the concept were analyzed, comparing the historical development and the causes of the progress of the United States with those of the Latin American republics. The author of the pamphlet recognises the progress achieved by the North American republic, finding two causes for its development: the efficiency of its colonial system and the quality, and growth, of its population. According to this author, while the republics that became independent from Spain had been colonized with the lowest and most detestable classes in Spanish society, the English colonies on the other hand had benefited from the noblest and most free-thinking people that sought to profess religious freedom. In the long run this, he reasoned, resulted in more virtuous political institutions. In fact, the author found no Manifest Destiny, but rather a distinct point of historical development that would mark the future of each of the regions.[74]

His comments on population growth were particularly interesting, for this Malthusian argument had been one of O'Sullivan's cornerstones in coining the concept. For O'Sullivan the American demographic trend of doubling its population every quarter century was irrefutable proof of America's need to expand across the continent, its Manifest Destiny, which imposed on the nation the need to procure new land for millions of future Americans on the basis of the land rights over what he understood to be inferior races.[75]

For the author of the preface, this population growth in the United States was not a sign of progress, something that was often pointed out in the US at the time, but a sign of ruin, since this population growth would be spurred on by strong immigration, which would bring new customs, languages and cultures to the American republic. This situation would eventually turn the United States into a 'Babylonian republic' where no national and cultural unity would be possible. Moreover, the preface questioned the supposed superiority of the United States political system, pointing to the persistence of slavery, which had been largely abolished in most of South America.[76]

73 José María Quijano Otero, *Memoria histórica sobre límites entre la República de Colombia i el Imperio del Brasil* (Bogotá: Imprenta de Gaitán, 1869), p. 323.

74 Anonymous, 'Destino manifiesto – área de la libertad – razas' in *Refutación al informe de la comisión del senado de Nueva Granada, sobre el tratado de amistad i límites de esta república con el Imperio del Brasil* (Bogotá: Imprenta de Ovalles i Compañía, 1857), pp. 3-5.

75 O'Sullivan, 'Annexation', p. 5; O'Sullivan, 'The True Title', *New York Morning News*, (December 27, 1845).

76 Anonymous, 'Manifest Destiny – Area of Freedom – Races', p. 4, p. 6.

The reason for the greater progress of the North American republic in comparison to its South American counterparts was the divergence in historical development. It was also due to the better geographical position of the US, and not due to a hypothetical Manifest Destiny. Even so, the author did not dismiss the concept altogether:

> The theory of *manifest destiny* and the *area of freedom*, the pretended aim of which is the armed conquest of the Southern hemisphere, and the extinction of every Latin element, in order to create the *one Yankee* republic, from Quebec to Chiloé and from the mouths of the Orinoco to the Bermejo Gulf in California, is an absurd theory so long as it is to be carried out by force; and a beautiful theory, easy and natural, so long as it is natural, and becomes in time what it is called to be: the great principle of the extinction of all government, except that of the district, under the solemn compact of a universal confederation.[77]

The editors of the Mexican daily *La Voz de la Patria*, a newspaper published in Guadalajara that had a Catholic orientation and social purpose with the aim of promoting faith, union and independence as principles that would guarantee the Mexican national identity, was equally critical of this theme. Like most of the Mexican press, this newspaper was deeply skeptical of the concept of Manifest Destiny; it was nothing but a threat to the territorial integrity of the country. However, in contrast to the predatory American Manifest Destiny, *La Voz de la Patria* introduced a Mexican Manifest Destiny. Mexico would be guided and protected by the Virgin of Guadalupe; as long as faith in the Virgin was present in the hearts of Mexicans, she would protect the country from future foreign interference and guide the nation in its national development.[78]

---

77 Ibid., p. 8. In the original: 'La teoría del *destino manifiesto* i de la *área de libertad*, cuya mira pretensiosa es la conquista armada del hemisferio del Sur i la estincion de todo elemento latino, a fin de crear la república *yankee única*, desde Quebec hasta Chiloe, i desde las bocas del Orinoco hasta el golfo Bermejo en California, es una teoría absurda siempre que se quiera llevar a cabo por medio de la fuerza; i una hermosa teoría, fácil i natural, siempre que ella fecunde por sí sola, i sea con el tiempo lo que está llamada a ser: el gran principio de la estincion de todo gobierno, escepto el del distrito, bajo el pacto solemne de una confederación universal.'

78 La fiesta de los días 8 y 12 de diciembre', *La voz de la patria: periódico católico y social*, Vol. I, N. 7 (18 December 1881), pp. 1-2; 'El día 12 de diciembre', *La voz de la patria: periódico católico y social*, Vol. I, N. 76 (14 December 1884), p. 1; 'El catolicismo en México', La voz de la patria: periódico católico y social, Vol. I, N. 101 (14 February 1886), p. 1.

Conclusion

As this chapter has shown, the concept of Manifest Destiny was the subject of a profound reception in Spanish-speaking countries during the years when the concept was active as a political term. Prior to O'Sullivan's coining of the term, Spanish literature had already formulated a version of the term as a rhetorical turn of phrase to dramatically express the concept of '*hado*', or fate. However, the popularity of the expansionist concept formulated by O'Sullivan in the mid-nineteenth century Texas and Oregon debates allowed this expansionist concept to replace previous autochthonous iterations.

This, however, did not imply a mere acceptance of the intellectual and discursive framework set out by American ideology. Spanish-speaking politicians and cultural elites carried out a deeply personal and creative reception of the concept, critical in many cases of its model of progress, and adapting a good part of the semantic core of the original to their circumstances, worldviews, and political projects.[79]

In most cases, Hispanic formulations of Manifest Destiny preserved the dichotomy between savagery and civilization typical of colonial discourses with the aim of justifying the domination and/or extermination of the native peoples of the Americas. The colonizing epic of the Anglo-Saxon frontiersman found its equal in the epic transmutation of the figure of the Spanish *conquistador*, celebrated both in Spain and by the South American creole elite. What in the United States was presented as a civilizing mission of a superior race, the Anglo-Saxon, in the Hispanic world found its counterpoint in the idea of the civilizing and evangelizing mission of the Spanish conquest, exchanging Anglo-Saxonism for Hispanism. Underlying both discourses was the racialist conception of a benevolent, culturally and racially superior empire, guided by the providential mission of exercising paternalistic control over backward peoples that were to be tutored and guided towards progress – or salvation, in the case of its more Catholic Hispanic variants. In both cases, republicanism played a central role in endowing Manifest Destiny with political content. While in the American case its Jeffersonian agrarian dimension would be more dominant, in the Hispanic case the republicanism of Manifest Destiny would be that of a system of liberties that tried to defeat monarchical despotism and the scourge of *caudillismo*.

While there are many points of connection between these two receptions, there are also notable differences. In the case of Hispanic discourses, the concept of Manifest Destiny was rarely linked to territorial

---

79 This creative appropriation of the concept did not completely break with the semantic core of the original concept. Michael Freeden, *Ideologies and Political Theory: A Conceptual Approach* (Oxford: Oxford University Press, 1996), pp. 47-95.

expansionism or imperialism. It had a marked civilisational and racial-cultural character, but much of its use was related to the longing for a South American unity that had not been achieved, in contrast to the United States, where this unity is found in federalism or, in the case of the Spanish intellectuals who advocated Hispano-Americanism, to the yearning to recover a lost imperial influence. There was also a greater thematic variety in the Hispanic versions of Manifest Destiny, as a concept that would convey the projects of failed national unity or political freedoms not in Spain and Latin America.

The process of reception and appropriation of the concept was not homogeneous. It was particularly popular in Argentina, Colombia, and Spain, but it was systematically rejected in Mexico and Cuba because of their greater exposure to American imperialism. It was significant that an author such as José Vasconcelos, whose thought was imbued with an American providentialism, made no mention of Manifest Destiny in a work such as *La raza cósmica*. Argentina was particularly prone to the creative adoption of the concept, both in its nationalist and Ibero-Americanist aspects. Its experience of nation-building with the colonization of the Pampas found certain echoes with the narrative of American expansion into the American West that animated the formation and use of Manifest Destiny.

This study has not covered all of the conceptual variants and uses of Manifest Destiny in the Spanish language. The vast majority of purely descriptive journalistic uses referring to American expansionism and imperialism in the second half of the nineteenth and first half of the twentieth century have been left out. However, as we have seen, alongside the passive reception of the term, a process of creative re-appropriation of the concept of Manifest Destiny emerged in the Hispanic world, which shows that, by the end of the nineteenth century, the concept had ceased to be an exclusively American term. Instead, it had become part of a broader political vocabulary of an era of imperialism and a symbol of Anglo-Hispanic identity and difference.

EDWARD JONES CORREDERA _____

When did Spain Go to Sleep?

An Empire Dead to the World

Introduction

We do not know what happened when the sun set on the Spanish Empire. There are no systematic studies of the night in an empire that stretched from Barcelona to Manila. One occasionally catches glimpses of its nocturnal life thanks to lampposts set by historians across these vast territories: in celebration of a military victory or the birth of a royal heir, luminary lights illuminated the nights of towns. Many enslaved peoples across other Atlantic empires saw their loved ones under the cover of dusk – in parts of the Spanish Empire, laws were established which decreed that an enslaved person found with a weapon at night would be sentenced to death.[1] In New Granada, before he printed and disseminated the Declaration of the Rights of Man and of the Citizen, Antonio Nariño was tasked with the implementation and supervision of a system of public lighting and created a legion of night-watchmen. Indeed, the most sophisticated study of the night in the Spanish Empire, and in the emerging Latin American republics, focuses on the rise of the night-watchman in Mexico – a comparative study of the rise of night-watchmen across this empire would yield hugely innovative insights on faith and fear in a Catholic empire.[2]

This was the first academic text I wrote as a doctoral student, and it remains surprisingly relevant today. My hope is that this chapter will foster interest in the comparative study of the night in the Spanish Empire and modern Latin America – for over the past three hundred years ministers and intellectuals used the study of the benighted Spanish Empire to compare it to other territories. The following pages will discuss

---

1 Joseph Clark, *Veracruz and the Caribbean in the Seventeenth Century* (Cambridge: Cambridge University Press, 2023), p. 239.
2 Nicole von Germeten, *The Enlightened Patrolman: Early Law Enforcement in Mexico City* (Lincoln: University of Nebraska Press, 2022).

Edward Jones Corredera • Universidad Nacional de Educación a Distancia

Supplicant Empires, ed. by Edward Jones Corredera, Habsburg Worlds, 8 (Turnhout: Brepols, 2025), pp. 167–189
BREPOLS ❦ PUBLISHERS   10.1484/M.HW-EB.5.145068

how the significance of this area of research is even greater than it may
initially appear, for ideas of the night shaped our understanding of Spanish decline. While foundational historiographical accounts have drawn
on the Black Legend and the logic of decline to synthesise overarching
narratives of early modern Spain, this chapter shows how discourses of
sleep and nocturnalisation in early modern representations of Spain were
far more salient than static concepts such as the Black Legend in the crystallisation of the idea of Spanish decline.[3] Decline provided a stable and
enduring name for a series of mercurial connotations. Mutable historical
associations of the nocturnal with deceit, laziness, and reveries formed a
conceptual constellation that facilitated the transition between early modern and modern understandings of Spain. Today, the influence of these
associations is so self-evident it may appear unremarkable. International
depictions of Spain frequently focus on the practice of the *siesta*, and the
move towards realigning Spain's clocks to GMT prompted *The Times* to
report: 'The three-hour lunch breaks and siestas have long been the envy
of northern Europeans but they are set to be consigned to history after
the Spanish prime minister proposed cutting the working day to bring
the country into the 21st century.'[4] In this context, decline, traditionally
associated with pre-modern Spain, lent historical credibility to modern
depictions of Spanish backwardness.

The reification of Spanish decline through the vocabulary of sleep
shaped the foundations of modern ideas of the Spanish nation. Between
the eighteenth and twentieth centuries, the reification of the idea of Spanish slumber proved to be sufficiently elastic to serve an array of political,
economic, and ideological interests.

This chapter considers the ways in which Spanish decline was reified
in Europe and the Iberian Peninsula through a historical exploration of
the imaginative repertoire inspired by the concept of sleep. Sleep and
nocturnalisation opened a space to connect 'the quotidian with the symbolic', and eighteenth-century associations of negligence and deceit paved
the way for Romantic visions of the Spanish nation and its modern self-
perception.[5] This study of the use of the concept of sleep and its ties with
'porous and policed peripheries' draws on conceptual history, a growing

---

3 Richard L. Kagan and Geoffrey Parker eds., *Spain, Europe, and the Atlantic World: Essays
   in Honour of John H. Elliott* (Cambridge: Cambridge University Press, 2002), John Lynch,
   Spain Under the Habsburgs: Spain and America, 1598-1700 (London: Blackwell, 1981), John
   Elliott, *Spain, Europe & the Wider World, 1500-1800* (New Haven: Yale University Press,
   2014).
4 Graham Keeley, 'Don't sleep it off: Spain set to drop the siesta', *The Times*, 4 April 2016.
5 Craig Koslofsky, *Evening's Empire: A History of the Night in Early Modern Europe* (Cambridge:
   Cambridge University Press, 2011), p. 1.

literature on early modern sleep, and a history of Spain's relationship with its past.[6] The result is a history of organicist visions of a nation colonised by fantasies and severed from its empire by the dream of reason.

The perils of the night: the nocturnal ambush of the slumbering Spanish Empire

In early eighteenth-century Spain, the night evoked the darker side of human nature.[7] Obscurity, the sleep-induced loss of consciousness, and the practice of using the cover of darkness to enact revenge, transformed the night into a precarious space. In 1734, a Spanish dictionary entry on the term 'night' emphasised the need for alertness at a time when confusion and darkness prevailed. Night was defined as 'the time of day when the sun drops below the horizon, and is therefore the time of darkness, confusion, and obscurity [*tinieblas y oscuridad*]'. The night, moreover, served as a metaphor for death, and 'to describe misperception, obscurity, or sadness, since these are the effects of the night'.[8] The expression, 'the dawn of night [*hacerse noche*]' was defined as 'a phrase to suggest something was lost, disappeared, or stolen'.[9] The night was a space governed by fear and confusion. Philip V's legal system enforced the same severe penalties for crimes committed at night as for those committed in uninhabited areas, since 'these conditions lessened the ability of the victims to defend themselves or receive aid from others'.[10]

Watchfulness and vigilance were further necessary since the night was the time for retribution.[11] The expression 'to ring *maitines*' denoted the practice of women stealing money from their husband's waist bags, and was 'expressed in this way because this activity is regularly carried out at the night, when the men are asleep'.[12] One of Philip V's earliest edicts

---

6 Ann Laura Stoler, *Duress: Imperial Durabilities in Our Times* (Durham: Duke University Press, 2017), p. 9. See Arthur Roger Ekirch, *At Day's Close: Night in Times Past* (New York: Norton, 2006); Koslofsky, *Evening's Empire*; Sasha Handley, *Sleep in Early Modern England* (New Haven: Yale University Press, 2016).

7 Earlier historical associations of this type can be found in Walter Mignolo, *The Darker Side of the Renaissance: Literacy, Territoriality, and Colonization* (Ann Arbor: University of Michigan Press, 1995).

8 *Diccionario de la lengua Castellana*. Volume 4. (Madrid: Imprenta de la Real Academia Española, 1734), p. 673.

9 *Diccionario de la lengua Castellana*. Volume 4, p. 114.

10 Ruth Pike, 'Capital Punishment in Eighteenth-Century Spain', *Histoire Sociale/Social History* 18 (1986), pp. 375-86. p. 380.

11 Similar historical associations were to be found in the cases of the White Boys in eighteenth-century Ireland, and the Ku Klux Klan in the twentieth century.

12 *Diccionario de la lengua Castellana*. Volume 4, p. 459.

was the ban on a popular form of nocturnal revenge – the duel.[13] But the night remained a lawless land, as captured by the the phrase 'the night is a cape for sinners: a phrase to explain that wrongdoers use the cover of the night and its confusion to hide their efforts and avoid being caught'.[14] In response, there was nothing less than a Bourbon colonisation of the night, which loomed large throughout the century, as arrests, apprehensions, and the famous banishment of the Jesuits in 1767, were all conducted at night.[15]

Sleep was, moreover, closely associated with the dangers of inaction. The 1734 dictionary's entry on sleep stated 'to sleep: v. n. to rest one's nature, said to happen when one loses their senses, to recover one's strength from fatigue or vigil'. The second definition specified that 'to sleep: v. the term also expresses one's disregard for the obligation to work, or the failure to apply themselves'.[16] In light of this context, political commentaries deployed the term *sleep* to indicate that the loss of consciousness exposed the individual and the Court to laziness, crime, and deceit. Many writings reflected the deep sense of crisis induced by the effects of the War of Spanish Succession and Philip V's subsequent bellicosity.[17] Philip V was nicknamed 'The Bewitched', as many felt his closest advisors and his wife had usurped the throne.[18] Early eighteenth-century political writings used the idea of sleep to convey deceit and to urge the King to act, with titles such as '*Madrid Asleep, called upon by this text to open her eyes*', '*Spain's Sleep and the King's Lethargy, and advices for his Majesty*', and '*Awake, the Majesty of Apollo*'.[19] In 1724, when Philip V stepped down from the throne, an anonymous pamphlet saw a character prompt his friend to '[...] wake up and you will see something that appears to be a dream. Reason is asleep, and delirium is awake'.[20] Another text criticised the political ambitions of a minister and asked the King of Spain to remain 'vigilant': 'You are the King of the New World and lord of many crowns,

---

13 Carmen Martín Gaite, *Love Customs in Eighteenth-Century Spain* (Berkeley: University of California Press, 1991), p. 99.

14 Gaite, *Love Customs*, p. 674.

15 Mario Martínez Gomis, "La noche y los noctámbulos en el siglo XVIII español", in *Fiesta, juego y ocio en la historia: XIV Jornadas de Estudios Históricos organizadas por el Departamento de Historia Medieval, Moderna y Contemporánea*. Edited by Ángel Vaca Lorenzo (Salamanca: Ediciones de la Universidad de Salamanca, 2003), pp. 147-71, p. 156.

16 *Diccionario de la lengua Castellana*. Volume 3 (Madrid: Imprenta de la Real Academia Española, 1732), p. 390.

17 Ricardo García Cárcel, 'La Opinión de los españoles sobre Felipe V después de la Guerra de Sucesión', *Cuadernos de Historia Moderna Anejos* 1 (2002), pp. 103-25 and I.L. McClelland, *Ideological Hesitancy in Spain 1700-1750* (Liverpool: Liverpool University Press, 1991).

18 Teofanes Egido López, *Opinión Pública y oposición al poder en la España del siglo XVIII (1713-1759)* (Valladolid: Universidad de Valladolid, 2002), p. 123.

19 López, *Opinión Pública*, pp. 59 and p. 68.

20 López, *Opinión Pública*, p. 147.

yet you fail to act and work accordingly [...] Does it never keep you up at night? Wake up, sir'.[21] The meaning of the term *awake* was multifaceted, as the word and its associations expressed 'the remembrance of a long forgotten memory', 'resurrection', and 'the act of remedying an error'.[22] In the 1740s, reformers frequently phrased their plans for reform in terms of their desire to awaken Spain, as in the case of José Campillo, who titled his political recommendations *Spain Awake*.[23] Marcelo Dantini suggested Spaniards had 'been blindfolded for over two centuries, and their senses perturbed';[24] José Carvajal y Lancaster referred to the most pernicious effects that haunted Spain as 'ghosts', and referred to the idea that Spain needed to 'resuscitate'.[25]

The discourse of sleep in economic writings reflected the fear that foreign merchants and European nations were exploiting the Spanish Crown. In his *Theory of Commerce*, the influential author of political economy, Jéronimo de Uztáriz, provided a definition of passive commerce which matched, word for word, contemporary definitions of sleep and resonated with concerns about potential nocturnal abuse. Uztáriz defined passive commerce as: 'lethargy that disables her [Spain's] natural strengths'.[26] Foreign commercial exploitation prevented Spaniards from enjoying the riches of the country, which were 'pitifully *usurped* by other Nations'.[27] In 1753, Carvajal bemoaned that Europeans had made a 'mental calculation' and decided to assign to Spain the responsibilities and costs of European trade, only to reap all subsequent profit.[28]

In this respect, Spanish political economists agreed with accounts of leading European intellectuals, who saw Spain's inaction as beneficial to the rest of Europe. Montesquieu characterised Spaniards as honest and easily deceived: 'The good faith of the Spaniards has been famous in all times. [...] The faithfulness they had of old they still have today. All the nations that trade in Cádiz entrust their fortunes to the Spanish; they have never repented of it. But this admirable quality joined to their laziness

---

21 López, *Opinión Pública*, p. 173.

22 *Diccionario de la lengua Castellana*. Volume 3, p. 218.

23 José del Campillo y Cossío, *Dos escritos Políticos* (Oviedo: Junta General del Principado de Asturias, 1993) and Ricardo García Cárcel, *De los elogios a Felipe V* (Madrid: CEPC, 2002), p. 69.

24 José Miguel Delgado Barrado, *Fomento portuario y compañías privilegiadas: los "Diálogos Familiares" de Marcelo Dantini* (Madrid: CSIC, 1998), p. 146.

25 *José de Carvajal y Lancáster: testamento político o idea de un gobierno católico (1745)*. Edited by José Miguel Delgado Barrado (Córdoba: Universidad de Córdoba, 1999).

26 Pablo Sanchez León, 'Science, Customs and the Modern Subject: From Emulation to Education in the Semantics of Spanish Enlightenment', *Contributions to the History of Concepts* 12 (2017), pp. 1-23, p. 6. Italics added for emphasis.

27 León, 'Science', p. 6.

28 José de Carvajal y Lancaster, *Testamento Político*. Biblioteca Nacional de España, mss/10446, 138–168, p. 141.

forms a mixture whose effects are pernicious to them; before their very eyes the peoples of Europe carry on all the commerce of their monarchy'.[29] Contemporary French definitions of sleep denoted similar associations with laziness.[30] In 1740, the French Academy's dictionary stated, 'To sleep, v. it figuratively means to act in a negligent manner, or to lose one's rights due to the failure to act correctly [...] we say figuratively that "a man does not sleep" to express that he not only avoids negligence, but tries to benefit from any situation he can profit from'.[31] Diderot's *Encyclopédie* drew on *The Iliad*'s warnings about sleep, described as the 'brother of death'[32] and further linked sleep with backwardness and stagnation: 'Ovid establishes Sleep's residence in the country of the Cimmerians, which the ancients believed was plunged into the thickest of shadows [...]. The only noise that one hears is that of the river of forgetfulness, which flowing over small stones, makes a soft murmur that invites rest'.[33]

The *Encyclopédie*'s entry on Spain claimed that '[u]nder Philip III, the great Spain was nothing but a corpse, and one which had more reputation than real strength [...] In this way, this beautiful kingdom, which used to elicit such terror in Europe, has gradually fallen into a decadence from which she will struggle to awake [*est par gradation tombé dans une decadence dont il aura peine a se relever*]'. The *Encyclopédie* expanded on Montesquieu's writings to suggest 'other nations carry out her commerce under her eyes, and it is truly beneficial for Europe that Mexico, Peru and Chile are owned by such a lazy nation'.[34] In Britain, Prime Minister Robert Walpole declared Spain was simply a 'canal through which all these treasures are conveyed over the rest of Europe'.[35] Exploiting its slumber, European merchants siphoned Spain's riches and reinforced its stagnation. A popular saying in the eighteenth century lamented this type of exploitation and denoted its resemblance with colonial abuses: 'Spain

29 Montesquieu, *The Spirit of the Laws* (Cambridge: Cambridge University Press, 1989), p. 313.

30 These contrasted with contemporary French associations of England with ennui: 'Jean-Bernard Le Blanc wrote in his *Letters on the English and French Nations* that the English suffered greatly from ennui but that they did not have a word for it'. See Marjo Kaartinen, 'Killing Time: Ennui in Eighteenth-Century English Culture', *Journal of Early Modern Studies* 6 (2017), pp. 133-55, p. 139.

31 *Dictionnaire de l'académie française, troisième édition*, Volume 1 (A-K) (Paris: Jean Baptiste Coignard, Impr. Du Roy & de l'Académie Française, 1740) p. 524.

32 Louis Jaucourt, "Sleep", in *The Encyclopedia of Diderot & d'Alembert Collaborative Translation Project*. Translated by Amy Keller (Ann Arbor: University of Michigan Library, 2004) Originally published as "Sommeil", *Encyclopédie ou Dictionnaire raisonné des sciences, des arts et des métiers* 15 (Paris, 1765), pp. 333-34.

33 "Sommeil", *Encyclopédie*.

34 Cited in Etienvre Françoise, 'Avant Masson, Jaucourt: L'Espagne dans l'Encyclopédie de Diderot et d'Alembert', *Bulletin Hispanique* 104:1 (2002), pp. 161-80, p. 167.

35 Arturo Giráldez, *The Age of Trade: The Manila Galleons and the Dawn of the Global Economy* (Lanham: Rowman & Littlefield Publishers, 2015), p. 174.

are the Indies of foreigners [Europeans]'.[36] Laziness, moreover, had long constituted an important trope in early modern European depictions of Amerindian barbarism.[37] Decline served as a way of distancing the decadent Spanish Empire, and its peoples, from Enlightenment mental maps of Europe.

Ministers under Philip V and Ferdinand VI believed Spain would awake if it enjoyed a period of peace and rebuilt its navy.[38] Foreign exploitation had induced the Spanish Empire into a state of sleep, and the wise management of imperial resources would restore its status in Europe. In the years between 1724 and 1754, Spain carried out naval reforms which led Benjamin Keene, the British ambassador to Spain, to warn his government of the threat the Spanish navy posed to British maritime expansion.[39] Carvajal, in turn, questioned the British and Dutch use of the term 'maritime powers' to refer to their naval capacity, and criticised their refusal to use this term for Spain 'when her naval power dominates Europe and more of the Americas than England and Holland combined'[40]. Philip V and Ferdinand VI sponsored erudite officials such as Jorge Juan, Antonio de Ulloa, and Bernardo Ward in their travels around Europe in search of measures worth emulating.[41] Reformers in Madrid subsequently studied Enlightenment policies and adapted many of them to address Spain's needs with an aim to – as the minister Marquis of Ensenada suggested – 're-learn that which we once taught' Europe.[42] Under Philip and Ferdinand, reformers designed the first cadastre of the peninsula, drafted reforms, and set up institutions such as the Royal Academy of History to host intellectual discussion.[43]

36 François Lopez, *Juan Pablo Forner (1756-1797) y la crisis de la conciencia española* (Valladolid: Junta de Castilla y León, 1999), p. 58.

37 Ruth Mackay, *"Lazy, Improvident People": Myth and Reality in the Writing of Spanish History* (Ithaca: Cornell University Press, 2006), p. 220.

38 Diego Tellez Alarcia, *Absolutismo e Ilustración en la España del siglo XVIII: El despotismo ilustrado de D. Ricardo Wall* (Madrid: Fundación Española de Historia Moderna, 2010), pp. 71-78.

39 José Luis Gómez Urdáñez, *El proyecto reformista de Ensenada* (Lleida: Milenio, 1996), p. 211.

40 Carvajal y Lancaster, *Testamento Político*, p. 25.

41 Alarcia, *Absolutismo e Ilustración*, p. 158.

42 Gómez Urdáñez, *El proyecto reformista de Ensenada*, p. 180; Edward Jones Corredera, *The Diplomatic Enlightenment: Spain, Europe, and the Age of Speculation* (Leiden: Brill, 2021), pp. 140-74.

43 See Rosa María Alabrús Iglesias and Ricardo García Cárcel, 'La cultura en tiempos de Felipe V', *Aula-Historia Social* 16 (2005), pp. 68-75.

The Enlightenment under Charles III: the origins of laziness as the source of decadence

The last years of Ferdinand VI's reign proved to be a bathetic end to a period of reform. In 1758, due to a severe depression, Ferdinand VI retired from power. Ferdinand's depression and his erratic behaviour were publicised and triggered a deep sense of unease across the Spanish Empire.[44] Many were relieved when Charles, the former King of Naples, arrived in Madrid and became the head of the Spanish Empire.[45]

In correspondence with his mother, Elisabeth Farnese, Charles III declared he would prove to be 'The Healer' (*El Curador*) of Spain.[46] Charles III chose as his ministers a set of Spanish officials who were hugely influenced by British and French Enlightenment writings. Isaac Newton's ideas of motion and reaction and Cartesian writings on cognition contributed to new understandings of the body and the self, and spurred the development of psychology and political economy.[47] These nascent disciplines reified the sense of a common good within national communities. Drawing on notions of motion, temperature, and climate, these thinkers developed ways to free labour from its past associations with baseness and sin.[48] The author of the *Fable of the Bees*, Bernard Mandeville, emphasised the role of balance in regulating the individual – 'the only thing then that can render the labouring Man industrious, is a moderate quantity of Money; for as too little will, according as his Temper is, either dispirit or make him Desperate, so too much will make him insolent and Lazy'.[49] Concerns that commercial expansion, luxury, and new goods would weaken the population's martial spirit and corrupt its ways encouraged thinkers to conceive of labour as a source of social regulation. Many thinkers believed the impact of labour would depend on the geographical and racial composition of communities.[50]

Through a physiological and climatological political theory, Montesquieu suggested Spaniards were subject to the same type of lethargy

44 López, *Opinión Pública*, p. 253.

45 López, *Opinión Pública*, p. 253.

46 Vicente Palacio Atard, *El tercer Pacto de familia* (Madrid: CSIC, 1945), p. 35.

47 Ann Thompson, *Bodies of Thought: science, religion, and the soul in the early Enlightenment* (Oxford: Oxford University Press, 2008), p. 69; Jan Goldstein, *The Post-Revolutionary Self: Politics and Psyche in France, 1750-1850* (Cambridge: Harvard University Press, 2008), p. 40.

48 William Sewell, *Work and Revolution in France: The Language of Labour from the Old Regime to 1848* (Cambridge: Cambridge University Press, 1980), p. 68.

49 Bernard Mandeville, *The Fable of the Bees or Private Vices, Publick Benefits*. Two Volumes. Volume 1 (Indianapolis: Liberty Fund, 1988), p. 147.

50 See William Max Nelson, 'Making Men: Enlightenment Ideas of Racial Engineering', *American Historical Review* 115:5 (2010), pp. 1364-394.

as their nation.[51] For Montesquieu, 'la servitude commence toujours par le sommeil'.[52] Subsequent Anglophone translations reflected the effective ambiguity of this statement. One work translated the phrase as 'slavery is ever preceded by sleep'.[53] Another defined it as 'servitude always begins with drowsiness'.[54] In Montesquieu's vision, Spain's inherent laziness, or sleep, forced Spaniards into a state of servitude and confusion. Montesquieu suggested that 'heat enervates the strength and courage of men' while 'there is in cold climates a certain strength of body and spirit that makes men capable of long, arduous, great and daring actions'.[55] From this principle, Montesquieu inferred that 'the heat of the climate can be so excessive that the body there will be absolutely without strength. So, prostration will pass even to the spirit [...] inclinations will all be passive, their laziness there will be happiness; most chastisements there will be less difficult to bear than the action of the soul, and servitude will be less intolerable than the strength of spirit necessary to guide one's own conduct'.[56] Spaniards were born into a fertile land that rendered them naturally lazy: 'what has naturalised servitude among the southern peoples is that, as they can easily do without wealth, they can do even better without liberty'.[57]

Under Charles III, the paradigm change in the deployment of the language of sleep in Spanish political writings demonstrated Montesquieu's indelible influence on Spanish enlightened thought. The leading minister under Charles III, Pedro Rodríguez de Campomanes, claimed previous Spanish reformers had failed 'to provide the necessary spurs to *wake her up* and encourage her to emulate the other active nations'.[58] Campomanes echoed Montesquieu when he stated 'this false *amour propre* of my nation is a pride born out of *weakness* and the *lack of labour*'[59]; and 'it is well known that all lazy nations are proud, for nothing appeals as much as *rest* and they contemplate work as *tiresome*. And when they come to learn the benefits of work, they would rather perpetuate their ways and mock the work they do not want to do'.[60] Campomanes and other intellectuals rejected Uztáriz's assessment of passive trade as the source of

---

51 Emanuel Rota, 'The Worker and the Southerner: The Invention of Laziness and the Representation of Southern Europe in the Age of the Industrious Revolutions', *Cultural Critique* 82 (2012), pp. 128-50.

52 Montesquieu, *De l'esprit des lois*. Volume 2 (Paris: Gallimard, 1995), p. 463.

53 Montesquieu, *Complete Works*. Volume 1 (Indianapolis: Liberty Fund, 2004), p. 307.

54 Montesquieu, *The Spirit of the Laws*, p. 242.

55 Montesquieu, *The Spirit of the Laws*, p. 278.

56 Montesquieu, *The Spirit of the Laws*, p. 234.

57 Montesquieu, *The Spirit of the Laws*, p. 355.

58 Pedro Rodríguez de Campomanes, *Bosquejo de política económica española: delineado sobre el estado presente de sus intereses*. Edited by Jorge Cejudo (Madrid: Editora Nacional, 1984), p. 150.

59 Campomanes, *Bosquejo*, p. 61.

60 Campomanes, *Bosquejo*, p. 144. Italics added for emphasis.

Spain's exhaustion, and assimilated Montesquieu's diagnoses. The political economist Lorenzo Normante declared the idle to be the true usurpers of Spain's wealth; their failure to work constituted a 'continuous robbery at the expense of the nation' and 'the idle' should be 'persecuted until they become laborious'.[61] Campomanes classified 'poor and backward peoples in three groups, "miserable", "barbarian" and "lazy", and included the Spanish in this striking third group, composed of those who, "though living in fertile countries, gather their fruits and metals uncut and sell them, without making any other use of them, at a vile price". The difference with barbarian nations –such as the inhabitants of "both Indies", who also reduced their exchanges to raw materials– laid in that lazy people were "civilised nations that live in the body of society"'.[62] Gaspar Melchor de Jovellanos, both a reformer and the author of some of the most influential works of political economy of his time, referred to the need to see Spanish labourers 'awake from their lassitude'[63] and emphasised the state's role in 'awakening the labourer to their true interests'.[64] Moreover, Jovellanos believed a lack of sociability resulted in laziness: 'Not an *alcalde* exists who does not establish a curfew, does not ban singing and charivaris [*cencerradas*], does not patrol and spy and, besides pursuing those who rob and swear, is not constantly chasing after those who merely sing and play [...] what other cause can there be for the despondency, the slovenliness, the fierce and unsociable character that mark the rustics of some of our provinces?'[65] Spanish decadence arose from within.

In 1766, the Revolt of Esquilache reaffirmed these views. The revolt began when the people of Madrid led a protest against Charles III's leading minister, the Marquis of Esquilache. The three main causes of discord arose from Esquilache's biopolitics:[66] the introduction of a new grain market, a decree banning certain ways of dressing, and in the case of Madrid, the introduction of a poll tax to finance public lighting.[67] 'The institutional sequels of 1766 were an overall reaffirmation of traditional corporations for the sake of underpinning the social order' and restrictions

---

61 William J. Callahan, *Honour, Commerce, and Industry in Eighteenth-Century Spain* (Boston: Baker Library, 1972), p. 58.

62 León, 'Science', p. 105.

63 E. J. Corredera, 'Labouring Horizons: Passions and Interests in Jovellanos's *Ley Agraria*', *Dieciocho* 38:2 (2015), pp. 267-90, pp. 283-85.

64 Corredera, 'Labouring Horizons', pp. 283-85.

65 Richard Herr, *Rural Change and Royal Finances in Spain at the End of the Old Regime* (Berkeley: University of California, 1988), p. 75.

66 Michel Foucault, *The Birth of Biopolitics: Lectures at the Collège de France, 1978-1979* (New York: Springer, 2008).

67 See José Andrés-Gallego, *El motín de Esquilache, América y Europa* (Madrid: CSIC, 2003).

on the press.[68] Following the revolt, the national 'awakening' would be strictly economic, since the people's wellbeing depended merely on 'moderate work to be able to eat, dress, afford a comfortable home, marry and have children'.[69] In his *Report on the Ley Agraria*, the most important economic text of the Spanish Enlightenment, Jovellanos conceived of the ideal labourer as a mere foot-soldier of the nation: 'In this peaceful age, why not employ the troops to build roads and canals, as they once did? Soldiers under Alexander, Sulla, and Caesar, humanity's greatest enemies, employed themselves in these useful trades during peace; why should we not expect the same from this army under the orders of a just king, full of peaceful virtues and caring towards his people? An army who labour their own happiness'.[70]

Two overlapping dimensions shaped the paradigm change in the use of sleep under Charles III. First, as José María Portillo suggested, these thinkers conceptually divorced Spain, as a European territory, from its empire, conceived of as a dispersed and untameable space.[71] In the pursuit of the integration of Spain within the civilisationary, enlightened European space, the Spanish Empire became a source of alterity, barbarism, and backwardness. The assimilation of Montesquieu's assessment was the second step of this discursive shift: Spaniards were ultimately indolent. Moreover, following the Esquilache Revolt, the awakening of the population was to be limited, strictly economic, and in the service of the nation. The political vision of Spain as an idle nation replaced the image of the Spanish Empire exhausted by foreign exploitation. Over the following decades, theories of constitutionalism, a revamped interest in Habsburg Spain, and a reactionary turn in favour of the role of religion in public life transformed the Spanish Enlightenment, yet the leading assumptions about the lethargic spirit of the nation remained unchanged.[72] Spanish laziness lingered as both a symptom and a consequence of Spanish decadence.

---

68 León, 'Science', p. 13. See also Pablo Sánchez León, 'Conceiving the Multitude: Eighteenth-Century Popular Riots and the Modern Language of Social Disorder', *International Review of Social History* 56:3 (2011), pp. 511-33.

69 Gloria Á. Franco Rubio, 'Captar súbditos y crear ciudadanos, doble objetivo de los "Amigos del País" en el siglo XVIII', *Historia Social* 64 (2009), pp. 3-23, p. 15.

70 Corredera, 'Labouring Horizons', pp. 284-85.

71 José María Portillo Valdés, *Crisis Atlántica. Autonomía e independencia en la crisis de la monarquía hispana* (Madrid: Marcial Pons Historia, 2006), p. 21.

72 Francisco Sánchez Blanco, "Dinastía y política cultural", in *Los Borbones: dinastía y memoria de nación en la España del siglo XVIII*. Edited by Pablo Fernández Albaladejo (Madrid: Marcial Pons, 2002), pp. 569-96, p. 594.

Nineteenth-century Spain: from a lazy nation to a decadent colony of dreams

The Spanish artist Francisco Goya titled his *Capricho 43* 'the dream/ the sleep of reason produces monsters' (*'el sueño de la razón produce monstruos'*). The title's ambiguity, between sleep as dreaming and sleep *qua* the suspension of sense and reason, has frequently served as a metaphor for Jovellanos' torment in the face of the Napoleonic invasion of Spain.[73] In this reading, Goya's portrait symbolised a fateful end to the dream of the Spanish Enlightenment at the hands of Napoleon. In 1809, Jovellanos' friend, the British intellectual Lord Holland, wrote to the Spaniard to remark upon Spain's inaction in the face of Napoleon's expansionism:

'Oh, how much precious time you have wasted! Bonaparte has now conquered Germany, and you have not yet been able to organise a meeting of the *Cortes* or establish the freedom of the press; while he has disbanded three or four hierarchies, you have failed to ensure the continuity of your own. The Enlightenment's ideals, patriotism, and the righteous ways, are all present in Spain; but without speed nothing can be done in this century. *Rest is not for the chariot of the Sun*; and Spain, having chosen such a glorious path, but a dangerous and difficult one, cannot afford to fall asleep along the way'.[74]

Lord Holland's remark denoted the sense of acceleration brought about by the Napoleonic Wars, an acceleration which encouraged leading Spanish political figures to search for new methods of reform.[75] In 1812, under siege, the *Cortes*, a self-proclaimed sovereign assembly with representatives from the Americas and Spain, drafted the Cádiz Constitution. The Cádiz Constitution rejected Enlightenment characterisations of Spain and defined the Spanish nation as one of 'Spaniards of both hemispheres'.[76] In 1814, however, King Ferdinand VII declared the constitution illegitimate, and at the Treaty of Paris, Spain was considered 'a second-class nation'.[77]

In this context, Goya's *Capricho 43* anticipated the nineteenth-century eruption of pan-European interest in Spain as a land of Romantic fantasy,

---

73 See, for example, John Dowling, 'The Crisis of the Spanish Enlightenment: Capricho 43 and Goya's Second Portrait of Jovellanos', *Eighteenth-Century Studies* 18:3 (1985), pp. 331-59.

74 Lord Holland to Gaspar Melchor de Jovellanos, 1 November 1809, in Gaspar Melchor de Jovellanos, *Obras completas*, Volume 5 (Oviedo: Centro de Estudios del Siglo XVIII, 2008), pp. 314-15.

75 Javier Fernández Sebastián, '"Riding the Devil's Steed": Historical Acceleration in an Age of Revolutions', in *Political Concepts and Time: New Approaches to Conceptual History*, edited by Javier Fernández Sebastián (Santander: Cantabria University Press, 2011), pp. 395-423.

76 The literature on this topic is extensive. See, for example, Josep Fontana, *La crisis del Antiguo régimen 1808-1833* (Barcelona: Crítica, 1979).

77 Raymond Carr, *Spain: A History* (Oxford: Oxford University Press, 2000), p. 1.

unblemished by the evils of civilization. As the Napoleonic Wars challenged the value accorded to eighteenth-century notions of progress, Spain's categorical decline morphed into an ambivalent sense of instability and decadence.[78] French statesmen feared their nation would suffer the same social atomisation as Spain, while British and German authors found it to be a source of poetic inspiration.[79] By the mid-nineteenth century, following two civil wars, Spain was in a state of social disarray. The reification of Spanish decline and decadence became a source of 'verification of psychological and sociological insights' on the political effects of religion and lethargy and, paradoxically, paved the way for the introduction of positivism in Spain.[80] In the late nineteenth century, *decadence* would be deployed by radical European authors hoping to pave the way for a new society, a use of this protracted narrative which would prove hugely influential in Spain.[81] But the century-long transformation from decline to lethargy began in the early nineteenth century when, building on eighteenth-century understandings of Spain's slumber, European and Spanish authors turned their attention to the dreams that occupied Spain's mind in her sleep.

During the Peninsular War, censorship of the press was abolished.[82] Between 1808 and 1814, pamphlets, songs, and popular texts fostered the growth of a Spanish national community from below, united against Napoleon.[83] The war prompted an outpour of popular writings that drew on dreams as rhetorical devices to envisage the future of the nation.[84] This literature provided a sense of common purpose and enabled Spaniards to process 'the fatigue' and 'the bucolic atmosphere of war'.[85]

During the war, propaganda drew on the old relationship between sleep and deceit. In 1808, Napoleon declared: 'Spaniards, after a long agony, your nation was about to perish. I have witnessed your ills, and I

---

78 Hayden White, *Metahistory: The Historical Imagination in Nineteenth-Century Europe* (Baltimore: Johns Hopkins University Press, 1975), p. 25 and Diego Saglia, *Poetic Castles in Spain: British Romanticism and Figurations of Iberia* (Amsterdam: Rodopi, 2000), p. 19.

79 Koenraad W. Swart, *The Sense of Decadence in Nineteenth-Century France* (The Hague: Martinus Nijhoff, 1964), p. 241.

80 Gonzalo Vicente Pasamar Alzuria, La configuración de la imagen de la 'Decadencia Española' en los siglos XIX y XX, *Manuscrits: Revista d'història moderna* 11 (1993), pp. 183-214, p. 198.

81 Swart, *The Sense of Decadence in Nineteenth-Century France*, p. 242.

82 Alejandro Pizarroso Quintero, 'Prensa y propaganda bélica 1808-1814', *Cuadernos Dieciochistas* 8 (2009), pp. 203-22, p. 212.

83 Emilio de Diego García, "La verdad construida: la propaganda en la Guerra de la Independencia", in Antonio Moliner Prada ed. *La Guerra de la Independencia en España (1808-1814)* (Barcelona: Nabla, 2007), pp. 209-54.

84 Jesús Martínez Baro, *La libertad de Morfeo: patriotismo y política en los sueños literarios españoles (1808-1814)* (Zaragoza: Universidad de Zaragoza, 2014), pp. 483-500.

85 Baro, *La libertad*, p. 19.

will remedy them […] you are not to blame for these, since your government is at fault […] what I want is for your grandchildren to proclaim: *He is the regenerator of our nation*'.[86] In 1809, the conservative Simón López wrote *Christian-Political Awakening (Despertador cristiano-político)*, a plea for Spaniards to ignore the heresies of reform; God willed Spain to victory, and Spaniards should 'open their eyes' to divine truth.[87] By contrast, the liberal *Gazeta* of Valencia stated: 'Awake Spain […] those panegyrists of your crops, your character and religion are the same who deceive you.'[88]

Spain's victory transformed the political vocabulary of sleep, as the emphasis shifted from economic to civic and patriotic ideals. Spaniards and Europeans would describe Spain's triumph against Napoleon as the 'awakening' of the Spanish nation.[89] Popular Spanish songs declared the Spanish nation 'awoke from her lethargy' to fight Napoleon and defend Europe, and many stamps, images, and texts depicted Spain as a sleeping lion that woke to battle the French eagle.[90] However, Spain's 'awakening' was disassociated from economic modernisation and failed to undermine notions of Spanish backwardness.[91] In 1828, the Spanish scholar Agustín Durán wrote: 'though foreign countries may be ahead of us in industry, we can at least take pride in preserving all the patriotic and religious enthusiasm that even he who dominated all of Europe [Napoleon] could not quell'.[92] Durán echoed the myth that Spain's society, deemed to be decadent, had prevented the fall of Europe to Napoleon. Yet Spain's Third State could not remedy the lack of industrial development. Throughout the nineteenth century, Spanish politicians hailed the people (*el pueblo*) as the heart of the nation, but many remained convinced of their igno-

---

86 Antonio J. Piqueres Díez, 'José I, "El Rey Regenerador". El discurso Josefino sobre la regeneración de España', *Cuadernos de Historia Moderna* 11 (2012), pp. 123-44, p. 124.

87 Simón López and Juan López Cancelada, *Despertador cristiano-político* (Madrid: Oficina de D. Mariano de Zúñiga y Ontiveros, 1809), p. 25.

88 Vicente León Navarro, 'La prensa valenciana ante la Guerra del Francés en 1808', *El Argonauta español. Revue bilingue, franco-espagnole, d'histoire moderne et contemporaine consacrée à l'étude de la presse espagnole de ses origines à nos jours (XVIIe-XXIe siècles)* 5 (2008) (Online) Footnote 19.

89 Gonzalo Butrón Prida, "Le modèle révolutionnaire espagnol en Italie au début des années 1820", in Jean-Philippe Luis ed, *La guerre d'indépendance espagnole et le libéralisme au XIXe siècle* (Madrid: Casa de Velázquez, 2017), pp. 177-91, p. 184; José Álvarez Junco, *Spanish identity in the age of nations* (Manchester: Manchester University Press, 2011), p. 49.

90 Pedro Rújula López and Jordi Canal, *Guerra de ideas: política y cultura en la España de la Guerra de la Independencia* (Madrid: Marcial Pons Historia, 2011), p. 298.

91 During the war, British soldiers depicted Spain as barbaric, and many self-identified with the French enemy. See Gavin Daly, '"Barbarity More Suited to Savages": British Soldiers' Views of Spanish and Portuguese Violence during the Peninsular War, 1808-1814', *War & Society* 35:4 (2016), pp. 242-58.

92 Roy Porter, *Romanticism in National Context* (Cambridge: Cambridge University Press, 1988), p. 269.

rance.[93] Furthermore, due to the recurrent use of this rhetorical praise 'the existence of a Spanish identity seemed so self-evident that no serious attempt was made to educate the masses in nationhood'.[94] Liberals would 'base their attempts at building a political edifice on the idea that people had been fighting for their sovereignty, but the conservatives had no compunction in claiming these anti-Napoleonic heroes were in fact fighting in defence of age-old traditions'.[95]

The curse of fantasy: the romantic spirit and the decadent spanish nation

Nineteenth-century Spanish politicians and intellectuals were invigorated by the renewed European interest in Spain's culture.[96] However, much of this interest focused on the poetic decadence of her Romantic spirit and, in particular, on her unrepentant martial spirit and religious fervour.[97] In *Childe Harold's Pilgrimage*, Byron appealed to the rebirth of the chivalric Spanish spirit when he suggested: 'Awake, ye sons of Spain! Awake, advance!/ Lo' Chivalry, your ancient goddess cries/ but wields not, as of old, her thirsty lance!'[98] The German literary critic Friedrich Schlegel suggested Spanish culture was in need of reform: 'living in an insular situation, they have slept through the eighteenth century, and how could they in the main have applied their time better? Should Spanish poetry again awake in old Europe [...] it would certainly have a step to make, from instinct to consciousness'.[99] Schlegel's insight indicated the myth of Romantic Spain drew on earlier assumptions about her inaction. In the nineteenth-century European gaze, Spain became a dreamscape, yet dreams were 'a source of creative work [...] more often seen as an inferior function, when parts of the mind were functioning "passively" or "automatically", as they do in insanity' and in the absence of reason.[100] Narratives of orientalism and escapism drew on the image of Spain as a land where 'the fumes of

---

93 Juan Francisco Fuentes, 'Mito y concepto de pueblo en el siglo XIX: una comparación entre España y Francia', *Historia Contemporánea* 28 (2012), pp. 95-110, p. 96.

94 Junco, *Spanish identity in the age of nations*, p. 113.

95 Junco, *Spanish identity in the age of nations*, pp. 110-11.

96 Diego Saglia, *Poetic Castles in Spain*, p. 19.

97 John Clubbe, "Byron and Chateaubriand Interpret Spain" in *Byron and Latin Culture: Selected Proceedings of the 37th International Byron Society Conference*. Edited by Peter Cochran (Newcastle: Cambridge Scholars, 2013), pp. 292-308, p. 306.

98 Clubbe, 'Byron', p. 58.

99 Michael Iarocci, *Properties of Modernity: Romantic Spain, Modern Europe, and the Legacies of Empire* (Nashville: Vanderbilt University Press, 2006), p. 25.

100 Tony James, *Dream, Creativity, and Madness in Nineteenth-Century France* (Oxford: Clarendon Press, 1995), p. 272.

oriental intermixtures gave it a wonderful degree of sublimity, and elevated a poetry, intoxicated as it were with aromatic vapours, far above the scruples of the sober west'.[101] Indeed, European views of Spain mirrored Montesquieu's depiction of Amerindian barbarity: 'nature, which has given these peoples a weakness that makes them timid, has also given them such a lively imagination that everything strikes them to excess'.[102]

The discourse of dreams and decline nonetheless remained influential in peninsular political assessments of the Spanish nation and its cultural life, as many spoke of the 'decadence' of Spanish theatre.[103] Between 1820 and 1823, Spain enjoyed a brief period of liberal reforms, which spurred cultural critics to suggest Spain, following years of war, was 'beginning to awake from a dream'.[104] In 1823, a French intervention restored Ferdinand VII as King of Spain. For many Spanish politicians, Ferdinand's return was another display of French domination and signalled the recurrence of absolutism.[105] In 1833, following Ferdinand's death, the struggle for power between liberals and conservatives led to the first of three civil wars, known as the Carlist Wars, and prompted nightmarish representations of the nation. The author Mariano José de Larra would suggest 'to write like Chateaubriand and Lamartine in the capital of the modern world is to write for humanity, a worthy and noble end for a worthy man [...] to write as we write in Madrid [...] is to weep, it is to search for a voice without finding it, as in an overwhelming and violent nightmare'.[106]

Throughout the nineteenth century, Spanish intellectuals disagreed over the role the discourse of dreams should play in ideas of national identity. The historian Antonio Gil y Zárate suggested that 'nowadays imagination delights itself in remembering and renewing the memories of the Middle Ages'[107]. However, others found the fantasy of Medieval Spain to be symptomatic with decadence, an overpowering form of intoxication of the senses, and ultimately, a source of laziness. Lucas Mallada referred to Spain's 'cursed fantasy' when he argued that 'the land of Don Quixote is a land of dreamers. With all that dreaming, we sleep a great deal; and though we do not drug ourselves with opium as the Chinese do, we see visions and perpetual illusions without stirring from our slumber'.[108] Some intellectuals would find in fiction the solution to Spain's problems. Miguel de Unamuno characterised the figure of Miguel de Cervantes as 'evidence

---

101 James, *Dream*, p. 24.

102 Montesquieu, *The Spirit of the Laws*, p. 235.

103 David Thatcher Gies, *El teatro en la España del siglo XIX* (Madrid: Ediciones AKAL, 1996), p. 5.

104 Mackay, *"Lazy, Improvident People"*, p. 238.

105 Junco, *Spanish identity in the age of nations*, p. 229.

106 Michael Iarocci, *Properties of Modernity*, p. 166.

107 Derek Flitter, *Spanish Romanticism and the Uses of History* (London: Legenda, 2006), p. 39.

108 Mackay, *"Lazy, Improvident People"*, p. 238.

of Spain's spiritual laziness', and Don Quixote's character as a source of inspiration for a national regeneration.[109]

After the loss of Cuba in 1898, the language of sleep frequently slipped into a medical discourse of lethargy, as the politician Francisco Silvela diagnosed Spain as 'being without a pulse' and Lord Salisbury deemed her a 'moribund nation'.[110] In the early twentieth century, Spanish intellectuals exploited the entangled political grammar of sleep and the intellectual pan-European deployment of decadence to galvanise reform. In line with European 'decadents' such as Schopenhauer or Nietzsche, Spanish reformers 'did not consider themselves decadent at all, but daring innovators intent on destroying the existing social and religious order'.[111] The loss of Cuba inspired Spanish intellectuals to conceive of ways to regenerate Spain, and many embraced the tension between the vigour of fantasy and the legacy of idleness in the Spanish *Volksgeist*. 'Events in *fin de siglo* Spain were envisioned variously as harbingers of hope or signs of millennial doom, but in either case as critical points or a stage of transformation integral to modernism'.[112] The diplomat Salvador de Madariaga drew on Romantic understandings of Spain as a land of impossible contradictions. In 1920, Madariaga stated: 'The Spanish character abounds in conflicting tendencies. [...] For in reality it is both resigned and rebellious, it is energetic and indolent [...] the combination [...] which we have observed in the Spanish character contributes to the richness and complexity of the famous Spanish indifference. Indifference, laziness, passivity, are but various appearances of passionate life quietly flowing'.[113]

Both Benito Pérez Galdos, one of the most widely read Spanish authors of the late-nineteenth century, and José Ortega y Gasset, the most important philosopher of the early twentieth century, saw Spain as 'a *sui generis* political entity uncontaminated by Europe'.[114] After the First World War, José Ortega y Gasset portrayed Spain's historical inaction as a source of vitality, untouched by the destructive tendencies of modernity, and a reservoir of energy for a weary Europe whose 'rationalism, democracy, mechanisation, industrialism, and capitalism' had never surfaced in Spain, and had begun to display 'a loss of vigour'. Spain's decadence, portrayed

---

109 Christopher Britt Arredondo, *Quixotism: The Imaginative Denial of Spain's Loss of Empire* (Albany: SUNY Press), pp. 132-33.

110 Joseph Harrison, "Introduction: the historical background to the crisis of 1898" in *Spain's 1898 Crisis: Regenerationism, Modernism, Post-Colonialism*. Edited by Joseph Harrison (Manchester: Manchester University Press, 2000), p. 5.

111 Swart, *The Sense of Decadence in Nineteenth-Century France*, p. 166.

112 Oscar E. Vázquez, *The End Again: Degeneration and Visual Culture in Modern Spain* (University Park: Pennsylvania State University Press, 2017), p. 1.

113 Mackay, *"Lazy, Improvident People"*, p. 251.

114 Raymond Carr, *Spain, 1808-1975* (Oxford: Clarendon Press, 1982), p. 105.

as fictional vitality, could breathe new life into 'European civilisation'.[115] Others, however, were less optimistic. In 1922, as social division grew, Unamuno declared: 'for some, life is but a dream. To others, life is nothing more than sleep. For those Spaniards who believe in the civil, historic con-science of the Spanish *patria*, life is but a nightmare'.[116] In 1923, General Primo de Rivera deployed this language when he carried out his coup d'état. The aristocrat blamed politicians, separatists, and communists for Spain's 'illness', and for driving her towards a 'tragic and dishonourable end'.[117] Rivera drew on a medical vocabulary to suggest the coup was a necessary but temporary step to 'return the nation to health' and claimed Spaniards suffered from 'aboulia' (the loss of volition).[118] By 1982, follow-ing the end of General Franco's dictatorship, King Juan Carlos I resumed the benign version of this narrative to portray Spain as a creative force in Europe and entreat European leaders to reject stereotypes: 'Spain, a nation rooted in Europe, is not only European; it is trans-European and has been configured as a modern nation since its formation. It is a Hispanic nation [...] Does this reduce its European essence? Quite the contrary, it strengthens it. For Europe is trans-European; it was created to transcend itself, shine on other nations and open up to them. A closed, egoistic Europe that looked down on others would be less European. By being true to its Hispanic character [...] Spain does not decrease its European nature but affirms it and actualizes it in a creative way'.[119]

Historiographical overview and conclusion: early modern Spanish decline and the Black Legend

'The name of the song is called "Haddocks' Eyes"'.
'Oh, that's the name of the song, is it?' Alice said, trying to feel interested.
'No, you don't understand', the Knight said, looking a little vexed. 'That's what the name is called. The name really is "The Aged Aged Man"'.
'Then I ought to have said "That's what the song is called?"' Alice corrected herself.

---

115 José Ortega y Gasset, *Obras Completas*, Volume Three (España invertebrada) (Madrid: Alianza, 1982), p. 123.
116 Victor Ouimette and José Luis Abellán, *Los intelectuales españoles y el naufragio del liberalismo: (1923-1936)* (Valencia: Pre-Textos, 1998), p. 109-10.
117 Alejandro Quiroga Fernández de Soto, *Haciendo españoles: la nacionalización de las masas en la dictadura de Primo de Rivera (1923-1930)* (Madrid: Centro de Estudios Políticos y Constitucionales, 2008), p. 75.
118 Soto, *Haciendo españoles*, p. 75.
119 Juan Carlos I, *Charlemagne Prize Reception Speech*, Aachen, 1982.

'No, you oughtn't: that's quite another thing! The song is called "Ways And Means": but that's only what it's called, you know!'

'Well, what is the song, then?' said Alice, who was by this time completely bewildered.

'I was coming to that', the Knight said. 'The song really is "A-sitting On a Gate": and the tune's my own invention'.

Lewis Carroll – *Through the Looking-Glass, and What Alice Found There* (1871)

In early modern Spain, decline constituted a familiar song without a clear name, or the name for a song beyond recall. Over the twentieth century, the Black Legend developed into the epithet for Spanish decline. A historiographical construct used to denote early modern European depictions of Hispanic barbarism, ignorance, and superstition, the Black Legend gradually became a catchphrase to glide over important historical nuances and shifting perceptions; sedimentary layers of the past best understood through careful, contextualised study. Seminal historiographical accounts have drawn on the Black Legend and the logic of decline to synthesise overarching narratives of early modern Spain.

Scholars have suggested 'the story of [Spanish] decline was plucked out of the air, rather than arrived at on the basis of evidence'.[120] However, the concept of Spanish decline belonged within a broader historically contingent political vocabulary. In this regard, 'the analytical tools we use to identify either historical continuities or, alternatively, profound ruptures from the past may be obstacles rather than openings'.[121] The study of orthodox narratives such as the story of decline, or the Black Legend, may obscure the durable influence of latent semantic strategies. Concepts with lives of their own may be fossilised into static terms for historiographical use. These concepts might, then, be stretched for analytical purposes, and projected upon the past. Historians frequently attribute the usefulness of terms such as decline or the Black Legend to their protracted elasticity: 'the utility of the "Black Legend" resides in its capacity to amalgamate heterogeneous propaganda campaigns against Spain [...] therefore this historiographical construct encapsulates the main historical stereotypes of said campaigns'.[122] The amalgamation of political campaigns against Spain would fail to account for the accumulating effects and shifting contexts that informed ideas of decline. Explorations into the history of the terminology

---

120 Kamen, *Imagining Spain*, p. 186.

121 Stoler, *Imperial Durabilities*, p. 5.

122 Javier Fernández Sebastián,""Los Desaciertos de Nuestros Padres". Los Liberales Y Los Orígenes Del Llamado "problema Español"", in *La Sombra de La Leyenda Negra*. Edited by María José Villaverde Y Francisco Castilla (Madrid: Biblioteca Nueva, 2016), pp. 483-510, p. 483.

used in contemporary studies may challenge historians to draw on multi-faceted approaches to the study of the past.

A few decades ago, scholars believed the first use of the term "Black Legend" emerged in 1914. In his work *The Black Legend and Historical Truth: Spain in Europe*, the historian Julián Juderias y Loyot defined the Black Legend as 'the legend of Inquisitorial Spain, ignorant and fanatical, incapable of standing side by side the most learned nations, prone to violent repression, enemy of progress and innovations.'[123] Yet, over the last decade, historians have found the first use of the term to be a response to the loss of Cuba.

In 1899, the writer Emilia Pardo Bazán delivered a speech at the Charras Salon in Paris to declare the end of Spanish rule over Cuba marked the loss of the legend that hailed Spain's 'messianic' role in the world.[124] 'Spain has lost everything in this storm, even her legend; and it is surprising to see the true physiognomy of a nation we long thought to be prone to attacks of desperate heroism, when in reality, she appears anaesthetised and shell-shocked.'[125] The perils of sleep characterised Pardo's analysis: 'For herein lies the problem. What will happen now to this diverse Spain we used to fantasise about, this Spain of impoverished blood, tired nerves, and with little cultivated intelligence? What will we reach for in order to save ourselves when we lived for so long off our heroic dead, now that we have been forced to bury them and look for our own identity?'

Pardo posited the age-old solution of labour as the answer to Spain's demons: 'A small, zealous minority confronts widespread indifference and aspires to *awake* Spain's vigour, displaying without fear the extent of the damage in an attempt to replace the legendary ideal with the idea of *innovation, labour* and overall *application.* [...] I have assumed the legend will fade and dissipate today, but I fear, however, that it will survive and may even *awake* as a threat – like those dragons with flaming mouths we see in paintings – in an attempt to devour those of us who seek the truth.'[126] Pardo's fears presaged Franco's deployment of said vision and warned of the seductive power of Spain's history of 'desperate heroism'. However, Pardo rejected the notion that patriotism was 'dead in Spain. I believe it to be *asleep*, and therefore I try to prompt it to *awake*.'[127]

Pardo was, however, equally critical of American historical accounts of Spain dating back to William Prescott in the 1820s, accounts which

---

123 Julián Juderias y Loyot, *La leyenda negra y la verdad histórica, contribución al estudio del concepto de España en Europa, de las causas de este concepto y de la tolerancia religiosa y política en los países civilizados* (Madrid: Revista de archivos, bibliotecas y museos, 1914), pp. 1-246, p. 15.

124 'La conferencia de Doña Emilia Pardo Bazán', *La Época*, 22 May 1899, pp. 2-3.

125 'La conferencia de Doña Emilia Pardo Bazán', pp. 2-3. Italics added for emphasis.

126 'La conferencia de Doña Emilia Pardo Bazán', pp. 2-3.

127 'La conferencia de Doña Emilia Pardo Bazán', pp. 2-3.

gained greater inernational prominence during the Spanish-American War. In July 1898, an article in *The Atlantic* titled "The Decadence of Spain" declared: 'In many respects the Spaniard is still living in the sixteenth century, unable to assimilate the ideas of the nineteenth, or to realise that his country is no longer the mistress of the sea and the dominating power of the land'.[128] Pardo criticised the American novelisation of the Spanish character at the expense of careful study of her contemporary national history:

> 'And my honesty allows me to condemn Spain's counter-legend, the *black legend*, divulged by this vulgar press that stains and offends the civilisation of the United States, and a thousand times more deceitful than the golden legend. The latter draws on tradition and history, and is based on our unbelievable feats of the past. By contrast, the *black legend* lies about our character, ignores our psychology, and replaces our contemporary history with a novel, in the style of [Pierre Alexis] Ponson du Térail, with attacks which do not merit our attention'.[129]

Pardo pointed to a dimension of these categorisations which frequently goes unnoticed: the myth of decline frequently risks distorting contemporary political dilemmas. In his study on Spanish decline, Henry Kamen concluded 'myth-making about the early modern history of Spain will persist because it is a direct consequence of the failure to create a homogenous national identity and a coherent, commonly shared historical memory'.[130] To portray the abuse of historical myth-making about decline and decadence as the direct consequence of Spain's politics complicates the study of histories that remain present. Kamen's faulting of Spanish political affairs reflects the effects of decline and decadence are 'past but not over', and are deeply embedded in historiographical readings of the modern nation.[131]

Shedding long-range light on the deployment of the language of sleep in the development of the Black Legend and the myth of decline offers an alternative explanation for the popularity of historical myth-making. Today, ideas of decline and decadence permeate the historiography of Spain due to their intuitive appeal, justified by centuries of 'partial reinscriptions, modified displacements, and amplified recuperations'.[132] By the mid-nineteenth century, the discourse of Spanish lethargy reconciled the impossible combination of the quotidian, the scientific, and the fantastic. In doing so, the discourse, paradoxically, cleared the way for Spanish

---

128 Henry Charles Lea, 'The Decadence of Spain', *The Atlantic*, July 1989.
129 Lea, 'The Decadence of Spain'.
130 Kamen, *Imagining Spain*, p. 210.
131 Stoler, *Duress*, p. 25.
132 Stoler, *Duress*, p. 27.

decline to become 'pure common-sense'.[133] In the transition to modernity, this commonsensical view of Spain enabled the transformation from empire to nation and the assimilation of positivism. The power of ideas of decline and decadence relies as much on their capacity to amalgamate historical trends as on their capacity to normalise backwardness and foreclose alternative interpretations.

Far from treating these terms as benign, historians should remain alert to their implications and their genealogies. Today's Spanish definition of *decadencia* reflects the historiographical challenges posed by this term. The Royal Spanish Academy defines *decadencia* through the verb *decaer*, 'said of someone or something which has lost the conditions or properties which constituted its strength, its benevolence, its importance, or its vigour', and 'said of a ship which has lost its route due to strong waves, winds, or currents'.[134] The first definition points to the term's inability to capture the intractable historical loss of ill-defined and historically contingent *positive* political conditions and properties of an empire or a nation. The second points to the implied sense of predestination and inevitability in many readings of early modern Spanish decline. Most importantly, it reinforces the sense that the Iberian Peninsula lost its north when it tried to rule the seas, only to be moored in a distant past.

In this context, concepts such as decline, decadence, and decay might be understood as reasonable intellectual carapaces capable of housing and reifying more diffuse and far less palatable views about nation-states, views that nonetheless remain lodged in modern self-identities. In this process, ties between otherwise distant concepts appear more sensible and acquire greater meaning through a historically constructed family resemblance. Historical research thus becomes an investigation into 'the inequities inscribed in how common sense is forged' and 'the anticipatory dangers in the conditional and future tense'.[135]

Today, the self-evident political grammar of sleep continues to exert a deep influence on visions of Spain. In 2010, the Spanish Ministry for Tourism released an advert that declared the *siesta* was 'a time for dreaming'.[136] In 2017, Jeroen Dijsselbloem, the then President of the Eurogroup, the European Union's body responsible for coordinating economic policies, proclaimed that 'during the crisis of the euro, the countries of the north have shown solidarity with [southern] countries affected by the

---

133 Javier Fernández Sebastián, '"Los Desaciertos de Nuestros Padres". Los Liberales Y Los Orígenes Del Llamado "problema Español"', in *La Sombra de La Leyenda Negra*. Edited by María José Villaverde and Francisco Castilla (Madrid: Biblioteca Nueva, 2016), pp. 483-510, p. 502.

134 Real Academia Española, *Diccionario de la lengua española* (Madrid: Online Edition, 2014).

135 Stoler, *Duress: Imperial Durabilities in Our Times*, p. 14.

136 Patricia Gosálvez, 'España en tres palabras: De "Spain is different" a "I need Spain"', *El País*, 16 June 2011.

crisis [...] but you also have obligations [...] you cannot spend all the money on drinks and women and then ask for help'.[137] Both the Spanish Ministry for Tourism and Dijsselbloem relied on the perception that Southern Europe was a land of the night, of idleness and fantasy. For many Spaniards, the term decline and its name, the Black Legend, remain epithets for a familiar song.

---

137 Mehreen Khan, Paul McClean, 'Dijsselbloem under fire after saying eurozone countries wasted money on "alcohol and women"', *Financial Times*, 21 March 2017.

PART 2

———

Testimonials

TAMAR HERZOG

Is Spain Exceptional?

Reflections on Thirty Years of Research and Writing

The question of whether Spain is, or at least was, exceptional has been debated for many centuries. Many answer this question in the affirmative with the goal of either congratulating or criticizing it. Others refute such categorizations either by claiming the non-existence of Spain, highlighting the presence of multiple Spain(s) or multiple Spanish kingdoms, or by insisting that it was an "ordinary" European country. Both Spaniards and foreigners engage in this debate. Despite constant disagreements, exceptionality often seems to carry the day. For many years, Spaniards marketed their country as exceptional in order to attract tourists. Those who visited, and foreign observers who wrote about it, frequently agreed.

Historians have not shied away from these debates. Though among them the current tendency is to assume similarity, at least with Southern Europe, very few insert the question of Spanish exceptionalism into a larger perspective by engaging in a true dialogue with the historiography of other countries and empires. In what follows, I ask what we stand to learn by doing so. Looking back on my trajectory of over thirty years of historical research and writing, I argue that we can indeed learn a great deal from this exercise. This task, I would note, benefits historians of Iberia and historians of other countries. To demonstrate my point, I observe a few examples among many of what can or perhaps should be done. These examples call upon historians to read widely not so much to compare historical experiences – after all, all historical experiences are both similar and distinct – but to reflect on the questions they ask. It is by asking questions and not only, nor even mainly, by supplying answers that we can approach the past more carefully.

The cases I examine all originate in my own work. They are the result of repetitively asking myself whether the investment in reading widely is worthwhile, and whether we can transform Iberian history in normative ways, in the sense that it would be read as a participant in a larger Euro-

Tamar Herzog • Harvard University

Supplicant Empires, ed. by Edward Jones Corredera, Habsburg Worlds, 8 (Turnhout: Brepols, 2025), pp. 193–204
BREPOLS ❧ PUBLISHERS   10.1484/M.HW-EB.5.145069

pean story and be considered as relevant by historians of Europe whose geographical focus is not the Iberian Peninsula. Could it become as iconic, for example, as France or Germany?

From Spain and Spanish America to Europe

In 2003 I published *Defining Nations: Immigrants and Citizens in Early Modern Spain and Spanish America*, a book that described the processes through which, during the early modern period in both Peninsular Spain and Spanish America, people were recognized or denied recognition as citizens of local communities (*vecinos*) and as Spaniards (*naturales*).[1] I argued that this recognition operated tacitly. Rather than being dependent on formal declarations, or on legal stipulations, it was rooted in practices that considered those locally integrated, and believed to be loyal to the community, as members. Loyalty could be manifested in multiple ways through residence, tax payment, local marriage, service in the militia, and so forth. I traced the operation of these rules at the local and municipal level and showed that they also influenced the identification of Spaniards. Spaniards were those who were tied to Spain and acted as Spaniards, with insertion into a Spanish (or Spanish American) local community being the best proof of their status.

This matrix allowed constant changes in the way people were classified as those who were citizens and Spanish could cease being thus because they were understood to have abandoned their integration in the community, for example, by immigrating elsewhere or serving another country. By the same token, those who were initially classified as outsiders could become insiders if they manifested the desire to do so (and their neighbors credited that they had). As a result of these views, behavior could become performative: it was by acting in certain ways that people could be recognized as members, but it was also the silence of those allowing them to do so that could enable their transformation. In other words, those who behaved as members and were allowed to do so could thereafter argue that they in fact were *vecinos* or *naturales*.

These processes transpired without royal or municipal intervention. Though royal and municipal authorities were called to settle conflicts regarding status, and they were sometimes requested to issue certificates that attested to status, their activities were not considered constitutive. Instead, they verified and formally attested who people already were. The question of who was who and who deserved which treatment was tacitly

---

1 Tamar Herzog, *Defining Nations: Immigrants and Citizens in Early Modern Spain and Spanish America* (New Haven: Yale University Press, 2003). Spanish and French translations are also available.

asked only when classification mattered, that is, when actors wanted to benefit from rights reserved for local citizens or Spaniards, or their peers wanted to bar them from doing so or, alternatively, force them to comply with the relevant duties. As a result, individuals could live for many years in the community without their status being questioned or verified. It was only when they pretended to do certain things (or their rivals wanted to stop them from doing so) or when other community members or the authorities wanted to force them to behave in certain ways that membership status was examined, discussed, and verified.

These rules operated somewhat similarly on both sides of the ocean. Though in the Americas there was a growing identification between the local and the Spanish community, with most Spaniards being recognized almost automatically as *vecinos* and many non-Spaniards easily excluded, the arguments that were used, and the dynamics that were unleashed, were not substantially different. Who was a *vecino* and which rights this person had were still questions that Spanish American communities debated in similar ways. In the Americas, being a Spaniard entitled individuals to benefits different than those one would enjoy in Spain – in Spain most discussions were focused on one's capacity to hold public office and ecclesiastical benefice, in the Americas officials analyzed one's capacity to engage in commercial activities– and therefore the identity of those discussing membership criteria was different, and so were their interests. This resulted in the targeting of a distinct set of individuals (mostly merchants, rather than local office holders as in Spain), and the use of specific arguments (regarding how to attest behavior in the case of merchants, considered to generally behave differently than other members), but it did not move the discussion in radically new directions.

These conclusions, summarized here far too briefly, could be construed as demonstrating that Spain and Spanish America were different. After all, historians of Europe have long argued that membership in European communities operated in radically different ways. Some pointed to the primacy of subjecthood in classifying people, thus stressing vertical rather than horizontal ties. Others distinguished between a European tradition that insisted on descent or, alternatively, on one's place of birth. Most suggested that the emergence of states led to the demise of local communities, as crowns gradually monopolized the definition of both people and territory. The general assumption was that elsewhere in Europe there were no ties between local and kingdom-wide membership, which operated separately with the latter trumping the former.

Yet, as I read the literature on other European countries, I constantly came across references that sometimes hinted, other times outright demonstrated, that their cases might have not been substantially different. True, those who studied their history concluded otherwise, but they had asked different questions, employed a distinct methodology, and often analysed different sources. Most importantly, they were less attuned to a history that did not focus on what social actors sought to accomplish but wished to understand how they went about doing so, reconstructing the rules that transformed their words and actions into social and juridical practices. Nor were they interested in a legal history that was not centered on royal or municipal decrees but instead, like linguists do when they observe speech, studied repeating practices to uncover the norms that underlie and structure them.

Convinced of the importance of the dialogue with historians working on other European states and empires, I concluded the book with a chapter asking, "was Spain exceptional?".[2] In this chapter I reviewed the literature on the Italian city states, France, and England from the perspective of what I had discovered in Spain and Spanish America. It soon became apparent that nowhere were arrangements precisely identical to what I had observed, but that many of the basic rules I had uncovered were broadly similar. In all three territories, for example, municipal communities were imagined as associations of free individuals who lived together under a common legal regime, where members were eligible for rights and in theory could be forced to comply with duties that non-members could not. Processes of incorporation into municipal communities were available and most demanded some corroboration for integration, such as property ownership, tax payment, marriage, or membership of a guild, before they made foreigners into insiders. Everywhere, there were plenty of indications that municipal membership also mattered in the evaluation of membership status in the wider community. In other words, although contemporary French and English jurists (and historians following them) insisted on the importance of subjecthood, the processes through which subjecthood was constructed and verified often forced the parties to examine the norms of integration in a local community. Curiously, such similarities across Europe were detected by some medieval historians, but they were considered irrelevant, or simply ignored, by most early modernists.[3]

What was most surprising about the affirmation that what was true in the Middle Ages, these similarities across Europe, ceased being thus in the early modern period was that the point of rupture was, according to most authors, the fourteenth century. For a legal historian, this is extremely significant. In our telling of European legal history, the fourteenth century was a period in which the European *ius commune* drastically expanded its geographical and ideological reach and gained substantial independence from the texts that initially formed its hard core. Many jurists working on

---

2 Herzog, *Defining Nations*, Chapter 8: "Was Spain Exceptional?", pp. 164-200.

3 Most notably, Susan Reynolds in *An Introduction to the History of English Medieval Towns* (Oxford: Clarendon Press, 1977) and *Kingdoms and Communities in Western Europe 900-1300* (Oxford: Clarendon Press, 1984).

this period were interested in affirming the autonomy of both communities and monarchs vis-à-vis emperors and popes. They came up with theories of jurisdiction (that is, of *iuris-dictio*, the ability to announce and implement norms) and they elaborated notions and mechanisms that could eventually support local and royal sovereignty. Among other things, jurists working in Italy observed the multiple ways Italian communes treated their citizens and allowed for the integration of immigrants. They came up with generalizations that, based on practices across multiple places, adopted a vision that explained them all. They thus proposed a doctrinal framework regarding the making and unmaking of citizenship that would thereafter dominate large parts of Europe.[4]

That the coming together of juridical ideas regarding citizenship in the fourteenth century, ideas that percolated throughout Europe as *ius commune* extended its reach, led to distinct practices across the continent and did not foster legal coherence, was (and is) an extremely puzzling conclusion, yet it survives criticism and continues to be affirmed today. Attempts to show the predominance of these pan-European juridical ideas, for example, in early modern France and England, were greatly criticized by more traditional scholars, who insisted on the particularity of their case studies. Yet, familiarity with these juridical ideas – which are often ignored – allows one to demonstrate their omnipresence. Whether directly citing them or not, across Europe (and definitely in the three cases I closely examined) what discussants and decision makers said strongly resonated with these doctrines.

Take England, for example, which most mistakenly assume was not affected by *ius commune*. Historians of England have long debated the meaning and extension of 'freedom': most argued it was a status related to economic activities that only existed in incorporated towns, where it gave members of guilds access to certain local rights and duties. Nonetheless, we also know that, although freedom might have operated in this way, it was also a condition accorded to the inhabitants of free towns that granted them the right to vote.[5] Depending on the payment of taxes and the establishment of domicile, which could easily be construed as manifestations of local integration, English jurists attested that even those who did not obtain a formal admission to the community could nonetheless

---

4 Particularly instrumental in this process were the works of Bartolus de Saxoferrato (1313-1357) and Baldus de Ubaldis (1327-1400) but many other jurists in Italy and elsewhere were engaged in the same creative activity.

5 See, for example, Jonathan Barry, 'I significati della libertà: la libertà urbana nell'Inghilterra del XVI e XVII secolo', *Quaderni Storici* 30:89 (1995), pp. 487-513. I find it extremely indicative that this piece was published in Italian, rather than English, and appeared in *Quaderni Storici*, the most important journal of history in Italy, rather than in the UK. Conclusions regarding what English jurists argued are based on my own research for *Defining Nations*; see references there.

be considered freemen and, indeed, municipal authorities could not reject them, nor deny them the right to vote. Eventually, entitlement to freedom would be understood as the birthright of all Englishmen and common law jurists would conclude that those who abandoned the community, or failed to comply with membership duties, could be construed as having relinquished their freedom. The jurisprudence of common law courts also determined that at stake were not truly objective facts – what people did – but their interpretation – why they did what they did. Behavior was to be interpreted so as to attest to intention. In summary, in seventeenth- and eighteenth-century England, a local freeman and an abstract national free-man coexisted side by side, along with the verification of freedom and the rights and duties attached to it – these practices had an incredibly strong resonance with *ius commune* and thus also shared extensive similarities with Spain. Furthermore, we also know that, from the late Middle Ages, English incorporated towns began excluding foreigners from the ranks of freemen. As a result, freedom not only became the birthright of all English-men but, over time, having freedom became identified with being English. The circle was now closed: all Englishmen were birthright freemen, and all freemen were English. Recent literature has also demonstrated that even English subjecthood was constructed in a somewhat comparable way. It was understood to be a contract into which foreigners could enter, if locals allowed them to do so, and which vassals could leave, and which implied a regime of rights and duties. Thereafter, complying or failing to comply with those duties could become proof, and a constitutive part, of one's condition as subject.[6]

The effort to engage in wide-ranging reading was partly motivated by pure curiosity, but it was also a means to question Spanish exceptionalism. Because I had uncovered these parallels and many others, I decided to add the already mentioned chapter ("Was Spain Exceptional?") in the book to showcase how the literature on Italy, England, and France could be read differently if one had the Spanish example in mind. The aim was not so much to engage in the debate on exceptionalism per se. Instead, I took up the challenge of demonstrating that Spanish history and Spanish historians can contribute to European-wide conversations. I was thus extremely pleased when historians who worked on areas beyond Spain and Spanish America found the book helpful. As I mentioned elsewhere, in the almost twenty years since it was published, it has been used by historians of the Jewish experience, the Netherlands, Portugal, Italy, France, and

---

6 Hannah Weiss Muller, *Subjects and Sovereign: Bonds of Belonging in the Eighteenth-Century British Empire* (New York: Oxford University Press, 2017). See my review of this book in *The William and Mary Quarterly* 75:1 (2018), pp. 179-82.

England.[7] Though some cited it to distinguish their case studies from mine, protesting that their cases were fundamentally different, many others showed that the questions I asked, the methodology I proposed, and even the conclusions I reached, were relevant to their case studies and indeed produced interesting and innovative results. There were even historians who found my findings valuable for the analysis of debates on citizenship in nineteenth-century California, on the making of the national census in the USA, as well as for studying attitudes and policies towards immigrants, minorities, and individuals of African descent more generally. Most pleasing for me was the conclusion of one author, according to whom my book had opened up alternative perspectives for analyzing the relations between citizenship and empire in Europe and beyond.[8] Somewhat recently, my work has also been instrumental in dreaming of another world, or at least another Europe, in which municipal rather than state loyalties and citizenship would carry the day.[9]

As pleasing as all this was, what I found most striking about these conversations was that they were not so much focused on the specific findings that I uncovered, but on the questions I asked, the sources I examined, and the methodology I employed. In many cases, it allowed scholars to move the conversation in new directions that indicated that there was an important story to be told about the relations between local citizenship and the emergence of states, which would portray the coming of the leviathan as the aggregation of many municipalities and their citizens, rather than their replacement. My work seemed to have also shed light on immigration and naturalization as the flip side of citizenship, showing that the same processes that excluded individuals were also responsible for identifying constituent members. It ultimately suggested that overseas expansion complicated these dynamics of identity but did not fundamentally change their nature.

While I may have convinced some of my readers that Spain was not altogether exceptional, or perhaps made them reconsider existing narratives about other countries by integrating Spain in their analysis, did I succeed in making Spain and Spanish American normative? In some cases I did but in many others I did not. Spain is still rarely enumerated among the case studies that most historians use to elucidate European history. Whether this is because it is considered exceptional or simply marginal to European-wide narratives, Spain continues to be, at least to some degree,

7 Tamar Herzog, 'Early Modern Citizenship in Europe and the Americas: A Twenty Year's Conversation', *Ler História* 78 (2021), pp. 225-37.

8 Frederick Cooper, *Citizenship, Inequality, and Difference: Historical Perspectives* (Princeton: Princeton University Press, 2018), p. 43.

9 Maarten Roy Prak, *Citizens without nations: Urban Citizenship in Europe and the World, c. 1000-1789* (Cambridge: Cambridge University Press, 2018).

an outsider. As a result of this impression, and because I believed that the way I proceeded in 2003 was not particularly successful, in 2018 I decided to adopt another strategy. Instead of studying Spain and Spanish America and showing that they can help us re-read the histories of other European countries, I turned my focus towards the drafting of a European-wide narrative in which Spain loomed large. The book, which described the history of law in Europe from ancient Roman times to the present, aimed to show that law itself, and not just particular legal solutions, has changed place, character, and means over time.[10] It also aimed to place the so-called continental (or civil) law side by side with English law, often stereotypically shorthanded as Common Law. Were these two systems truly distinct? Since when and in what ways?

In this long narrative, whenever I needed specific examples for European-wide processes, I deliberately turned, when I could, to Spain. Describing the emergence of provincial Roman Law, the mixing of Roman with Germanic law, and the Christianization of Roman Law, Spain could serve as an example. The same was true of the persistence of some elements of Roman Law in the early middle ages, or of efforts by European monarchs first to encourage the use of *ius commune* in their territories and then to attempt to control it. Paradoxically, perhaps because they were familiar with my trajectory, Spanish legal historians who reviewed the book were disappointed that there were no additional references to Spain. Other reviewers, on the contrary, did not notice the provocation at all: throughout the book they may have repeatedly read about Spain as an example of broader European processes, but they did not pay attention to this aspect of the work. I therefore came to the conclusion that this method – perhaps far too implicit despite being profoundly subversive – was not particularly helpful either. A hidden Spain was the same as no Spain.

From other empires to Spain

While I found it hard to convince historians of other territories that familiarity with Spanish and Spanish American history may be helpful, I certainly found the dialogue with other historiographies incredibly enriching. This was clearest to me as I was writing *Frontiers of Possession: Spain*

---

10 Tamar Herzog, *A Short History of European Law: The Last Two and a Half Millennia* (Cambridge: Harvard University Press, 2018). Translations are available in Spanish, French, Italian, Korean, and Mandarin, and forthcoming in Portuguese and Farsi.

and Portugal in Europe and the Americas.[11] Traditionally, the history of the territorial formation of Spain and Portugal in both the Iberian Peninsula and the Americas tended to center on royal designs. It had concentrated on studying treaties between monarchs, including negotiations, implementation – successful, partial, or failed – and violations, sometimes in the form of large-scale violence, even open war. Yet the literature most particularly of British North America but to some degree also of French America, told a radically different story regarding how European intrusion into the continent operated. This was a story in which the state was mostly absent and in which colonists, habitually identified as 'settlers', played a major role. The North American literature described how colonists gradually encroached upon new territories, and how they confronted the indigenous populations, winning them over, allying with them, expelling them, fighting against them, or attempting (and often succeeding) in annihilating them. Thus, while historians of Spanish America who looked for state and state-sanctioned activities tended to treat the Americas more or less as a single unit, assumed that the hegemony of Spain was never seriously contested and thus relations with indigenous peoples and other European powers were not central to these narratives – while they departed from convictions regarding striking differences between Europe and the Americas by insisting, for example, on the existence of a phantasmagorical *derecho indiano* legislated by the king for the empire and distinct from the law both in Spain and elsewhere in Europe – historians of British and French colonialism did the opposite. They paid close attention to local dynamics, focused on local legal and political arrangements; they imagined a colonial commonwealth made of active individuals who operated on the margins of states, put relations with natives and with other European powers at the center of their analyses, and portrayed a dynamic of extreme fragmentation, with each colony operating differently, each place unique, and each encounter exceptional. Of course, not all historians told the same story, and some were more attuned to certain things than others, but the image that emerged, and was sanctioned in textbooks and manuals, largely corresponded with these portrayals – at least this was the case until recently.

Awareness of the literature on British and French America and, mainly, of the questions it asked, and its presuppositions, made my inquiry into Spanish and Portuguese archives extremely different than I had initially imagined.[12] It was no accident that for a long time I referred to the

---

11 Tamar Herzog, *Frontiers of Possession: Spain and Portugal in Europe and the Americas* (Cambridge: Harvard University Press, 2015). Translations are available in Portuguese, Brazilian-Portuguese, and Spanish.

12 See the section, in Herzog, *Frontiers of possession*, titled "South and North: Writing Imperial Histories in a Prenational Age", pp. 255-60.

manuscript of *Frontiers of Possession* as the "Richard White book". After all, this book was partially inspired by the many conversations I had with Richard, who was a friend and a colleague at Stanford, where I used to work, and whose book, the *Middle Ground*, revolutionized the literature on colonial North America in the early 1990s.[13] It was by conversing with Richard that I realized how powerful historical narratives set us on a given course, often without us being aware of it or at least aware of the consequences. I came to ask myself, what would happen if I asked my sources the same questions that historians of Britain and France asked theirs and if, instead of looking for royal longhand, we inquired into how a plethora of individuals with a wide array of interests, often in opposition to one another, nonetheless gradually defined the contours of their communities and their territorial extension. What if we approached the study of the formation of colonial territories through the analysis of the relations between Europeans and indigenous peoples, and between the various European powers, and asked the question of who often instrumentalized indigenous peoples, and who could also be instrumentalized by them? Thus, rather than asking, as others have done, if Anglo and Spanish America were different, a question that does not truly liberate us from the existing narratives but rather tends to confirm and perpetuate them, I wanted to apply the methodology of one to the study of the other.

Adopting the tools of a foreign historiography as my own, I gradually discovered that if we parted from the same assumptions, asked the same questions, and used the same source material in comparable ways, we would ascertain that more often than not it would be difficult to distinguish English from Spanish and Portuguese methods of expansion. We would also learn to observe the activities of Spaniards and Portuguese peoples from a different perspective, and think about them in new ways.

It is therefore not surprising that, as I read the sources, rather than seeing the state, or concentrating on state agents, I discovered a colonial Latin America where frontier diplomacy, with both indigenous peoples and other Europeans, was vital in the construction of norms, where temporary solutions became permanent, and where multiple actors, but rarely the state, were involved in establishing presence, taking possession, arguing for rights, and fighting against rivals. The territorial formation of both Spain and Portugal in the Americas, I concluded, was the result of multiple activities by countless agents who, while they went about accomplishing different tasks and defending their own interests, also defined the territories of their communities and states. Among these agents were farmers, noblemen, clergymen, friars, missionaries, settlers, governors, municipal authorities, and military men who explored, settled, and used different

---

13 Richard White, *The Middle Ground: Indians, Empires, and Republics in the Great Lakes Region, 1650-1815* (Cambridge: Cambridge University Press, 1991).

spaces, while they vocally and often violently rejected similar activities carried out by their neighbors, both indigenous and European. These confrontations were neither planned nor controlled by states. They occurred when the situation required it, that is, when the interested parties wanted to let their animals pasture, or when they wanted to collect wood, establish residence, trade, or convert or control the local populations. Though cacophonic and haphazard, this persistent struggle between individuals and groups, rather than fixed by inter-polity agreements or war, led to territorial formation.

Moving on from asking where the border was, or ought to have been, as many have done before me, I asked how claims were made, how they operated, and when and why they were successful. Which were the precise mechanisms and processes that countless individuals and groups embraced to establish territorial presence? What was remembered, and what was forgotten? And how did group membership and identity formation affect these dynamics? If it were not for reading the literature on North America, I would have probably abided by an analysis (also featured in *Frontiers of possession*) of how contemporaries understood the various treaties between Spain and Portugal, and how they argued about their correct interpretation and implementation. It would have been a worthwhile study, but it would have been vastly different than the one I ultimately undertook.

Why it matters

Obviously, constantly looking at our sources from a different perspective and questioning traditional narratives is an important task in and of itself. Obviously, reading widely can teach us many things and give us plenty of new ideas. Yet, with these short comments I wish to advocate for the urgency of transcending national divisions. Global historians have long insisted on the importance of looking at exchanges and the dynamic relations between different areas of the globe. They have advised us against observing places, societies, people, and processes as if they existed in a vacuum and disconnected from a wider context. They have suggested that anything and everything can be interdependent and entangled, at least to a degree. Yet, the search for a global history, which has often generated exciting new questions and innovative methodologies, has rarely translated into conversations between the various historiographical traditions. Paradoxically, one could argue that there are national schools of global history – or even that global history is done differently in different countries. These distinctions are extremely powerful because, whether we are fully conscious of them or not, they are ensconced in the traditions of the nation state and in how its politicians and intellectuals used (and misused) the past. If it is time to study history without being constrained by a priori geographical or political divisions, even a priori periodizations, as many have rightly sustained, it is also time we consider how looking through a particular prism, that of an earlier national historiography, colors our understanding of the past. The question as one studies Spain, then, should not be whether it is exceptional or not, but how its history and its historiography can help us comprehend Europe and its historical experiences in new ways.

Interviews

Basque History: Hyper-Local and Hyper-Global

Amanda L. Scott, **Pennsylvania State University**

What has been the most significant change in the field of Iberian history since the start of your career?

Honestly, I'm not sure I have had a "career" in Iberian studies long enough to really answer a question involving a long-look back on the field! However, even in the last few years, I do think that the field is getting distinctly more global. As I will discuss below, Basque historiography has always been quite polarized between hyper-local (studies of villages) or hyper-global (studies of Basque emigration over centuries). Nonetheless, outside the field of Basque studies, I do think that some of the more recent work on race and empire is starting to push even some of the more conservative strands of historiography to seriously broaden how we think about participation and identity in early modern Iberia. New monographs by Nick Jones and Erin Rowe provide spectacular visual and cultural examples of how Black Iberians shaped Golden Age culture.[1] Outside the Iberian Peninsula, work by Miguel Valerio and Cécile Fromont have likewise helped amplify the voices and central contributions of the Black Atlantic, and indeed, make the art and literature of the Golden Age all the more relevant to the present.[2] On the other hand, unfortunately, I do not see Basque studies keeping pace with these expanding frameworks. Though I see numerous references to the sale of enslaved Africans in the

---

1 Nicholas R. Jones, *Staging Habla de Negros: Radical Performances of the African Diaspora in Early Modern Spain* (University Park: Pennsylvania State University Press, 2019); and Erin Rowe, *Black Saints in Early Modern Global Catholicism* (Cambridge: Cambridge University Press, 2019).

2 Miguel A. Valerio, *Sovereign Joy: Afro-Mexican Kings and Queens, 1539-1640* (Cambridge: Cambridge University Press, 2022); and Cécile Fromont, *Images on a Mission in Early Modern Kongo and Angola* (Cambridge: Cambridge University Press, 2022).

Supplicant Empires, ed. by Edward Jones Corredera, Habsburg Worlds, 8 (Turnhout: Brepols, 2025), pp. 205–230

BREPOLS ❧ PUBLISHERS   10.1484/M.HW-EB.5.149996

diocesan and civil archives in the Basque Country and Navarre, this facet of the Basques' role in the early modern Iberian Empire remains largely ignored.

Of course, to be fair, this also has to do with the fact that there are very few scholars outside of the Basque Country and Navarre that are currently working on any aspect of the early modern Basque Country, let alone a racial dimension. This hasn't changed much since I began working in this region about a decade ago. This is further unfortunate, since (as I will discuss further below), the Basques were so deeply involved in early modern exploration and conquest. Moreover, the archives in the Basque Country and Navarre are some of the richest and most complete in all of Iberia, maintaining impressive jurisdictional organization and overlap. Closer to home in the US, we also have a gem of a research library at the Center for Basque Studies at the University of Nevada, Reno. This collection is decisively more modern and anthropological, but also holds numerous manuscripts and rare books, and I would love to see more researchers exploring its rich holdings and contacting its generous staff.

The records are similarly rich and under-utilized in archives in the Basque Country and Navarre. In Pamplona the entire records of the Diocesan criminal court are preserved going back as far as the mid-sixteenth century through the twentieth century, in addition to parish records, benefices, and diocesan administration matters. The diocesan tribunal heard cases ranging from crimes involving the clergy, to marriage disputes, to inheritance disputes (and correspondence) with the New World. The same people appear simultaneously in the secular jurisdictions; the Royal Archive of Navarre holds an equally impressively complete collection of a thousand years of criminal, administrative, and demographic records. Their utility is further enhanced by the also substantially complete notarial records. The potential of these records is immense – especially when put together with complementary records from elsewhere in Europe, Spain, and the Americas – but I rarely see other American scholars at these archives. I hope to see this change in the coming years.

What are the main challenges facing the field today?

Basque history has obviously long been closely connected to study of the Atlantic world, with some older work such as that by José Aramburu, José Azcona, and Javier Pescador standing out in particular.[3] These studies

---

3 José Miguel Aramburu Zudaire, *Vida y fortuna del emigrante navarro a Indias (siglos XVI y XVII)* (Pamplona: Gobierno de Navarra, Departamento de Educación y Cultura, 1999); José Manuel Azcona Pastor, *Possible Paradises: Basque Emigration to Latin America* (Reno: University of Nevada Press, 2004); and Juan Javier Pescador, *The New World Inside a Basque Village* (Reno: University of Nevada Press, 2003).

provided clear examples of how Atlantic emigration was far from one-directional, something that is at once a given to scholars of early modern Iberia, but also easy to forget.[4] Importantly, and particularly in the case of Pescador, studies of Basque emigration and its effects at the local level have been influenced by microhistorical studies of local communities, in a style perhaps more associated with French and Italian historiography than other local studies of early modern Spain. Iberian studies have long struggled with striking a comfortable balance between hyper-local studies and extremely detached birds-eye view perspectives. However, studies of the effects of emigration on gender, economy, and social structures at the community level have provided an important avenue for considering tensions between the local and the emerging early modern global world.[5]

As scholars of the early modern Basque Country and Navarre are eager to constantly remind us, the Basques were present in all the major early modern explorations; indeed, the importance of whaling and deep sea-fishing may even mean that they reached North America in the fifteenth century. Later, their expertise in mining, shipbuilding, and navigation also placed them at the center of imperial expansion. They established themselves across the empire, becoming important parts of colonial society in Peru, New Spain, the Philippines, and elsewhere. The money these *Amerikanuak* sent back is still strikingly visible today in the civic architecture of even the smallest town squares across the Basque Country. In this sense, the relationship between American colonial enterprises and the comfort of the modern Basque Country is inescapable. On the other hand, these visible reminders prioritize the Atlantic world of the Basque Country, and there has been a lot less interest in the Pacific dimension.

Overall, I believe the field (including both Iberian and Basque studies) is heading in a decisively Pacific direction. Some new works by Christina H. Lee and Sarah E. Owens hint at what this turn has in store, particularly in so far as a key thread is the transnational dimension of lived religion.[6] We desperately need new social histories of the Manila galleon trade and the Manila Inquisition, as well as more work on the ways in which Iberian religious houses maintained contact with their sister institutions in Asia.

---

4 Especially, Ida Altman, *Transatlantic Ties in the Spanish Empire: Brihuega, Spain, and Puebla, Mexico, 1560-1620* (Stanford: Stanford University Press, 2000); Ida Altman, *Emigrants and Society: Extremadura and Spanish America in the Sixteenth Century* (Berkeley: University of California Press, 1989); and Óscar Álvarez Gila and Juan Bosco Amores Carredano, *Del espacio Cantábrico al mundo americano: Perspectivas sobre migración y retorno* (Bilbao: Universidad del País Vasco, 2015).

5 For a related study in Galicia, see Allyson Poska, *Women and Authority in Early Modern Spain: The Peasants of Galicia* (Oxford: Oxford University Press, 2005).

6 Christina H. Lee, *Saints of Resistance: Devotions in the Philippines under Early Spanish Rule* (Oxford: Oxford University Press, 2021); and Sarah E. Owens, *Nuns Navigating the Spanish Empire* (Albuquerque: University of New Mexico Press 2017).

In all these studies, however, the experience of the individual remains paramount: I firmly believe that without an empathetic grounding in lived experience, any global or transnational study suffers from dislocation.[7] In the case of the Basque Country, new Pacific directions will likely involve close studies of testamentary bequests originating in the Philippines, the communities that those testators built, and the economic networks of Asian emigrants. Modern Basque studies on the trauma of exile (coined as the "Ulysses Syndrome") could also provide a useful entrance into considering the ways in which emigrants remembered, misremembered, and invented memories of the world they left behind.[8] In this sense, the Iberian Empire as a framework remains relevant, as it helps us ground individuals who traveled throughout the Empire, building lives permanently or transitorily, and crafting altered perceptions of lives they could never return to as immigrants.

What new directions in the field do you find the most generative?

Though I lamented above that there is little interest (or awareness) among English speaking researchers concerning the wealth of Navarrese and Basque archives, there are a few exceptions, and there has been some absolutely fantastic new work in the areas of children, family, and early modern Catholicism.

The Upper (Spanish) Pyrenees were home to one of the most consequential witch-hunts in the early modern period, which was most famously treated by Gustav Henningsen in his 1980 classic, *The Witches' Advocate*. The Basque witch-hunts are typically characterized as peripheral anomalies; things that only could have happened on the edges of a non-Hispanized part of Spain. Moreover, it has been extremely difficult for historians of early modern Catholicism, witchcraft, and social history to move past Henningsen's opus, which dominated the narrative for decades. Specifically, Henningsen argued that the Spanish witch-hunt was a turning point for both early modern witch-hunting culture, as well as the Spanish Inquisition. Guided by the "enlightened" jurist Alonso Salazar Frías – who Henningsen saw as coming to doubt the existence of witches and thereby leading the Inquisition into a more modern direction involving proof, evidence, and confession – the Spanish Inquisition ceased (for the most part) to prosecute witches.

---

7 Or to put it in the words of Carlo Ginzburg, 'there can be no global history without a deep knowledge of the local'. See 'Our Worlds, and Theirs: A Reflection on the Historian's Craft, Today', in *Historical Knowledge: In Quest of Theory, Methodology and Evidence*, edited by Susanna Fellman (Newcastle: Cambridge Scholars Publishing, 2012), pp. 97-119.

8 Joseba Atxotegi ed., *Ulysses Syndrome: The Psychology of Basque Migrations* (Reno: University of Nevada, 2020).

In a comparative context within the larger continental field of witchcraft studies, this was a provocative and seductive argument. However, recent revisions by Lu Ann Homza and Rochelle Rojas in the Spanish Pyrenees (and Jan Machielsen in the nearby French Pyrenees) have produced solid new work challenging how we understand early modern witch-belief in the Pyrenees.[9] Specifically, these three scholars are pushing us to look more closely at the local jurisdictional contexts that gave rise to the accusations, and the ways in which the unique social dynamics of early modern Basque communities were particularly prone to witch-accusations. Moreover, as Homza argues, villagers actively sought out legal aid in their witchy disputes, using various criminal, diocesan, and inquisitorial jurisdictions at will when it served their needs better. In this way, Homza shows witch-beliefs and witch-prosecutions were anything but top-down, and even Salazar's skepticism had more to do with concern over procedure than it did over the veracity of witchcraft. Indeed, it was the villagers themselves that were the true witches' advocates.

Some of these new studies echo much older historiographical and anthropological treatments on European witchcraft, though with attention to communal dynamics, and particularly in Homza's case, emotions and family, these new treatments of Basque witchcraft are decisively modern. Homza pays close attention to the role of children in the hunts, placing them provocatively front and center in how criminal accusations unfurled and struck home.[10] Though there has often been a notable methodological gap between English-speaking scholars working on the Basque Country and Basque and Spanish scholars, here at least there is some important cohesion. Navarrese scholars Jesús María Usunáriz and Amaia Nausia Pimoulier, for instance, have both cast a feminist lens on the wealth of the Pamplona archives, producing excellent work on witches, trans-Atlantic familyhood and courtship, widowhood, and the social history of insults.[11]

All told, however, I think that there is ample space for more attention to the early modern Basque Country, from social, religious, and global

9 Lu Ann Homza, *Village Infernos and Witches' Advocates: Witch-hunting in Navarre, 1608-1614* (University Park: Pennsylvania State University, 2022); and Rochelle Rojas, 'The Witches' Accomplice: Toads in Early Modern Navarre', *The Sixteenth Century Journal* 51:3 (2020), pp. 719-40. Rojas also has a book forthcoming on this topic, as does Jan Machielsen. See Jan Machielsen, *The Basque Witch-hunt: A Secret History* (London: Bloomsbury Academic, 2024).

10 See also Lu Ann Homza's forthcoming source reader on child witches, *The Child Witches of Olague* (University Park: Pennsylvania State University, 2024).

11 See, among other works, Jesús María Usunariz Garayoa, 'Cartas de amor y cartas de emigrantes como prueba judicial en España (siglos XVI–XVIII)', in *Hispanic Research Journal: Iberian and Latin American Studies* 16:4 (2015), pp. 296-310; Cristina Tabernero Sala and Jesús María Usunáriz Garayoa, *Diccionario de injurias de los siglos XVI y XVII* (Kassel: Reichenberger, 2019); and Amaia Nausia Pimoulier, *Ni casadas ni sepultadas Las viudas: una historia de resistencia femenina* (Tafalla: Txalaparta, 2022).

perspectives. Basque studies have largely been carrying on in their own distinct track within as well as alongside broader Iberian historiography, but the wealth of the archives means that they are a perfect space to push for a more prominent role of the periphery in studies of Spanish church, state, and society. I don't think that the field suffers from Castilian-centrism in the same ways as it used to, but there is still often the assumption that border areas are peripheral. The diversity of early modern Iberia and its colonies belies this characterization, of course, but a wider lens that captures the rich social history of the edges, placing it into comparative context with the rest of Europe or the world in its own right (and not as a placeholder for Castile) suggests an exciting potential for the field.

Towards a Global History of the Iberian World

Thiago Krause, **Wayne State University**

What has been the most significant change in the field of Iberian history since the start of your career?

From my vantage point as a Brazilian historian, one of the most significant evolutions in the field in the past twenty years has been the increasing integration of European and overseas histories within a unified framework. While empires have traditionally been recognized as pivotal to the development of early modern Iberia, they were often tacitly portrayed as fundamentally distinct from, and perhaps even less central than, their European counterparts. This perspective stemmed from a nineteenth-century understanding of the colonial past, which itself was a reinterpretation of earlier eighteenth-century dynamics, emphasizing a dichotomy between colonies and metropolises. Fortunately, a serendipitous convergence of scholarly endeavors by historians such as António Manuel Hespanha, who emphasized the necessity of interpreting sixteenth- and seventeenth-century politics on its own terms, and Bartolomé Yun-Casalilla, along with predecessors like Vitorino Magalhães Godinho, who illuminated the intricate connections between imperial and European economies, has catalyzed a shift in recent historiography. This shift moves away from the divisive narratives introduced by the era of independence, focusing instead on highlighting the connections and shared characteristics between both sides of the Atlantic. This integrative approach is particularly pronounced in the Luso-Brazilian context, owing to the expansive growth of the field in Brazil and the demographic asymmetry between the two nations. While this reevaluation of historical perspectives promises to enrich our understanding of the early modern era, its relevance appears to be more pronounced for the first two centuries than for its latter part, when overseas territories started to be perceived in a more subordinate manner, as both Pedro Cardim and Kirsten Schultz have recently shown.

How have comparative approaches to the study of history informed your own work on Iberian spaces?

In my exploration of society and politics in seventeenth-century Salvador da Bahia, then Brazil's capital, the comparative approach proved indispensable for two primary reasons.

Firstly, juxtaposing the local elites of Salvador with their counterparts in Portugal revealed striking similarities in rhetoric, aspirations, and conceptions of their relationship with Lisbon, but also an increasing divergence after the 1670s. This parallelism was particularly pronounced in Salvador's adoption of *ancien régime* social vocabulary. By the mid-seventeenth century, local elites had fashioned themselves as a distinct nobility, a status that was recognized and accepted by the Crown and royal officials. This acceptance was largely facilitated by robust communication channels between the center and periphery, which, in Salvador's case, were more robust than those maintained by all but the largest Portuguese cities, and may have even surpassed them.

Secondly, when comparing Salvador's local elites with their counterparts in the Americas and Western Europe, it became evident that many faced analogous challenges related to taxation and warfare. However, the responses to these challenges varied significantly based on institutional, social, and economic contexts. From William Beik's examination of Languedoc to Alejandro Cañeque's studies on Mexican politics, a consistent theme emerged: collaboration between the Crown and localities was crucial, often at the expense of marginalized societal groups.

In my ongoing collaborative research on the global history of Salvador da Bahia (1580-1763) with Christopher Ebert, the comparative perspective remains central. We aim to contextualize Bahian connections within broader trans-imperial frameworks. Questions we are exploring include: Was Salvador's development more or less influenced by trans-imperial networks? Did the activities of Dutch, English, French, and even Italian traders in Salvador – both directly and indirectly – mirror those in other Atlantic regions? Additionally, which other American locations were linked to Asia, and how might these connections shed light on Salvador's role in sustaining the *Carreira da Índia*?

As research on the Caribbean, Pacific, and Atlantic dimensions of the Iberian World has gradually grown more connected to, and in dialogue with, regional, trans-imperial, and postcolonial strands of history, is the framework of Iberian Empires still relevant to the study of the past?

Oceanic and global perspectives have revolutionized historical scholarship, challenging traditional methodologies and undermining the limitations of methodological nationalism. These approaches highlight the anachronistic and often restrictive nature of nation-state-centric analyses. However, it's essential to recognize that during the early modern era, a significant portion of commercial, social, and political interactions –excluding high-level diplomacy and warfare– occurred within the framework of imperial structures.

As such, the Iberian Empires remain crucial subjects of study in their own right. This is particularly true for their institutions, which defined the parameters for nearly all societal phenomena, even if these parameters were frequently disregarded or challenged. Therefore, while global and oceanic perspectives offer invaluable insights, they should not lead us to completely abandon imperial frameworks.

What are some recent works on Iberian history that demonstrate the merits of comparative approaches to the study of the past?

In the realm of cultural and political history, Giuseppe Marcocci's contributions have been instrumental in adopting a global perspective to explore the cultural and intellectual landscape of the early modern Iberian world. His work, exemplified in *Indios, cinesi, falsari* (2016), later translated into English as *The Globe on Paper* (2020), offers invaluable insights into this complex historical tapestry. Similarly, Angela Barreto Xavier's *Religion and Empire in Portuguese India* (2022, originally published in Portuguese in 2007) provides a comprehensive analysis of the social, political, and religious dynamics of Goa by juxtaposing them with subsequent South Asian empires. Pedro Cardim, meanwhile, has consistently positioned the Portuguese experience within broader Iberian and European contexts and, in recent years, has expanded his scope to include Brazil, offering comparative insights into other European empires. Jean-Frédéric Schaub's work on the history of race also adopts a comparative approach, challenging conventional narratives.

In the field of social and economic history, Paolo Calcagno's research on Genoa-Lisbon commercial ties serves as a critical reminder of the Mediterranean's significance as a focal point for comparison in Iberian history. Leonardo Marques and Fabricio Prado are at the forefront of publishing innovative research that bridges the South Iberian Atlantic with the Anglo-American world during the eighteenth century and the Age of Revolutions. Bartolomé Yun-Casalilla, meanwhile, embraces the challenges posed by Global History by continuing to explore the Iberian Empires through a comparative lens to elucidate divergent economic trajectories. Robert DuPlessis' *The Material Atlantic* (2015) is another seminal work that integrates the Iberian World into a broader narrative of textiles and fashion in the early modern Atlantic, focusing on themes of adaptation, circulation, and the production of inequality.

What new directions in the field do you find the most generative?

The global turn in Iberian History is an ongoing process, building on a rich intellectual lineage that includes figures like Fernand Braudel and Magalhães Godinho. While Atlantic History has been a transformative influence, encouraging trans-imperial perspectives and broader, less parochial approaches, the field faces new challenges and opportunities.

Moving forward, a key challenge will be to continue harnessing the power of comparative analysis to situate inquiries within larger historiographical debates while also identifying specific connections and interactions. While the pressures of a publish-or-perish culture can make time-consuming tasks like language acquisition and archival research more daunting, the accelerating pace of digitization in primary source collections and the advent of innovative technologies, such as Handwritten Text Recognition (HTR), offer promising avenues for advancing the field.

These technological advancements not only facilitate remote access to archival materials but also streamline the process of ordering reproductions and analyzing handwritten documents. As a result, they hold the potential to make the ambitious task of crafting global histories of the Iberian world more feasible and accessible to scholars, thereby enriching our understanding of this complex and interconnected historical landscape.

The Science of Modernity

Juan Pimentel, **Centro de Ciencias Humanas y Sociales (CSIC)**

What has been the most significant change in the field of Iberian history since the start of your career?

I think the most significant change has been the acceptance and assimilation of the Iberian past within broader histories. Spain was not that different (the idea of 'Spain is different' was a tourist slogan of the 1960s, a marketing strategy that drew on orientalist and exoticizing ideas, in line with the ideas of Georges Bizet or Washington Irving). Following the deconstruction of the meta-narratives of the Scientific Revolution, it turned out that Europe was not as modern, nor was Spain as different, as we thought.

How have comparative approaches to the study of history informed your own work on Iberian spaces?

The Atlantic turn has known various interesting iterations, as in the case of the great British Hispanist John Elliott, or the Ecuadorian historian based in the United States, Jorge Cañizares-Esguerra. Others were not quite so interesting. In many cases the Septentrional outlook, and the moralizing sense of cultural superiority of Northern Europe and the United States, have been cast upon the Iberian cultures. This can be seen in the bibliographies that some North American and British historians draw on; they are absolutely solipsistic. They are condescending towards the past of those Latin peoples and that which is not produced in their academic contexts.

On the point about other possible areas of comparison, the Iberian World offers a rarely traveled research path: the Portuguese expansion in Asia. It is incredible how little the histories of the two Indies, the occidental and the oriental, have been compared. The oriental world offers an interesting comparative way to understand the Iberian expansion in the New World. Here I am thinking specifically of the study of Kapil Raj, *Relocating Modern Science.*

What are the main challenges facing the field today?

Honestly, I have never considered myself as a historian of the Iberian World, since my research topics were always translations and always incorporated sources, actors, and bibliographies that were not Iberian. Only when working abroad, and particularly from the United States and the United Kingdom, do you end up seeing yourself as they see you, as a specialist of the Iberian World. National identities are always constructed in the process of entering into communication with other ones. Is the field of the Iberian World still relevant? No more and no less than others. It helps us to visualize our work, but I consider myself more of a historian of science than a historian of specific cultural contexts. Knowledge circulates and nature is transnational. Its historians circulate too.

What are some recent works on Iberian history that demonstrate the merits of comparative approaches to the study of the past?

As I said before, Jorge Cañizares-Esguerra is a reference, though his work has a strong meaning in the American context: he is a vindicating voice of subaltern Latin America who is trying to be listened to in the USA. His work, in this sense, is more local (American) than global (European). ¿Have recent studies on gender, race, and religion changed my thoughts on the Catholic faith in the Iberian world? Not very much, to be honest.

I think the emphasis on the Catholic dimension of Iberian world is over-sized by Anglo-American historiography. It is an easy label to mark a soft 'Black Legend', very trendy now and then in some contexts.

What new directions in the field do you find the most generative?

The new directions in my field – the history of science, more than Iberian studies – have been shaped some time ago – the material turn, the visual turn, cultural history, global history, the social construction of fact, and the great fall of tradition. By contrast, in the last few years the number of topics that occupy our interest has increased exponentially to include studies of gender, environmental history, and climate crisis. The fragmentation of these stories, and the dissolution of the great narratives of the mid-twentieth century produces nostalgia among the nostalgic. I am one of them, in part, like many historians and lovers of the past. But I doubt my generation will establish another great narrative: we demolished the old one. Perhaps the next generation will respond to this collection of fragmented, local, and micro approaches that have dominated the literature over the past twenty or thirty years. But I am not sure, they seem busier trying to find a job than changing a paradigm. As Tony Judt declared, ill fares the land.

Towards a Comparative Global Environmental History

Maria Gago, **Universidade Nova de Lisboa**

What has been the most significant change in the field of Iberian history since the start of your career?

As a historian of the late Portuguese Empire, I would say that the most significant change had to do with the question of "backwardness". During my PhD, I studied the history of Angola's coffee and how it became a global commodity after World War II. I was interested in understanding the role that scientists had played in this story. I examined the practices of the botanists and agricultural scientists that engaged with this cash crop between 1898 and 1961. I remember spending much of my time making sense of a literature that described the Portuguese Empire as unsophisticated, retrograde, backward. Because this went against what I saw in my sources – an empire that followed its British, French, and Belgian homologues in terms of the chosen forms of colonial governance, the scientific networks and institutions on which it relied, the labor regimes, the market circuits, but not in terms of scientific practices – I saw very few differences in terms of the process of empire building when I compared the Portuguese cases. As far as the twentieth century is concerned, there are two explanations for this historiographical bias.

The first is specific to the twentieth century and has to do with the fascist experience of *Estado Novo*, the political regime that ruled Portugal between 1933 and 1974, led by the dictator António Salazar. The second has to do with the theme of this book, the idea that Iberian Empires were not able to follow the process of European modernization and modern capitalism, which somehow made them incapable of reinventing themselves later in time. Indeed, I didn't need concepts like "Iberian history" or "the Iberian World" to write my story. But I needed this literature to make sense of the preconceived ideas about the empire I had chosen to study. I think that the state of the discussion nowadays is very different. Scholars do not talk about the "backwardness" of the Portuguese Empire like they did when I started my PhD. I think here the "global turn" in the historiography has played an important role in changing the field. In being forced to put the Portuguese Empire in wider contexts, historians gained distance from national narratives and ended up unveiling similarities with other empires. I could cite several scholars who have contributed to the deconstruction of this historiographical bias. In my case I was particularly influenced by two: the historian of science and technology Tiago Saraiva, who kickstarted a debate about the relationship between science and fascism in the Portuguese context, demonstrating the key role that scientists played in the making of the *Estado Novo*; and the historian Miguel Bandeira Jerónimo, who has initiated a discussion about the end of the Portuguese Empire and the international, transnational, and inter-imperial dynamics that shaped this historical process. It is no coincidence, of course, that both scholars felt the necessity of rethinking modernity on their own terms. Saraiva made the case for an "alternative modernity", one that could explain the development of scientific practices under the authoritarian regime of Salazar, both in metropolitan and colonial spaces; Jerónimo in turn put forward the idea of "repressive developmentalism" as an essential trait of Portuguese late imperial rule.

Is there a more fruitful comparative perspective on Iberian history than the one offered by the Atlantic turn?

I have to say that I was never convinced by the Atlantic turn and that I prefer the idea of writing "connected histories" to the comparative perspective. Of course, this is intimately related with the kind of history that I do. My work is about following an object of scientific inquiry – let's say, a coffee plant – and analyzing it through the lens of scientific practices. How it emerged as an artifact, how it moved from one place to the other, how it remained rooted to certain spaces and localities. When

Sanjay Subrahmanyam proposed the model of connected histories (as opposed to the comparative histories) he had in mind disciplines such as philology and hoped to probe and integrate scattered archives. What I do is use the methodologies of the field of the history of science and technology to trace these connected histories. Specifically, I use a firm engagement with the materiality of these objects that I am following. I am interested in understanding how the materiality of the things we produce, use, co-inhabit, live in – things like crops, machines, viruses, forests – shaped the making of the human world, and what the role of scientists was in the process. This engagement with materialism – new materialism to be more precise – can be very surprising in terms of the connections that it can reveal between different geographies and imperial spaces, but also in putting together different temporalities, timescales, and chronologies. Let me illustrate what I am saying with an example from my work on Angola's coffee. Basically, what I do is to analyse how a coffee species indigenous to the northern rainforests of Angola (a species called Robusta coffee) was transformed into a stable commodity and entered the global market. I show how this circulation was not a fluid movement but a highly negotiated one, orchestrated by Portuguese and American scientists involved in the process of Angola's coffee standardization on both sides of the Atlantic. In discussing the concessions that the Portuguese Empire made to the Americans, I am connecting the histories of European imperialism, Portuguese fascism, and American hegemony. But I also show that this story of circulation cannot be fully understood without also understanding the series of extensive adaptations that the Empire had to make to the environment in which this coffee crop was produced – the cloud forests of Northern Angola, where, before being planted, Robusta coffee plants used to grow spontaneously. And to understand these adaptations one must go back to the early nineteenth century, when European planters, the creole elite and the African chiefs started their first agricultural experiments. Moreover, one must also be able to play with different timescales if we want to take seriously the ecology of the cloud forests and how it shaped the making of colonial Angola. Highly interesting work, using crops to connect different historiographies and in so doing contributing to rethinking narratives of global circulation, is being experimented at the Max Planck Institute for the History of Science: see the project "Moving Crops and the Scales of History".

What new directions in the field do you find the most generative?

As a historian of science, I would say that one of the most generative directions has to do with the project of decolonizing the practice of history, which in the tradition of postcolonial studies has been forcing historians to revisit imperial historiographies and to bring to light actors that were somehow ignored by those narratives. See for instance what is happening with the history of the sciences of ecology and the figure of Alexander Von Humboldt. For many years, there was a consensus among historians of science about the pioneering role that the German naturalist had played in the history of ecological thought, how he had been at the center of an epistemic turn in the history of natural sciences, how he had contributed to a new understanding of how geology, botany, zoology, etc., are related to each other. The publication of Andrea Wulf's book *The Invention of Nature* in 2015 is the culmination of this vision. Today, this narrative is being completely turned upside down. Based on extensive work on non-European archives, a group of scholars of the Iberian World is putting forward the project "The Invention of Humboldt", a postcolonial critique of the traditional narrative on the German naturalist. The project, led by Mark Thurner and Jorge Cañizares-Esguerra, has demonstrated the extent to which Humboldt's major works were inspired in the work of his Latin American peers, namely the naturalist Francisco José de Caldas. It shows how Humboldt silenced them, for instance, by not citing them when he should. These are very interesting times to produce a new history of science. I think we are about to bear testimony to the fall of many European scientists whose authority we were used to taking for granted. And I think that this epistemic zone where the history of science meets Iberian history is an especially fertile field.

A second direction has to do with current debates on the Anthropocene and how they are inspiring historians to write history in different ways. I have to say that, in my opinion, this is the most generative direction in whatever field of history we are talking about – Iberian history included. Not that long ago, I was chatting with a professor of the early modern period, someone whose work I really admire, and I was starting to talk about this theme when I listened him saying something like this: "for us, working in the early modern period, these debates are not that interesting because we are dealing with a world that precedes the world of environmental degradation and ecological collapse that the concept of Anthropocene is concerned with". I could not disagree more. Firstly, because one of the possible beginnings for the Anthropocene – the alleged period when humans became a major geological force, since it literally means the "epoch of man" – is precisely the beginning of European imperialism in the Americas, with the environmental destruction of this continent and its global biological upheaval. Let's not forget the foundational work of environmental history, Alfred Crosby's *Ecological Imperialism*. To reduce the discussion of the Anthropocene to the modern world seems to me a strange imposition. Secondly, the most interesting outcomes of these debates are not the historical considerations about when the Anthropocene began, but the historiographical implications of this very same idea. What does it mean to write history if we accept that we are a major geological force? Should we continue to write about the history of human power over nature (that is, how empires, capitalism and globalization are connected to the present ecological collapse)? Or should we start producing historical narratives that emphasize the more-than-human dependencies that are necessary for humans to survive? For Dipesh Chakrabarty, putting together these "global" and "planetary" histories is the biggest challenge historians are facing today. It seems to me that Iberian history has a lot to offer in this direction.

Chocolate over Coffee: Sociability and Food History in the Spanish Atlantic

Marta Manzanares Mileo, **Universidad Autónoma de Madrid**

What aspect of Iberian history has remained unchanged since you started your career?

As an early career historian working on sugar, I witnessed an unprecedented wave of interest in the history of food and cooking. Influenced by the 'material turn', a growing number of scholars have persuasively shown how food offers a unique insight into colonial policies, social identities and hierarchies. A case in point is the seminal work of Sidney Mintz, *Sweetness and Power*, which revealed how the increased production of sugar cane in large plantations in the Americas and the Atlantic slave trade transformed consumer practices and tastes for sugar in Western Europe.[12] While the British Atlantic has received much attention from this scholarship, we still know little about the place of sugar across the Spanish Empire in the early modern period, that is, before Cuba became the major sugar producer in the Atlantic in the 1800s.[13] Indeed, the Spanish case presents us with a distinctive geographical and temporal context, a point that has often been overlooked in the early modern history of sugar.[14] Spaniards

---

12 Sidney W. Mintz, *Sweetness and Power: The Place of Sugar in Modern History* (New York: Penguin, 1986).

13 Manuel Moreno Fraginals, *The Sugarmill: The Socioeconomic Complex of Sugar in Cuba, 1760-1860* (New York: Monthly Review Press [c. 1976]).

14 For the Spanish Caribbean, see, among others: Juan Giusti-Cordero, "Beyond Sugar Revolutions: Rethinking the Spanish Caribbean in the Seventeenth and Eighteenth Centuries" in *Empirical Futures: Anthropologists and Historians Engage the Work of Sidney W. Mintz*, ed. by George Baca, Aisha Khan, and Stephan Palmie (Chapel Hill: University of North Carolina Press, 2009), pp. 58-83; Alejandro de la Fuente, "Sugar and Slavery in Early Colonial Cuba", in *Tropical Babylons: Sugar and the Making of the Atlantic World, 1450-1680*, ed. by Stuart B. Schwartz (Chapel Hill: University of North Carolina Press, 2004), pp. 125-62.

had established small slave-based sugar plantations in the Caribbean, the coastal valleys in Peru and the lowland regions in Mexico as early as the sixteenth century; nonetheless, their production was mainly intended to meet the demand of local and regional markets in the Atlantic. In contrast to other European powers in the Atlantic World, the Spanish mostly relied on sugar imports from abroad, until Cuba, after the uprising of Saint-Domingue, emerged as the major sugar producer. This is why Josep M. Fradera and Christopher Schmidt-Nowara have defined the Spanish Monarchy as a 'colonial pioneer and plantation latecomer'.[15] Moreover, sugar cane cultivation flourished in the Iberian Peninsula, especially in the Andalusian coast (Motril), and Valencia (Gandia, Oliva), although these small sugar mills became loss-making enterprises due to deforestation and high taxation by the turn of the eighteenth century. Hence the particularities of the sugar economies across the Spanish Empire were hardly comparable to other European contexts of sugar production and trade. These specificities must therefore be considered in further historical analyses of sugar in the early modern world.

How have comparative approaches to the study of history informed your own work on Iberian spaces?

Comparative approaches helped me raise awareness of the diversity of uses and meanings of sugar in Iberian spaces, particularly in its role as sweetener of the newly introduced hot beverages (chocolate, coffee, and tea). Scholars have long recognized how these foodstuffs created new spaces and practices of consumption and sociability across Western Europe.[16] However, the prevalence of coffee, and later tea, in England has often been presented as representative of a uniform European paradigm, without considering the diversity of social meanings and uses of sugar across early modern Europe. By the eighteenth century, authors like Antonio Lavedán pointed to these national differences in the consumption of hot beverages. In 1796, Lavedán claimed that 'the use of tea in Spain was not as widespread as in England, Holland and the East Indies'.[17] Indeed, it was chocolate, rather than coffee and tea, that prevailed in eighteenth-century Spain, whilst its consumption decreased in Northern Europe. By the second half of the eighteenth century, chocolate consumption became a sign

---

15 Josep Maria Fradera and Christopher Schmidt-Nowara eds., *Slavery and Antislavery in Spain's Atlantic Empire* (New York: Berghahn Books, 2013), p. 1.

16 Among a substantial historiography, see: Mintz, *Sweetness and Power*; Wolfgang Schivelbusch, *Tastes of Paradise: A Social History of Spices, Stimulants, and Intoxicants* (New York: Vintage Books, 1993); Woodruff D. Smith, 'Complications of the Commonplace: Tea, Sugar, and Imperialism', *The Journal of Interdisciplinary History* 23:2 (1992), pp. 259-78.

17 Antonio Lavedán, *Tratado de los usos, abusos, propiedades y virtudes del tabaco, café, té y chocolate* (Madrid, 1796), p. 159.

of cultural and national identity in Spain.[18] Here, it is also important to note the dissimilar impact of chocolate within the Spanish Empire. A good example could be the significant quantities of sugar used to sweeten *mate*, rather than chocolate, in many parts of the viceroyalty of Peru and Río de la Plata. As Sydney Mintz and Claude Fischler remind us, a preference for sweetness is seen as universal among human beings, but meanings and uses are historically specific, as they are influenced by political, economic, and social factors.[19] In this regard, the study of culinary uses and tastes for sugar may prove useful in developing comparative approaches between different empires, and within different regions within the Spanish Empire.

What are the main challenges facing the field today?

One of the main challenges in the historiography of sugar in the early modern world is perhaps moving beyond general assumptions on sugar economies, colonialism, and imperial strategies in the Atlantic. Stuart Schwartz cautioned that the model of export-oriented sugar plantation and consumer metropolis may not be appropriate for the early sugar plantation production across the Iberian Atlantic prior to 1650.[20] Although some economic historians made important inroads on sugar plantations in New Spain, Peru and the Spanish Caribbean in the 1970s and 1980s, as of yet a comprehensive history of sugar in the Spanish Atlantic has not yet been written.[21] To date, most of the studies focus on specific regions of colonial Latin America, yet very few works have attempted to establish transnational and/or transatlantic comparisons and connections.[22] Comparing different sugar production regions within the Spanish Atlantic, and with those of other colonial powers, can complicate and expand upon the

---

18 Irene Fattacciu, *Empire, Political Economy, and the Diffusion of Chocolate in the Atlantic World* (London: Routledge, 2020).

19 Mintz, *Sweetness and Power*; Claude Fischler, *L'Homnivore: le goût, la cuisine et le corps* (Paris: Éditions Odile Jacob, 2001), chapter 10.

20 Schwartz, *Tropical Babylons*, pp. 1-26.

21 One important exception is the Special Issue on sugar industry in the Americas published in *Revista de Indias*: 'La industria azucarera en América', *Revista de Indias* 65:233 (2005). For case studies, see: Fernando B. Sandoval, *La industria del azúcar en Nueva España* (Mexico: Universidad Nacional Autónoma de México, Instituto de Historia, 1951); Ward Barret, *The Sugar Hacienda of the Marqueses del Valle* (Minneapolis: University of Minnesota Press, 1970); Nicholas P. Cushner, *Lords of the Land: Sugar, Wine, and Jesuit Estates of Coastal Peru, 1600-1767* (Albany: State University of New York Press, 1980); A. Scarano, *Sugar and Slavery in Puerto Rico: The Plantation Economy of Ponce, 1800-1850* (Madison: University of Wisconsin Press, 1984); Fraginals, *The Sugarmill*.

22 Some exceptions are Juan Martínez-Alier, *Haciendas, Plantations and Collective Farms: Agrarian Class Societies, Cuba and Peru* (London: F. Cass, 1977); and more recently, Schwartz, *Tropical Babylons*.

main historical narratives of sugar in the Atlantic World. To do that, a major challenge would be how to overcome the long-standing national and linguistic divide between historiographies.

Have recent studies on gender, race, and religion changed the way you think about the structuring role of the Catholic faith in the Iberian World?

An extensive scholarship on gender, race and religion in colonial Latin America has provided me with a fruitful framework to think about the gendered and social meanings of sugar across the Spanish Atlantic.[23] Most of the studies focusing on the sugar plantation system usually highlight class and race in their analysis, while the gender dimension of sugar has been comparatively underexplored. Indeed, sugar epitomizes hierarchies of gender and of racial discrimination on both sides of the Atlantic. The historian Kim Hall has convincingly shown that ideologies of gender and race were entangled in relation to the production and consumption of colonial commodities, especially sugar, in seventeenth-century England.[24] Yet, Hall's work has raised important questions which remain unanswered for the Iberian spaces.

The focus on sugar opens a window into how ideas of gender, class, race and religion were closely intertwined across the Iberian Atlantic. For instance, colonial convents were important venues for imposing religious and gender ideologies, but also for developing hybrid culinary practices merging European, Indigenous and African ingredients and cuisines. Thanks to the historians of female monasticism in colonial Latin America, we know that religious women greatly contributed to shaping a taste for sugar with their 'heavenly desserts' on both sides of the Atlantic.[25] More generally, recent studies have stressed the agency of women of different ethnic and social backgrounds in shaping local food trades and creating creole cuisines in colonial Latin America.[26] Yet, women's contributions are

---

23 See, among others, Nora E. Jaffary ed., *Gender, Race and Religion in the Colonization of the Americas* (Aldershot: Ashgate, 2007); Sarah E. Owens and Jane E. Mangan eds., *Women of the Iberian Atlantic* (Baton Rouge: Louisiana State University Press, 2012).

24 Kim F. Hall, "Culinary Spaces, Colonial Spaces: The Gendering of Sugar in the Seventeenth Century", in *Feminist Readings of Early Modern Culture: Emerging Subjects*, ed. by Valerie Traub, M. Lindsay Kaplan, and Dympna Callaghan (Cambridge: Cambridge University Press, 1996), pp.168-90.

25 Among a vast literature, see, for instance: Asunción Lavrín, *Brides of Christ: Conventual Life in Colonial Mexico* (Stanford: Stanford University Press, 2008); and Kathryn Burns, *Colonial habits: Convents and the Spiritual Economy of Cuzco, Peru* (Durham: Duke University Press, 1999).

26 See, for instance: Kimberly Gauderman, *Women's Lives in Colonial Quito: Gender, Law, and Economy in Spanish America* (Austin: University of Texas Press, 2003); Jane E. Mangan, *Trading Roles: Gender, Ethnicity, and the Urban Economy in Colonial Potosí* (Durham: Duke

often neglected in the historiography of sugar. In this regard, a transatlantic gendered analysis, as suggested by Susan Amussen and Allyson M. Poska, may prove useful to further the historical analysis of the entangled transculturation of food and religious practices across the Spanish Empire.[27]

What new directions in the field do you find the most generative?

In recent years, many historians have reflected on how microhistorical approaches can contribute to the field of global history in order to overcome generalisations of universal historical processes.[28] These works have stressed the importance of considering local experiences of the material world in broader narratives of colonialism, power relations, and empire. Global microhistorical approaches can help us gain a more nuanced understanding of the complex social landscape of the production and trade in sugar on both sides of the Atlantic. Historians of food in the Iberian World have increasingly focused on the agency of historical actors, especially of non-European peoples, in the so-called Columbian Exchange.[29] From elite cooks to food retailers and street vendors, all of them promoted and provisioned foreign food commodities, and thus participated in broader processes of political, economic and social change. Spanish, creole, and indigenous peoples, and enslaved and free African women and men played a key role in the production and marketing of sugar, although this is an area of study that merits more academic attention. A shift in the focus of research from macro-historical analyses of export-oriented sugar plantation systems to an examination of the everyday practices of ordinary people can greatly enrich the ways we look at the place of sugar in the early modern world at all levels. Finally, new directions for the history of sugar must integrate an interdisciplinary dialogue with scholars in fields such as anthropology, archaeology, and environmental history, to explore the multifaceted dimensions of sugar, including its environmental impact, material culture, and social practices. Likewise, collaboration between historians working on different regions and languages will contribute to overcoming the dominant divide between national historiographical traditions.

University Press, 2005); Karen B. Graubart, *With Our Labor and Sweat: Indigenous Women and the Formation of Colonial Society in Peru, 1550-1700* (Stanford: Stanford University Press, 2007).

27 Susan D. Amussen and Allyson M. Poska, 'Restoring Miranda: Gender and the Limits of European Patriarchy in the Early Modern Atlantic World', *Journal of Global History* 7:3 (2012), pp. 342-63.

28 John-Paul A. Ghobrial, 'Introduction: Seeing the World like a Microhistorian', *Past & Present* 242:14 (2019), pp. 1-22; Francesca Trivellato, 'Is There a Future for Italian Microhistory in the Age of Global History?', *California Italian Studies* 2:1 (2011).

29 Alfred W. Crosby, *The Columbian Exchange: Biological and Cultural Consequences of 1492* (Westport: Greenwood, 1973).

After the Nation

José María Portillo Valdés, Universidad del País Vasco

What has been the most significant change in the field of Iberian history since the start of your career?

To me the most relevant change that has emerged since I became interested in this topic in the late 1990s has to do with the historiographical questioning of the nationalist perspective. With a few exceptions, like Tulio Halperin, the historiographical orthodoxy took for granted that the only interesting space was the national. It was not only true for the period after the conformation of the new Latin American nations but also for colonial history, and for the study of the crisis of the Spanish monarchy and the independence of Latin American territories. In the last decade of the 20th century, starting with the works of François-Xavier Guerra, Antonio Annino, Jamie E. Rodríguez and Luis Castro Leiva, a new perspective permitted the historiography in the first decade of the new century to criticize nationalist chronicles of the birth of the new Latin American nations.

In 2008, around the bicentennial celebration of the crisis of 1808 and the proliferation of the first autonomous governments and constitutional texts, historians became more interested in an Atlantic perspective that provided a new reading of the whole process of the disintegration of the Spanish Empire. It was no longer viewed as the epiphany of nations that were already in existence and which seemed to be waiting in the wings for the right moment to take control of the territory. A notable number of studies showed how nations were actually defined during the crisis of the monarchy as alternative types of sovereign bodies, and how other possibilities of imagining the former monarchical space were also debated and given serious consideration.

The first Spanish American nations were therefore not as nationalist as the existing historiography has supposed. In my opinion, the de-nationalisation of the study of the period running from late eighteenth century to the third decade of the following century cleared the way for the relevance of a more interconnected history to come through. Accordingly, this has allowed historians to re-evaluate the meaning of the crisis of the Spanish Empire and the transformation of these territories into new republics.

*How have comparative approaches to the study of history informed your
own work on Iberian spaces?*

Some historians, like Roberto Breña, have been reluctant to apply the term
Atlantic history to the study of Iberia. For these scholars, the Atlantic
history forged in the sixties and seventies of the last century had a clear
North Atlantic flavour and evoked the kind of historical changes usually
clustered under the label of Atlantic revolutions. Other historians, myself
included, preferred to retain the term Atlantic history in the case of the
Iberian world, above all when it came to the revolutionary period.

I would argue that, in fact, the Iberian World experienced a more
Atlantic history than, say, the United States or France. Undoubtedly, the
American and the French Revolution had an Atlantic dimension since they
were both a consequence of an imperial crisis in the Atlantic. The Iberian
monarchies, in addition, also shared constitutional experiences. Not only
did the Spanish and Portuguese constitutions of 1812 and 1820 envisage
Atlantic united nations, but there was a symbiotic relationship between
the various political experiments on both sides of the ocean. Historians
exploring other themes, like war or economics, have further insisted on
the relevance of the Atlantic space to better understand what happened in
individual territories.

One could therefore conclude that the crisis of empire, along with the
long process of dismantling its structures, were both Atlantic histories.
It is true that there was a tendency among Hispanic statesmen to define
particular national spaces and that, as the Spanish Empire was sundered
and new republics in the Americas, and in the Portuguese and Spanish
polities in Europe, took shape, the shared Atlantic space for political, social
or economic histories shrunk. Overall, I would suggest that the Atlantic
perspective provides a useful framework to study the decades following
the independence of the Latin American territories: the effective dissolution of the empire was connected with recognition, debts, diplomacy,
commerce, and social links that persisted for decades.

*As research on the Caribbean, Pacific, and Atlantic dimensions of the
Iberian World has gradually grown more connected to, and in dialogue
with, regional, trans-imperial, and postcolonial strands of history, is the
framework of Iberian Empires still relevant to the study of the past?*

With regard to this question, I would like to begin by stating that I feel
that we should try to find a balance between different levels of observation.
We have seen different historiographical approaches from local to global
but, at least in relation to the Iberian World, I would insist on the idea
of interconnected histories. You can get interested in some local processes
and focus your historical account on them, but it will be more enriching if

you also try to find the ties that link individual examples to other similar cases or to wider historical processes.

It is also important to specifically reassess the relationship between national and Atlantic histories. I would not discard the relevance and convenience of a national perspective when we narrate the processes that led precisely to a world composed by nation-states. Political discourses of the era of the birth of the modern world rely extensively on ideas of the nation. It is also true that sources, and very often resources, used in research are also "national". Hence, as historians, we have to reflect this "national moment" in our accounts: it would be a mistake to substitute the nation and the "national" with an Atlantic perspective as though the nation had no relevance in the construction of this framework. However, like I said before, the consolidation of an Atlantic perspective on the Iberian process of nation-building constitutes one of the most important steps taken by historiography in the last few decades. Perhaps we should think about some sort of Atlantic history (or histories) of the nations in the Iberian World, that is, a history, for example, of Chile that can explain how Chile was formed as a nation in an Atlantic context. There are a large number of historical processes that fit very well within this perspective, including those mentioned before, such as the history of public credit, commerce and, of course, the history of political ideas, state formation or constitutional development.

From the perspective of an Atlantic history of nations, I think that it is possible to address some of the historiographical challenges we face today more efficiently. If my generation was obsessed with nations, states, and constitutions, younger historians are more interested in reconstructing the politics of social developments, like the place of women in private and public spaces, the social history of slavery and its relations to an earlier form of capitalism, or the history of culture and many other fields where politics and society merge.

What are some recent works on Iberian history that demonstrate the merits of comparative approaches to the study of the past?

All these fields of interest that have to do with what we can call a social history of the political are particularly well suited to a comparative approach. The best examples are the history of slavery in the context of liberal, representative and capitalist states, gender history and, of course, the history of the relationship between Catholic religion and politics which continued to be both as Atlantic as it was national.

What new directions in the field do you find the most generative?

I would say that the period following the independence processes is less known to us from a comparative or Atlantic perspective. This is somewhat paradoxical because it is a period frequently studied by national historiographies and, consequently, very detailed in some aspects, above all with regard to political history. But, at the same time, from the 1830s on it seems as if the Atlantic literally disappears and everything turns national. On the whole, there is a historiographical challenge in restoring the Atlantic dimension of many historical aspects that have, to date, been considered exclusively from a national point of view.

Comparative Iberian Histories

José Javier Rodríguez Solís, Universidad Autónoma de Madrid

What has been the most significant change in the field of Iberian history since the start of your career?

The most striking aspect for a young researcher like myself has been the initiation into a discipline that was on the move, one that had already made the transition from the national to the Atlantic and then to the global. As a result, we have witnessed an integration of Iberian studies within global frameworks of interaction and discourses. This evolution has taken place in recent decades and has been reflected in articles, international congresses, and research centers that have made Iberian studies a basic research area of modernity.

In 2012, the strength of this shift became clear when, in a monographic issue of the journal *Espacio, Tiempo y Forma. Series IV* on the Iberian Monarchies – *Las Monarquías Ibéricas (1580-1715): Barroco y Globalización* – Pablo Fernández Albaladejo titled his text "*Siameses unidos por la espalda: memoria compartida de dos monarquías*". The metaphor alluded to the challenges posed by new trends in global history to the study of Spanish and Portuguese historiography. Albaladejo discussed the importance of the seminal works carried out in legal history by authors such as António Manuel Hespanha or Bartolomé Clavero, and in journals such as *Penélope* or *Lér História*. The deconstruction of the modern state, which started in the 1980s, paved the way for new formulations of empire. Ever since, the process by which historiographical comparativism has been gaining weight has allowed the introduction of global perspectives. These promoters of new questions about the Iberian past have included, in addition to a renewed interest in political history, scholars studying the Pacific Ocean, collective identities, the different trends arising in cultural history, and the study of miscegenation through the scholarship on postcolonial and gender studies. These new currents have contributed to the study of global processes that shaped Iberian spaces by foregrounding subjects that had traditionally been relegated to the background, including women, indigenous people, and enslaved people. All these changes have brought new topics and contexts to the fore of academic debate, making it possible to establish Iberian studies as a globalized space full of new research opportunities.

How have comparative approaches to the study of history informed your own work on Iberian spaces?

The comparative history of Portugal and Spain in the context of the Union of Crowns (1580-1640) constitutes the basis of a Hispanic Lusitanianism which shaped the seminal works of Fernando Bouza, like *Portugal en la Monarquía Hispánica (1580-1640)*, and Rafael Valladares, including his *La conquista de Portugal. Violencia militar y comunidad política en Portugal*, or Pedro Cardim's *Portugal unido y separado*, among others. This consolidated trend serves as a basis for the study of a period in which, while avoiding the derivations of nationalist discourses on either side of the border, it is possible to carry out a reflexive analysis of a shared political culture typical of a context that gave rise to political frameworks in which the construction of unions and revolutions generated more flexible or malleable discourses than those that emerged in the modern era.

In the field of Portuguese and Castilian historiography of the sixteenth and seventeenth centuries, in particular, this is particularly clear thanks to the comparative perspective applied to the different kingdoms. The comparison of the histories written in the context of the Union of Crowns yields results that are more local than national. At the same time, historiographical discourses were imbued with dynastic and, above all, confessional, connotations that distanced them from our national, or state-based, present. They highlighted the exchange of topos, common ideas and shared readings without this conditioning the particular Portuguese or Castilian interest of their authors. The result was different visions of the historical narrative that made Hispania both Castilian and Lusitanian. And all this took place without undermining a broader European contextualization which found that similar processes were underway in the kingdoms of France, England, or the Holy Empire.

What are the main challenges facing the field today?

The global projection of the Iberian Empires may continue to be relevant insofar as they are a sufficiently broad and complex framework for study. But this must consider not only comparison as a research method, but also the interconnection with other contemporary realities such as Anglo-Saxon America or Pacific territories. This work can be extended to studies that do not necessarily seek to write a global history, but that implement its principles. In this sense, research such as Jorge Cañizares-Esguerra's *How to write the History of New World* (2002) or Serge Gruzinski's *Le quatre parties du monde. Histoire d'une mondialisation* (2004) still serves as a reference for those who wish to develop the study of Iberian studies in this global context. All of them are necessary when it comes to recovering languages and discourses that highlight dimensions, either from American or Atlantic studies, that raise new questions and answers. In other words, it is also a matter of avoiding the "nationalizing" tendencies of global history in which national identities take precedence over historical subjects and overshadow the connections and relationships of its actors.

What new directions in the field do you find the most generative?

The contribution of a renewed Atlantic history that conceives the Euro-American subject jointly and globally has really boosted the field. Recent works such as *La nación imperial* (2015) by Josep María Fradera or *Historia conceptual del Atlántico ibérico* (2021) by Javier Fernández Sebastián, the recent work published by José María Portillo, *Una historia atlántica de los orígenes de la nación y el estado* (2022) exemplify this shift. This concep-tualisation of constitutionalism depicts it as a global phenomenon with a mutable national component at its core. This would oscillate between the eighteenth-century notion of the *"nación literaria"*, a participant in the European Republic of Letters, and its transmutation in the context of the imperial crisis of 1808, where concepts such as sovereignty and emancipation took center stage in political discussions. The result is a complex context of interconnections on both sides of the Atlantic that resulted in the emergence of the modern concepts of "nation" and "state" in the nascent American republics as well as in the Spanish constitutional monarchy, key in the configuration of the Atlantic world of the nineteenth century.

What are some recent works on Iberian history that demonstrate the merits of comparative approaches to the study of the past?

Many of these books are collaborative, such as *Polycentric Monarchies. How did Early Modern Spain and Portugal Achieve and Maintain a Global Hegemony?* (2014). Out of research centers such as the Centro de Hu-manidades (CHAM) at the Universidade Nova de Lisboa, new studies and research have regularly benefited from the comparative and global study of the Iberian worlds. This is evidenced by titles such as *Repensar a identidade. O mundo ibérico nas margens da crise da consciência europeia* (2015) or

"Por toda la Tierra". España y Portugal: globalización y ruptura (1580-1700) (2016), all of which point to the direction of travel of the field. All of them report the discourses and languages – religious, juridical, ethnic, national or linguistic – that shaped the identity traits of those monarchies that were debated and questioned not only from the Peninsula, but from Europe, America and Asia.

A study of one of those interior margins of the Iberian world is *People of the Iberian borderlands. Community and conflict between Spain and Portugal (1640-1715)* (2022) by David Martín Marcos. It shows the development of the peninsular border between Portugal and Spain, and tries to highlight the symbiotic dynamics of these spaces. In these spaces, clear ideas of sovereignty found conceptual constraints, giving rise to connections between the communities on both sides that in many cases prioritized the local and proximity over the "national", or those forms of power projected from the courts of Madrid or Lisbon.

Notes on the Contributors

Bethany Aram is Associate Professor of History at Pablo de Olavide University. She directed the research project 'ArtEmpire' (ERC CoG 648535) funded by the European Commission (Horizon 2020), and is the author of *Juana the Mad: Sovereignty and Dynasty in Renaissance Europe* (Johns Hopkins University Press, 2005).

Pedro Cardim is Associate Professor of History at the Universidade Nova de Lisboa. He has published numerous books on Iberian and Portuguese history and, most recently, he has co-edited, with Nuno Gonçalo Monteiro, the volume *Political Thought in Portugal and its Empire, c. 1500-1800* for Cambridge University Press.

Maria Gago is a Postdoctoral Fellow at the Universidade Nova de Lisboa. She is a historian of science and technology who is interested in the global history of crops. She is associate editor of *HoST: Journal of History of Science and Technology*.

Tamar Herzog is the Monroe Gutman Professor of Latin American Affairs at Harvard University, Radcliffe Alumnae Professor, and an Affiliated Faculty Member at the Harvard Law School. Her most recent single-authored book is *A Short History of European Law: The Last Two and a Half Millennia* (Harvard University Press, 2019), and she recently co-edited, with Thomas Duve, *The Cambridge History of Latin American Law in Global Perspective* (Cambridge University Press, 2024).

Edward Jones Corredera is Assistant Lecturer at the Universidad Nacional de Educación a Distancia. He is the author of a number of books, the most recent of which is *Odious Debt: Bankruptcy, International Law, and the Making of Latin America* (Oxford University Press).

Thiago Krause is Associate Professor at the Departments of History and African American Studies of Wayne State University. He has published a number of books on the Portuguese Empire, with a focus on Brazil, and is currently co-writing, with Christopher Ebert, a global history of Salvador da Bahia (1580-1763).

Marta Manzanares Mileo is a Ramón y Cajal Fellow at the Universidad Autónoma de Madrid. She is the author of *Dolços i confiters a la Catalunya moderna* (Eumo, 2021) and her article "Sweet Femininities: Women and the Confectionery Trade in Eighteenth-Century Barcelona" won the 2022 Sophie Coe Prize in Food History.

David Martin Marcos is Associate Professor of History at the Universidad Nacional de Educación a Distancia. He is the author of a number of books, the most recent of which is *People of the Iberian Borderlands: Community and Conflict between Spain and Portugal, 1640-1715* (Routledge, 2023).

Fabien Montcher is Assistant Professor of History at Saint Louis University. He is the Director of the University's Center for Iberian Historical Studies and the author of *Mercenaries of Knowledge Vicente Nogueira, the Republic of Letters, and the Making of Late Renaissance Politics* (Cambridge University Press, 2023).

Juan Pimentel is Research Professor in the History of Science at the Centro de Ciencias Humanas y Sociales, or CSIC. He is the author of many books, including *The Rhinoceros and the Megatherium: An Essay in Natural History* (Harvard University Press, 2017).

José María Portillo Valdés is Professor of History at the University of the Basque Country. He has published many books on constitutionalism in the Hispanic World, and his most recent work is *Una historia atlántica de la nación y el Estado. España y las Españas en el siglo XIX* (Alianza Editorial, 2022).

Marcos Reguera Mateo is a Researcher at the University of the Basque Country and a journalist. His first book *El Imperio de la democracia en América. John L. O'Sullivan y la formación del concepto de Destino Manifiesto*, will be published by Fondo de Cultura Económica in 2025.

José Javier Rodríguez Solís is a doctoral student at the Universidad Autónoma de Madrid. The title of his thesis is *Escrita y vista, manuscrita e impresa: la Monarquía de España de Pedro Salazar de Mendoza*.

Amanda L. Scott is Associate Professor of History and Women's, Gender, and Sexuality Studies at Pennsylvania State University. She is the author of a number of articles on gender and faith in the Iberian World, and her first book was *The Basque Seroras: Local Religion, Gender, and Power in Northern Iberia, 1550-1800* (Cornell University Press, 2020).